THE CLASSICAL SUBLIME

A. Paillet and G. Vallet, engraving, frontispiece to the Traité du sublime, *in Boileau's* Œuvres diverses *(Paris, 1674).*

NICHOLAS CRONK

THE CLASSICAL SUBLIME:
FRENCH NEOCLASSICISM AND
THE LANGUAGE OF LITERATURE

ROOKWOOD PRESS
Charlottesville
2002

ISBN 1-886365-22-9

This book is printed on acid-free paper.

EMF CRITIQUES

EDITORS
Anne L. Birberick and Russell Gamin

COORDINATING EDITOR FOR THIS VOLUME
David Lee Rubin

COPY EDITOR
Marie Hertzler

PRODUCTION
Angel Applications

COVER DESIGN
Dallas Pasco

TABLE OF CONTENTS

List Of Illustrations

for my mother and father

and in memory of
Nicholas John
(1952-1996)

ACKNOWLEDGEMENTS

I am deeply grateful to Marian Jeanneret, to Denys Potts, and to the late Robert Shackleton for their supervision of the thesis upon which this book is based; and also to my D.Phil examiners, Peter Bayley and Peter France. For their friendship and unflagging encouragement, I am enormously indebted to David Rubin, and to my colleagues at St Edmund Hall, Ken Segar, Chris Wells, and the late Richard Fargher. For their practical as well as scholarly expertise, I also wish to thank very warmly Madeline Barber, Russell Goulbourne, Peter Damian-Grint, and my copy editor Marie Hertzler. The superb staff of the Taylor Institution Library, Oxford have given unstinting help over many years, and I am extremely grateful to them. St Edmund Hall and the Oxford Faculty of Modern Languages have given financial assistance. Andrew Kahn has been generous in support and assistance of every other kind.

This book is dedicated to my mother and father, whose loving support has sustained me throughout, and to the memory of Nick John, who proof-read the earliest drafts.

REFERENCES

Page references in parentheses in the text are to the editions described in the Bibliography.

References to Boileau are, unless indicated otherwise, to the appropriate volume in the seven-volume edition of Charles-H. Boudhors (1934-43).

The following abbreviations are used in references to Longinus:

OS On sublimity, trans. D. A. Russell, in *Ancient Literary Criticism*, ed. D. A. Russell and M. Winterbottom (Oxford, 1972)

OTS On the sublime, ed. with introduction and commentary, D. A. Russell (Oxford, 1964)

TS Traité du sublime, trans. Boileau, ed. Ch.-H. Boudhors (1942)

THE CLASSICAL SUBLIME

Introduction

'French classicism' remains an oddly elusive concept, not least because there appears to be an unbridgeable divide between the undisputed greatness of the literature produced in the 1660s and 1670s and the apparent triviality of much of the poetic theory produced in the same period. A modern literary critic analysing Racine's poetry is very likely to refer to the rhetorical tradition within which Racine was working, but most unlikely to turn for illumination to contemporary poetic theory. The old-fashioned notion of Boileau as the archpriest of a rationalist cult of rules has still not been entirely superseded or discredited.

There has, amazingly, been no comprehensive study to replace René Bray's *La Formation de la doctrine classique en France* (1927), and although E. B. O. Borgerhoff made a pioneering attempt to debunk the supposed rigidities of classicism in *The Freedom of French Classicism* (1950), this study does not deal directly with questions of poetic theory. The single most important study of classical poetic theory since Bray is surely Jules Brody's *Boileau and Longinus* (1958). This work undertakes a meticulous comparison of Boileau's translation of 'Longinus' with the Greek original, and moves on to a penetrating analysis of Boileau's use of certain key critical terms. (For the sake of simplicity, 'Longinus' or Pseudo-Longinus will be referred to henceforth as Longinus.) In showing, for example, how *raison* describes for Boileau not a rational norm but an intuitive principle, Brody presents a complex and sophisticated picture of Boileau's critical thought surpassing all previous studies.

In *La Formation de la doctrine classique*, Bray makes no mention either of Boileau's translation of Longinus or of the term *le sublime*, and Brody's study in effect added a new text and a new term to the canon of French classical criticism. In a paperback history of French classicism published in 1984, for example, Roger Zuber and Micheline Cuénin conclude their chapter on 'la doctrine et l'esthétique classiques' (an interesting shift from Bray's 'doctrine classique') with a section on *le sublime*: to describe the poetic theory of French classicism without discussion of *le sublime* no longer seems possible. But as *le sublime* has increasingly come to be treated in recent studies as an integral component of classicism, so too there has been a growing tendency to emphasise the continuity of French, even European, debate about the sublime from the late seventeenth century to the early nineteenth, thereby compromising the particular function of *le sublime* within the poetics of French classicism.

The implications of Brody's argument and method are far-reaching, but he quite explicitly refrains from situating his newly restored picture of Boileau's thought in a broader context. The aim of the present study is to complement Jules Brody's *Boileau and Longinus* by attempting to situate the *Traité du sublime* in the critical debate of

i

the 1670s and so explain its remarkable success. The term *le sublime* quickly acquired wide currency, so much so that a generation later it became a defining source of contention in the *querelle des Anciens et des Modernes*. Of course, Boileau's translation played an important and influential role in spreading the name of Longinus, in France and beyond. But it is a common error to consider Boileau's *Traité du sublime* primarily as a contribution to some history of 'the sublime', as if this were a coherent concept existing indendently of time, place and language. Boileau 'invents' *le sublime* as a critical term, rather as Bouhours three years earlier had 'invented' *le je ne sais quoi*: both were attempts to define a theory of poetic language in a specific context, within the confines of a number of quite particular linguistic and philosophical constraints. Boileau published his translation of Longinus in 1674, together with the *Art poétique*: the two works were purposefully conceived as a critical diptych and in Boileau's lifetime were always published, and read, together. Of the two complementary works, it is the *Art poétique* which has most occupied modern commentators; yet it was the *Traité du sublime* which generated most immediate comment (and which was the more prominent on the title-page of the *Œuvres diverses*). Speaking through, and hiding behind, the voice of 'Longin', Boileau is able to be more outspoken in the *Traité du sublime* than in the *Art poétique*. It is only an apparent paradox that this 'translation' of a classical text is perhaps the most innovative text of French classical poetic theory.

1: THE CONSTRAINTS OF CLASSICISM

> Mediation, which is the immediacy of all mental communication,
> is the fundamental problem of linguistic theory, and if one chooses
> to call this immediacy magic, then the primary problem of lan-
> guage is its magic. (Benjamin)[1]

'J'ai songé qu'il ne s'agissoit pas simplement ici de traduire Longin', writes Boileau, introducing his version of Longinus, 'mais de donner au Public un Traité du Sublime, qui pût estre utile' (44). To understand what Boileau might mean by a 'use-ful' treatise, we need first to understand the problems that beset poetic theory in the 1670s. Many scholars have set out to describe the 'pre-history' of the classical language by identifying the various influences which combined to determine its development. Roger Zuber, for example, demonstrated the decisive importance of certain translators in shaping 'le goût classique', and more recently Marc Fumaroli has shown how the language of the classical generation emerged as a middle way between conflicting Jesuit and Gallican traditions of eloquence. These studies are of course concerned with the practice rather than with the theory of the literary language, and when we turn to the history of poetic theory in this period, we are faced by a rather different methodological problem. Various developments in linguistic and aesthetic thinking come to a head in the decade or so in which Boileau was evolving his ideas about poetry, and it is the aim of this chapter to attempt to identify some of the constraints which operated on the formulation of a satisfactory theory of poetic language in the 1670s.

I. THE CLASSICAL SIGN

A theory of poetry necessarily presupposes a theory of language, and there can have been few periods when matters of language and grammar were more keenly discussed than in seventeenth-century France. The achievement of the grammarians and language-theorists was considerable, and the Port-Royal *Grammaire générale et raisonnée* of Lancelot and Arnauld (1660) is judged by modern linguists to mark an important turning-point in linguistic history. The sixteenth century had dreamed of recovering the original language which had united mankind before the Fall. This adamic tongue had been characterised firstly by its universality, and secondly by its transparency, which is to say that it presupposed an absolute affinity between words and things. 'Chascune espece estoit venue en la présence d'Adam, et leur avoit imposé les noms, non point à la volée, mais par cognoissance certaine,' writes Calvin. This link between word and object had been obscured since the Fall, but it was still assumed to be present: 'Quant aux noms qu'Adam a imposez, je ne doute point qu'il n'y eust tres bonne raison en chascun, mais l'usage d'iceux, comme beaucoup d'autres bonnes choses est aboli.'[2] For the Renaissance, therefore, words enjoyed an occult quality, being considered not as signs designating some separate reality, but rather as the very signature of that reality and so in correspondence with its innermost nature. It was such a theory of language which enabled the cabalists to demonstrate the secret connections between cosmic architecture and the structures of the Hebrew language.[3]

Although classical rhetoricians such as Cicero and Quintilian observe a distinction between *res* ('things', 'subject-matter') and *verba* ('words', 'figures'), 'their integration in an ideally abundant discourse is always recommended,' writes Cave, 'as is the priority of *res*'.[4] Discussing *De duplici copia verborum ac rerum*, a handbook on how to write copiously, Cave shows how Erasmus blurs further the distinction between *res* and *verba*:

> To render *res* itself as 'idea' would be to confuse, or rather over-simplify the issue. In some contexts, it is true, *res* could be defined as the extra-linguistic reality apprehended by the mind and reproduced in the form of *verba*; in this sense, according to the classic mimetic model, words copy or represent the objects of thought. But in the *De copia*, [...] this reassuring hierarchy is disturbed, if not inverted. *Res* do not emerge from the mind as spontaneous 'ideas'; they are already there, embedded in language, forming the materials of a writing exercise.[5]

Such a view of language still prevails in Claude Duret's *Trésor de l'histoire des langues de cet univers* (1613): 'Adam imposa les vrayes et propres appellations de toutes choses' (243). This notion that words are the secret ciphers of reality privileges language over any other form of communication, and in a fascinating passage, Duret draws out the full consequences of this position:

> Car ainsi comme toutes [les Idées de toutes les Creatures formees et à former] se cognoissent par leur droite appellation, laquelle ne nous peut estre representee que par la parole, ou l'Escriture; dont la peinture et sculpture avec tels autres arts qu'on appelle imitatrices, sont comme une branche et dependance: par consequent outre ce que l'escriture est plus spirituelle que la parole, et les mots escrits plus preignants pour nous manifester l'essence de la chose qu'ils representent, que les proferez de vive voix, d'autant qu'on y insiste plus [...]. (26)

What is striking here is Duret's claim that the 'imitative arts', as he terms them, such as painting and sculpture, are subsidiary to, and so apparently inferior to, language. It is the written word which comes closer to a full penetration of reality than any of the other so-called dependent arts; the Horatian tag has been reversed: *ut poesis pictura*. Within this theoretical framework, it would be absurd—literally unthinkable—to question the efficacy of language in communicating reality. (Even to pose a problem in terms of 'the communication of reality through language' is of course to presuppose a different episteme.) Discourse, in this view, does not stand apart from the world; it is inscribed in it.

Such a view was already conservative in the early seventeenth century when Duret was writing; Dubois describes the gradual demythification of language, notably under the impulse of scientific and medical thought, and he quotes Laurent Joubert, for example, who uses the empirical evidence of aphasia to argue that language is acquired rather than innate.[6] In the realm of rhetorical and logical theory, Ramus (Pierre de la Ramée) is generally held, especially since the pioneering work of Ong, to mark a crucial turning point. Fundamental to Ramist method is a distinction between dialectic (dealing with *res*) and rhetoric (dealing with *verba*). '*Things*,' writes Ong, 'are constituted not in opposition to the mind, but in opposition to the word',[7] and he further explains the epistemological underpinning of this theory: 'The Ramist corpuscular epistemology, supposing that knowledge consists of sets of mental items, thereby implied one-for-one correspondence between terms and things'.[8]

Thus the notion that language in some sense inhered in reality gave way in the seventeenth century to the idea that words were merely tokens, man-made and arbitrary, designating an external and separate reality. This broad theory of language which sees words as surrogates for ideas or things we may call *nomenclaturist*: it postulates a complete divorce between *res* and *verba*, and conceives of language as a nomenclature, a set of verbal tokens which stand in for the 'real thing'.[9] With this theory, interest shifts away from the word itself—witness the Renaissance fascination with arcane etymologies—and refocuses on the relationship linking word to world, hence the seventeenth-century's preoccupation with the function of imitation.

Nomenclaturism brings in its wake renewed interest in the theory of the sign, a theory with a long medieval tradition behind it, but one which had been eclipsed by the rather different linguistic interests of Renaissance humanism. Modern interest in the classical theory of the sign has been fired by Foucault's analysis in *Les Mots et les choses* (72-81), but, because of his broadly-based classical episteme, his description conflates the ideas of the Port-Royal, Berkeley and Condillac. The aim here is to focus more narrowly, within this general framework, on the detail of the debate at the moment of classicism, for it is specifically among the writings of the Port-Royal authors that discussion of the nature of the sign re-emerges. The semantic theory propounded by Arnauld and others has been studied elsewhere by Donzé and Gniadek,[10] and their analyses pay tribute to the sophistication of the Port-Royal's semantic theory, aspects of which—the arbitrariness of the sign, for example—are thought to have influenced Saussure. It will be useful here to supplement their discussion by emphasising two aspects which they rather overlook: (i) the way in which debate about the sign intensified in the course of the 1660s and 70s, and (ii) the role within that debate of Bernard Lamy's *Rhétorique*.

Donzé and Gniadek describe the semantic theory of the Port-Royal all of a piece, conflating remarks in the *Grammaire* and in the different editions of the *Logique*. It is in the Port-Royal *Grammaire* (1660) that we find the first discussion of the sign in the seventeenth century, only briefly, but Lancelot and Arnauld drive home their point in the second sentence of the book, which opens thus: 'La Grammaire est l'art de parler. Parler, est expliquer ses pensées par des signes que les hommes ont inventés à ce dessein' (7). Later we read:

> Ainsi l'on peut définir les mots, des sons distincts et articulés, dont les hommes ont fait des signes pour signifier leurs pensées. C'est pourquoi on ne peut bien comprendre les diverses sortes de significations qui sont enfermées dans les mots, qu'on n'ait bien compris auparavant ce qui se passe dans nos pensées, puisque les mots n'ont été inventés que pour les faire connaître. (22-23)

The same theoretical position is assumed, though not really discussed, by Arnauld and Nicole in the first edition of *La Logique ou l'art de penser* (1662), where the term 'signe' is used some half dozen times. In their preamble the authors speak of 'paroles' as 'signes', remarking 'nous ne pouvons faire entendre nos pensées les uns aux autres, qu'en les accompagnant de signes exterieurs', and concluding that 'il est necessaire dans la Logique de considerer les idées jointes aux mots, et les mots joints aux idées' (38). Later there is mention of 'l'accord que les hommes ont fait de prendre de certains sons pour être signes des idées que nous avons dans l'esprit' (42). Nomenclaturism is taken for granted in the first edition of the *Logique*, but it is not accorded detailed treatment.

This changes radically with the fifth edition of the *Logique* ('Cinquième édition reveuë et de nouveau augmentée', 1683), the last significant revision which the authors made to their text. Two entire chapters are now added on issues relating to the sign: 'Des idées des choses, et des idées des signes' (I, 4), and 'Des propositions où l'on donne aux signes le nom des choses' (II, 14). Arnauld and Nicole now elaborate a fully-fledged theory of the sign as a bipartite entity:

> Quand on considere un objet en lui-même et dans son propre être, sans porter la vûe de l'esprit à ce qu'il peut représenter, l'idée qu'on en a est une idée de chose, comme l'idée de la terre, du soleil. Mais quand on ne regarde un certain objet que comme en représentant un autre, l'idée qu'on en a est une idée de signe, et ce premier objet s'appelle signe. C'est ainsi qu'on regarde d'ordinaire les cartes et les tableaux. Ainsi le signe enferme deux idées, l'une de la chose qui représente, l'autre de la chose représentée; et sa nature consiste à exciter la seconde par la premiere. (52-53)

In Saussurean terms, we might say that this theory describes a sign comprising *signifiant* and *référent*: it draws no distinction whatsoever between *signifié* and *référent*.

As we shall see later, this absence of a notion of a *signifié* proves a crippling restraint, for example when theorists of the period attempt to describe the process of metaphor, since they are unable properly to distinguish between denotation and connotation.

The difference, then, as concerns sign theory between the 1662 and 1683 editions of the *Logique* is a dramatic one. In the intervening period there had appeared the work which is without doubt the most original and most influential rhetoric of the century, *De l'art de parler* by the Oratorian Bernard Lamy. First published in 1675, it quickly went through a bewilderingly complicated series of different editions, being rebaptised *La Rhétorique ou l'art de parler* from 1688 ('Troisième édition') onwards and reaching a fourth edition in 1701.[11] The work is clearly infused with the principles of cartesianism and the Port-Royal, and the *Rhétorique*, coming after the *Grammaire* and the *Logique*, would logically seem to form the third wing of a Port-Royal triptych, yet it has never been accorded as much attention as the other two works. It is not surprising, then, that neither of the treatments of Port-Royal sign theory cited above even mentions the *Rhétorique*. The first two editions of Bernard Lamy's work (1675 and 1676) in fact make only brief reference to the notion of the sign: 'La parole est un assemblage de sons de la voix que les hommes ont établis pour être les signes de leurs pensées'.[12] In the third (1688) edition, however, this sentence in the opening chapter is replaced by a lengthy paragraph discussing the nature of the sign:

> Les hommes auraient pu marquer ce qu'ils pensent par des gestes. Mais, comme on a dit, la facilité qu'il y a de parler les a porté [*sic*] à n'employer pour signes de leurs pensées que des paroles, lorsqu'ils ne sont point contraints de garder le silence. On appelle signe une chose, qui outre cette idée qu'elle donne quand on la voit, en donne une seconde. Comme lorsqu'on voit à la porte d'une maison une branche de lierre; outre l'idée du lierre on conçoit qu'on vend du vin dans cette maison. On distingue deux sortes de signes: les uns sont naturels, c'est-à-dire qu'ils signifient par eux-mêmes, comme la fumée est un signe naturel qu'il y a du feu, où on la voit. Les autres, qui ne signifient que ce que les hommes sont convenus qu'ils signifieraient, sont artificiels. Les mots sont des signes de cette sorte.[13]

It is interesting that Bernard Lamy thought it necessary in 1688 to incorporate some discussion of the sign into the introductory chapter of his rhetoric, and his description of the sign seems indebted to the fifth edition of the *Logique*, published five years earlier. It would appear then that the initial conception of the *Rhétorique* (1675) was decisively shaped by the first appearance in the 1660s of the *Grammaire* and *Logique*, and that when Arnauld and Nicole radically revised their work in 1683 by including extended treatment of the sign for the first time, Bernard Lamy then followed suit in 1688 with a major overhaul of his renamed *Rhétorique*. He adds nothing of significance to what Arnauld and his collaborators had already said; on the contrary, his discussion of the sign is derivative and, compared with his source, simplistic. But because his work was less theoretically sophisticated than that of his Port-Royal predecessors, it was accessible to a wider and different audience; it may also, because of its long-standing popularity with the public, provide us with a more accurate insight into generally received opinion about poetic language. The *Rhétorique*, constantly reprinted throughout the final quarter of the seventeenth century and well into the eighteenth, had no serious rival as a guide to the classical *art de parler*, and it must have played an appreciable role in publicising and popularising the new semantic theory of the Port-Royal.

In the period between 1660 (the *Grammaire*) and 1683 (the fifth edition of the *Logique*)—precisely the period which literary historians have traditionally described as the high-water mark of classicism—there was thus a sudden and extraordinary rebirth of scholarly interest in the nature of the linguistic sign. This new preoccupation of logicians and grammarians has a decisive influence on successive editions of Lamy's *Rhétorique* and make it a very different work from any of the French rhetorics published earlier in the century; and this in turn prompts us to speculate about the possible wider literary repercussions of the Port-Royal's semantic theory.

This semantic theory, with its rediscovered emphasis on the notion of word as sign, radically realigns the seventeenth century's understanding of what language is. The very concept of the sign presupposes an awareness that discourse is an essentially separate entity from the reality to which it is understood to refer, an awareness that there exists, very crudely, a 'gap' between *res* and *verba*, between things and words. Indeed it must be a defining characteristic of the sign that it is different from the object which it designates, as the authors of the *Logique* had seen: 'Tout signe demande une distinction entre la chose représentante et celle qui est représentée' (53). But this idea is anticipated by Descartes, in an extraordinary passage of *La Dioptrique* in which he explores the apparent paradox that the perfection of a sign depends on its not resembling too well the object which it represents (and it is interesting to find him using the word *signe* in advance of the Port-Royal authors, even though he does not apply the term specifically to language):

> Nous devons considérer qu'il y a plusieurs autres choses que des images, qui peuvent exciter notre pensée; comme, par exemple, les signes et les paroles, qui ne ressemblent en aucune façon aux choses qu'elles signifient [...]. Il faut au moins que nous remarquions qu'il n'y a aucunes images qui doivent en tout ressembler aux objets qu'elles représentent: car autrement il n'y aurait point de distinction entre l'objet et son image: mais qu'il suffit qu'elles leur ressemblent en peu de choses: et souvent même, que leur perfection dépend de ce qu'elles ne leur ressemblent pas tant qu'elles pourraient faire. (I:684-85)

Descartes thus anticipates, by implication at least, the dislocation that was about to occur between language and the world.[14]

It would be no exaggeration to describe the re-emergence of sign theory as the single most critical development in seventeenth-century linguistics. 'La théorie du signe linguistique joue en effet,' says Donzé, 'aussi bien dans la *Grammaire* que dans la *Logique*, un rôle dont l'importance semble avoir échappé aux historiens qui se sont occupés de ces deux ouvrages' (48). The point is worth emphasising, if only because its importance is so easily underestimated.[15] Such a sea change in the general understanding of language has important repercussions for poetic theory.

II. MISTRUST OF METAPHOR

The classical preoccupation with clarity is a familiar, but none the less odd, phenomenon.[16] Rapin's voice is typical: 'La diction doit estre claire pour estre intelligible: car un des plus grands défauts du discours est l'obscurité.'[17] The rhetorician Bernard Lamy is equally opposed to the slightest obscurity which might tax the reader's ingenuity: 'On dit qu'un stile est doux lorsque les choses y sont dites avec tant de clarté, que l'esprit ne fait aucun effort pour les concevoir.'[18] Such views are a culmination of a movement which had begun early in the century when 'enfin Malherbe vint';[19] Pierre de Deimier, a contemporary of Malherbe, is unyielding in his attack on poetic obscurity:

> L'obscurité est un des plus grands vices qui se treuvent en la Poësie
> […]. C'est pourquoy d'escrire obscurement, et de ne vouloir pas
> estre entendu c'est une mesme chose: Et voire, je diray qu'à bon
> droict c'est mieux faire de n'escrire point, que d'escrire
> expressement avec des termes obscurs pour detenir cachees en
> tenebres les raisons et l'intelligence de ce que l'on escrit. Il vaudroit
> donc mieux ne rien faire, que d'escrire ainsi parmy les nuages de
> l'obscurité: Car un subject discouru de la sorte ne faict qu'amuser
> vainement le temps et la patience des lecteurs.[20]

This is uncompromising, but in the first half of the century there was some opposition to Malherbe's views on metaphor, from Mlle de Gournay, for example, or from Théophile de Viau: 'Malherbe a tres bien fait, mais il a fait pour luy'.[21] The highly metaphorical baroque prose style reached a climax in France with such authors as Nervèze and Des Escuteaux during the first two decades of the seventeenth century, when Malherbe and Deimier were just beginning to propagate their new ideas. Thereafter the ornate style came increasingly under attack, for example from such authors as Sorel and Tallemant des Réaux, and *parler Nervèze* became in time a term of abuse. In Furetière's *Nouvelle allégorique* (1658), *la Princesse Rhétorique*, aided by her prime minister *Bon Sens*, confronts a battalion of metaphors and—ironically enough—allegories under the prolix command of Nervèze and Des Escuteaux (7,16); the use here of such terms as 'raison' and 'bon sens' is revealingly eloquent of the rationalism underlying the shift to greater simplicity and a less figurative style. This tendency grew ever more prominent as the century advanced and as one norm of simplicity was progressively outstripped by another, so that Guez de Balzac, who must have seemed almost austere to his earliest readers, came in his turn to be deemed overly ornate for the more sensitive palates of the 1670s.

The possible impact of cartesian philosophy on literary thinking has long been the subject of widespread, and often confusing debate. Emile Krantz was perhaps the first (in 1882) to argue extensively the thesis that Descartes, though not himself having written on aesthetics, was none the less the effective originator of the 'classical aesthetic'. In a famous article of 1896, on the other hand, Gustave Lanson denies the existence of any aesthetic system in Descartes's thought and asserts that the philosopher exercised no significant influence on subsequent literature. In this context, it is useful to bear in mind the distinction which C. Beyer makes (1943) between Descartes's own doctrines and an 'esprit cartésien'. It would clearly be a gross overstatement to suggest that Descartes's thought gives definitive shape to the poetic theory of his century; but it seems equally implausible to believe that the Cartesian preoccupation with clear and distinct ideas can be entirely separated from the speculations of the poetic theorists. (This leaves open the question of direct influence: the two currents of thought may have developed in parallel from similar origins.) The attack on ornament does not originate with cartesianism—Deimier predates Descartes—but it may well have been reinforced by it. At the beginning of the third *Méditation*, Descartes asserts uncompromisingly that clarity is a criterion for the establishment of truth: 'Je puis établir pour règle générale que toutes les choses que nous concevons fort clairement et fort distinctement, sont toutes vraies' (II, 431). From here the jump is not great to the statement which we find in Bernard Lamy's *Rhétorique* that clarity is 'le caractère de la verité' (441).

III. MISTRUST OF POETRY AND RHETORIC

It is not altogether surprising, then, that a movement which had begun at the beginning of the century as an attempt to prune poetry of its worst excesses should have ended up questioning the very status of poetry. The various aspects of this onslaught on poetry and rhetoric (the two cannot be distinguished, since at the heart of the movement is a discussion about metaphor) have been described elsewhere.[22] The debates of this period concerning the nature of poetry can best be exemplified through a comparison of two works published at a distance of ten years.

Guillaume Colletet, a founder member of the Académie française, writes in his 'Discours de la poésie morale et sententieuse' (1658) that poetry, because it is divinely inspired, serves to divert our attention from ourselves and thereby bring us closer to God:

> Il n'y a point d'homme, pour peu qu'il ait utilement feüilleté les
> bons livres, qui ne sçache que la veritable Poësie est un don du
> Ciel, qu'il ne communique pas indifferement à tous ses Sacrez
> Mysteres; [...] en un mot qu'il faut se separer de soy-mesme,
> s'eslever au dessus de sa propre nature, et n'avoir pour objet que

celuy dont nous sommes la vivante Image. C'estoit à peu pres la
pensée de ce grand Oracle du dernier siecle, Pierre de Ronsard.
(17-18)

Evidently Colletet does not feel the need in 1658 to defend poetry; on the contrary, he
assumes confidently that his view is generally shared ('il n'y a point d'homme [...]
qui ne sçache'), and it is especially interesting that he should invoke the authority of a
poet of the Renaissance to support this (essentially Renaissance) justification of po-
etry on moral grounds.

Certainly Colletet shares more common ground with the Pléiade than with Ber-
nard Lamy, who only ten years later was to publish a devastating attack on poetry
which denies categorically Colletet's central thesis. The title of the opening chapter of
Lamy's *Nouvelles Réflexions sur l'art poétique* (1668) is eloquent enough: 'La Poësie
est une peinture parlante de ce qu'il y a de plus beau dans les Creatures; elle fait
oublier Dieu, dont ces Creatures sont l'image.' For Colletet it had been the prime
purpose of poetry to release men from the confines of their own natures, to uplift them
and so bring them closer to their Creator: poetry, in this view, is a liberating force. For
Bernard Lamy, however, poetry ensnares and enslaves us. It appeals through the art-
ful use of language to our baser instincts, to our hearts over our heads, to emotion over
reason. The allure of poetic imagery thus entices fallen man away from contempla-
tion of God's creation, and 'les hommes charnels' fail to comprehend that the beauties
that they admire in their fellow creatures are but feeble reflections of the beauties of
the Almighty. The devices and conceits of poetry are false beauties which serve only
to sustain men in their error: 'Nous sommes à peu prés comme un amant passionné,
qui se cache les defauts de la personne qu'il aime, et qui s'attache aux ornemens
qu'elle emprunte de l'art pour la trouver plus aimable' (14-15). (Lamy's own use and
choice of imagery is of course pleasingly problematic.)

Accusations of immorality had long been levelled at the theatre, but these too
acquire a new vehemence in the second half of the century with the attacks of Nicole
and Bossuet.[23] Rhetoric was open to attack on precisely the same grounds of immo-
rality as poetry and theatre. Gradually all imaginative literature became vulnerable to
the charge of immorality, a process which would culminate in the poetic theory of the
Moderns. In *De la recherche de la vérité*, published in the same year as the *Traité du
sublime*, Malebranche mounts a swingeing attack on 'la force de l'imagination' of
certain authors, including notably Montaigne, whose eloquence is painted as distinctly
sinister:

Ce n'est point en convainquant la raison qu'il se fait admirer de
tant de gens, mais en leur tournant l'esprit à son avantage par la
vivacité toujours victorieuse de son imagination dominante. (284)

The abbé d'Aubignac eulogises the powers of rhetoric in his *Discours
académique sur l'éloquence* (1668), and speaks of the orator as a Hercules, dragging
his audience in his wake by the strength of the chains attached to his tongue: the

image is entirely conventional—and for d'Aubignac evidently unproblematic—but it was soon to become contaminated. Debate about the nature and moral status of rhetoric, and of literature more generally, will figure as an important element of the *Querelle* between Ancients and Moderns.

IV. MISTRUST OF LANGUAGE

Daniel Mornet's *Histoire de la clarté française* chronicles the inexorable rise of the classical literary language as an unrivalled and unproblematic instrument of communication. His ideological assumptions are not unexpected—he is a pupil of Lanson—but they have proved surprisingly durable. 'Le langage classique se fait invisible ou presque. Il est en tout cas devenu si transparent à la représentation que son être cesse de faire problème […]. A la limite, on pourrait dire que le langage classique n'existe pas. Mais qu'il fonctionne':[24] not all literary critics have agreed with the view, reiterated here by Foucault, that classical authors regarded language as entirely unproblematic. Odette de Mourgues, for example, remarks on the 'semantic instability' of the vocabulary of such authors as La Rochefoucauld and Pascal; and Peter Bayley speaks of an underlying preoccupation with what he calls 'a poverty of language' in La Rochefoucauld's *maximes*.[25] If the *Maximes* flirt with the idea of linguistic duplicity and ambiguity, this theme is explored with much greater profundity, Bayley suggests, in *La Princesse de Clèves*, and he concludes:

> If there is a crisis of language at this period, and if these writers turn it into the substance of their enterprise, that meditation on language reinforces—at the same time as it expresses—the bafflement, blockage, powerlessness that we discern generally in French classicism.[26]

There is evidence, too, already in the seventeenth century, of a preoccupation with language's representative function. For example, it is in this period that the first projects for a system of universal writing begin to emerge, starting in 1627 with Jean Douet's *Proposition présentée au roy, d'une escriture universelle, admirable pour ses effects tres-utile et nécessaire à tous les hommes de la terre*. In the first place, the idea of a universal language was attractive because it promised to provide an alternative means of international communication at a time when Latin was declining in prestige (Descartes was the first major French philosopher not to write exclusively in Latin); and it was further argued that a universal language would be easier to learn, more harmonious even, than existing languages. There was, however, a second factor which greatly stimulated interest in universal language schemes in the later part of the century: this was the hope evinced by certain scholars that a 'scientific' language might be constructed in such a way that it would be more directly representative of the natural world, thereby avoiding the obscurities of existing languages.[27] The universal languages of the seventeenth century were conceived of as scientific taxonomies, in which each object is analysed into its component parts, each of which is then accorded a distinguishing term or mark. The growth of universal languages in the seventeenth century was a rational response to the perceived inadequacies of the natural languages, inadequacies brought about by 'the information explosion (including science) experienced in the Renaissance', and secondly by advances in printing and literacy which made possible 'the collection and transmission of vast amounts of information'.[28] Hence the need to develop a more 'scientific' language:

> The requirements of logic and of science are such that terms must be unequivocable. In the seventeenth century, however, it was generally felt that natural language was not isomorphic with nature or reality—that words and things did not properly match—an attitude which is not surprising in the multi-cultural, multi-lingual context of Renaissance humanism.[29]

In the course of the seventeenth century, however, as aristotelian essentialism came to be questioned, the taxonomies came to be seen as representations of ideas in our minds, but not necessarily as representations of nature. 'The isomorphic relation between language and nature, once considered ideal and attainable, is more or less impossible';[30] and so the interest in universal languages declined.

In 1629 Mersenne sent to Descartes a prospectus by an unidentified author for a universal language scheme, to which Descartes replied with a critique of the project. What is needed instead, he suggests at the end of his letter, is a universal language based on more strictly philosophical criteria. For this, it would be necessary to find a means of distinguishing and classifying ideas to make them clear and simple ('claires et simples'—the essentialist model is evident here), for only then, he says, would a scientifically-based language be feasible:

> J'oserais espérer ensuite une langue universelle, fort aise à apprendre, à prononcer et à écrire, et ce qui est le principal, qui aiderait au jugement, lui représentant si distinctement toutes choses, qu'il lui serait presque impossible de se tromper; au lieu que, tout au rebours, les mots que nous avons n'ont quasi que des significations confuses, auxquelles l'esprit des hommes s'étant accoutumé de longue main, cela est cause qu'il n'entend presque rien parfaitement. Or je tiens que cette langue est possible, et qu'on peut trouver la Science de qui elle dépend, par le moyen de laquelle les paysans pourraient mieux juger la vérité des choses, que ne font maintenant les philosophes. Mais n'espérez pas de la voir jamais en usage; cela présuppose de grands changements en l'ordre des choses, et il faudrait que tout le Monde ne fût qu'un paradis terrestre, ce qui n'est bon à proposer que dans le pays des romans. (I:231-32)

Already in the *Regulae* (c.1628), Descartes had spoken of the obscurity of expression which impedes philosophical thought;[31] here he goes further and declares that the understanding of most men is blunted because so few words possess precise meanings, and he evokes the admittedly impossible ideal of a perfectly transparent language which reflected reality so precisely that it would be impossible to fall into error.

Descartes returns to this question in the *Principia philosophiae* (1644; French trans. by abbé Picot, 1647), where he describes language as one of the causes of error. Men are obliged to attach their ideas to certain words in order to be able to express them, he argues, and so it is the words they remember rather than the things ('choses'). It is almost impossible for us to conceive clearly of an object apart from the word used to designate it:

> Ainsi tous les hommes donnent leur attention aux paroles plûtot qu'aux choses; ce qui est cause qu'ils donnent bien souvent leur consentement à des termes qu'ils n'entendent point, et qu'ils ne se soucient pas beaucoup d'entendre, ou parce qu'ils croient les avoir entendus autrefois, ou parce qu'il leur a semblé que ceux qui les leur ont enseigné en connaissent la signification, et qu'ils l'ont apprise par même moyen.[32]

The suggestion here is that it would be preferable to be able to communicate thoughts directly, and that the recourse to language is considered a regrettable necessity. As it is, we are obliged to use words to designate our thoughts, even though these words end up dominating the thoughts they supposedly represent. But if Descartes states that men employ terms which, 'bien souvent', they do not understand, he at least leaves a loop-hole: it is presumably possible for the conscientious philosopher to weigh his words more carefully and so try to avoid the obscurities into which most men fall. Little attention has been paid to Descartes's views on the philosophical problems posed by the question of linguistic clarity; and although over the years Descartes's reflections on the nature of language and communication grow more detailed as they come to be based on a theory of speech, the principal contention that language is an imperfect vehicle of expression remains.

Descartes's views on language were not without influence. The suggestion put forward in the *Principia* that words come to dominate the ideas they are supposed to represent and so lead to obscurity is taken up by Arnauld and Nicole in the *Logique*:

> Nous avons déja dit que la necessité que nous avons d'user de signes exterieurs pour nous faire entendre, fait que nous attachons tellement nos idées aux mots, que souvent nous considerons plus les mots que les choses. Or c'est une des causes les plus ordinaires de la confusion de nos pensées et de nos discours. (83)

The argument, highly reminiscent of Descartes, is here expanded more fully as the authors go on to discuss the ambiguities of such terms as 'vertu', 'âme', 'sens', and 'sentiment'. Like Descartes, too, they recommend that the best means of surmounting this confusion is to define terms with care as they occur (86-90).

If we turn to the other cartesian thinkers of the 1660s, we find interest in the idea that eloquence has purely physical causes. Louis de la Forge, for example, argues in his *Traité de l'esprit de l'homme* (1666) that if we wish to express ourselves clearly, we must first discern with precision the subject of our speech:

> La netteté est la meilleure et la plus avantageuse de toutes les qualitez de l'Imagination; Et il n'y en a point qui contribuë tant au raisonnement et l'éloquence: Car quoy que nous ayons l'avantage d'avoir la conception prompte, nous ne saurions pourtant jamais, ny nous bien exprimer, ny bien raisonner, si nous ne concevons nettement les choses dont nous voulons discourir. Cette qualité fait les Orateurs, quand elle se rencontre avec la promptitude, comme elle fait les Savans, quand elle se trouve avec la force. (270)

La Forge does not discuss here the nature of language as such, but the very fact that he insists on the need to distinguish clearly the object of discourse in order to be able to express oneself adequately suggests that the role of language is not to be taken for granted. These ideas are further developed by Gerauld de Cordemoy in his *Discours physique de la parole* (1668). He likewise insists that eloquence has a purely physical basis:

> Je reconnois que la peine, que quelques-uns ont à concevoir, ou à s'expliquer, n'est pas un défaut de l'Ame; et que cette merveilleuse facilité qu'ont d'autres à s'exprimer, ne vient que d'une heureuse disposition du cerveau, et de toutes les parties, qui servent à la voix ou aux mouvemens du corps. (198)

La Forge had earlier emphasised the need for *netteté* in establishing the object of our speech, where *netteté* had been conceived of as a quality of the imagination. Cordemoy, however, is concerned rather to catalogue the ways in which eloquence is dependent on certain physical predispositions in the speaker: the ability to discern precisely what must be presented to one's audience; the ability to arrange one's material in the clearest and most natural order; the ability to find the precise word ('trouver aisément le mot, par lequel chaque chose est proprement signifiée dans la langue dont on se sert')—all these are attributed not to intelligence but to purely physical factors (242). Cordemoy remarks upon the disparity between the immaterial nature of thought, and the material vehicle through which it finds expression: it is clear here that the Cartesian dualism of body and soul is underpinning the inadequacy of language. Cordemoy states explicitly what Descartes had already implied, that the recourse to signs in the communication of thought is a regrettable necessity:

> Nos esprits mêmes auroient entr'eux une communication plus aidée, si l'étroite union qu'ils ont avec le corps, ne les obligeoit indispensablement à se servir de signes. Le même raisonnement

me fait aussi connoître que la peine, que nous avons dans les
entretiens, n'est pas de concevoir la pensée de ceux qui nous parlent,
mais de la démêler des signes, dont ils se servent pour l'exprimer,
qui souvent ne luy conviennent pas. (199)

In *De la recherche de la vérité* (1674-75), Malebranche sets out in the first five books to analyse the sources of human error, before describing in the final book the most effective method for establishing truth. Although there is no particular section devoted to problems of language, Malebranche does touch on the subject in several chapters. Like Descartes before him, he appreciates that the precise definition of terms is an essential prerequisite to a lucid philosophical discussion; but he goes further than Descartes in his analysis of the causes of 'l'équivoque des termes', arguing that we can never precisely define such concepts as pleasure or pain since all men experience these things differently, and that therefore many words are inevitably ambiguous.[33] Malebranche's arguments are full of interesting perceptions about the nature of language: as, for example, his remark that obscurity of vocabulary stems in part from the fact that we are obliged to employ terms condoned by usage, terms which do not necessarily correspond exactly to our individual feelings and emotions (II:223).

If Malebranche did not address himself primarily to the issue of language, a Jesuit contemporary, le Père Besnier, wrote a short book entirely devoted to the question of why human languages differ one from another. The central claim of *La Réunion des langues, ou l'art de les apprendre toutes par une seule* (1674) is that all human languages are linked together and that all are based on human reason. In seeking to explain why differences exist between languages, Besnier, referring to 'la Philosophie nouvelle', employs many familiar cartesian arguments. He argues, for example, that since words are the reflections of thoughts, and that since each nation conceives of objects in a slightly different way, words will acquire particular meanings in each language; words, like plants, cannot be exported (35, 39). The study of the origin of ideas shows that there are few objects of which we can have precise conceptions: 'C'est par là que je feray connoistre, qui sont les objets dont nous avons des idées propres, et combien il y en a peu' (36). For most of the time we are obliged to communicate through 'des images étrangères', or figurative speech, because there is no exact term at our disposal. Besnier does not discuss explicitly the shortcomings of language, but it is all the more revealing that there is, underlying many of his comments, the assumption that speech does not very often convey wholly the ideas which we wish to express.

A very minor author in comparison with some of the others considered here, Besnier none the less illustrates the extent to which Cartesian thinking had by the 1670s permeated received views about the nature of language. We have seen how a whole series of writers—Arnauld and Nicole, La Forge, Cordemoy, Malebranche, and Besnier—take up and discuss ideas which we first located in the writings of Descartes, and it seems legitimate to speak of a cartesian tradition of debate about language's representative function. Descartes regards language as a potential source of error, and at the beginning of the second *Méditation*, he considers the possibility of a 'malin génie' which wilfully deceives and deprives us of all certainty (II:417-20); this hypothesis is dismissed, however, and nothing ultimately can undermine Descartes's faith in the notion of clear and distinct ideas. Not all his contemporaries were quite so sanguine, though. Gassendi, for example, wonders about how precisely one is able to recognise clear and distinct ideas:

> Mais remarquez cependant que la difficulté n'est pas de savoir si l'on doit concevoir les choses clairement et distinctement pour ne se point tromper, mais bien de savoir comment et par quelle méthode on peut reconnaître qu'on a une intelligence si claire et si distincte, qu'on soit assuré qu'elle est vraie, et qu'il ne soit pas possible que nous nous trompions. ('Cinquièmes Objections, contre la Quatrième Méditation', in Descartes, II:756)

By 1674, which saw the publication of *De la recherche de la vérité* and of *La Réunion des langues*—and, of course, of the *Traité du sublime*—, Malebranche and Besnier are both going beyond simply saying that language can be a possible source of error (which had been Descartes's position), and are arguing that many or even most words are inevitably ambiguous, and that language is thus inherently and ineluctably imprecise. The cartesian tradition of debate about language evidently acquires an increasingly sceptical tone in the second half of the century. When Odette de Mourgues remarks in passing on 'l'instabilité sémantique' of certain texts in the classical canon, she is alluding to a phenomenon which was entirely familiar to writers of the time, and a phenomenon whose roots run deep into contemporary concern about the relationship of thought to language.

It has been widely assumed that Enlightenment speculation concerning the inadequacies of language derives uniquely from Locke's *Essay* (1690, French trans. 1700). François Lamy, for example, in the heat of the *Querelle*, invokes the authority of Locke in his attack on rhetoric: 'Mais enfin c'est M. Loke Anglois, qui a eu soin de dire que la Rhétorique est un puissant instrument d'erreurs et de fourberies'.[34] In the same way Condillac, in his *Essai sur l'origine des connaissances humaines*, later describes Locke as a pioneer: 'Les mots sont l'objet du troisième [Livre],' he writes, 'et [Locke] me paraît le premier qui ait écrit sur cette matière en vrai philosophe' (103). If we examine Locke's arguments, however, it becomes evident that there are many parallels with the cartesian tradition. The following is a typical instance of Locke's style of argument in the *Essay*:

> Besides the Imperfection that is naturally in Language, and the obscurity and confusion that is so hard to be avoided in the Use of Words, there are several *wilful* Faults and Neglects, which Men are guilty of, in this way of Communication, whereby they render these signs less clear and distinct in their signification, than naturally they need to be. (490 (III, 10, 1))

The idea that language is inherently imperfect, as well as the implication that the remedy to this situation is to be sought with the users of the language, are already familiar arguments from Descartes; even the vocabulary ('clear and distinct') has cartesian overtones. Of course, the discussion of language occupies a much more prominent position in Locke than in any of his French contemporaries, and the reasons motivating the discussion of language are different: at least some of the Cartesians come to discuss language as an example of the dichotomy between spirit and matter, whereas Locke's reasons are rather those of the empiricist who needs to clear the ground by defining his terms at the outset of an argument.

Perhaps the importance of Locke in this debate is not so much that he initiated discussion of language in France, but rather that he helped reinforce a current of thought which was already established. When Helvétius considers in his turn the problem of the abuse of words, he begins by praising Locke's treatment of the topic, but then goes on to remark that Descartes anticipated Locke in his criticism of the Peripatetic philosophers who cloaked their thoughts in obscurity:

> D'après Descartes et Locke, je vais donc prouver qu'en métaphysique et en morale, l'abus des mots et l'ignorance de leur vraie signification est, si j'ose le dire, un labyrinthe où les plus grands génies se sont quelquefois égarés. (*De l'esprit*, 42 (I: 4))

Helvétius, at least, is conscious of the common ground which they share in their concern about language's referential function.

Culler, strengthening an idea put more tentatively by Foucault, asserts that there is greater confidence in the representative function of language among French classical writers than among their English contemporaries.[35] Closer study of the cartesian debate about language, however, shows this interpretation to be untenable. There exists widespread doubt, at least among French philosophers, about the capacity of language to imitate reality adequately. Yet, as Culler rightly points out, La Rochefoucauld himself does not explicitly discuss language as a source of error. So to what extent did philosophical discussion in France about the inadequacies of language have any impact on the theory or practice of writing? To help answer this question it is necessary to turn to the grammarians and rhetoricians of the period.

Writing in the mid-century, Vaugelas draws a clear distinction between 'pureté' and 'netteté', the former being concerned with vocabulary and syntax and grounded often on social criteria, and the latter concerned with the arrangement of words and 'tout ce qui contribuë à la clarté de l'expression' (*Remarques*, 567). 'Pureté' is thus the term used to describe polite or correct usage, and 'netteté' to describe language which successfully communicates the writer's thoughts. These are considered as two quite separate qualities of language, so that a writer might in theory possess one without the other. However, whereas the number of those who possess 'netteté' without 'pureté' is, he says, 'almost infinite', there are very few indeed in the opposite position of possessing 'pureté' without 'netteté'. In other words, Vaugelas considers it rare for a writer to be unable to express adequately his thoughts: language itself is not generally problematic. On the other hand it is all too frequent to find an author who expresses himself clearly but 'incorrectly', hence the prescriptive bias of Vaugelas's work, with its constant emphasis on 'Usage' (578).

Among writers on linguistic matters in the following, classical generation, Bouhours was one of the most admired and most influential, and he has often been considered a disciple of Vaugelas. The *Entretiens d'Ariste et d'Eugène* (1671) contain a description of the qualities required in poetic language: 'facilité', 'une extréme pureté' on the one hand, and on the other 'une grande exactitude', 'des paroles [...] pleines de sens' (91). It is evident that 'pureté' is not being used here to describe a linguistic-social norm, the sense in which Vaugelas had employed the term; for Bouhours 'pureté' is more a synonym for 'simplicité' or 'naïveté'. Furthermore Bouhours freely admits that 'pureté' and 'précision' are qualities which are very difficult to combine, so that his whole approach to literary language differs fundamentally from that of Vaugelas; it is doubtful, indeed, whether Vaugelas would even have understood the sense of Bouhours's demand for 'des paroles pleines de sens'. The representational function of language is no longer assumed by Bouhours as it had been by Vaugelas.

Further evidence of shifting attitudes can be found in Lamy's *Rhétorique*. In a chapter devoted to the question of 'netteté', Lamy cites several of the arguments and examples of Vaugelas's own article on the same topic; then he takes another of his examples, but this time in support of a wholly new argument, namely that clarity is impeded by an accumulation of superfluous words:

> Le second vice contre la netteté est un embarras de paroles superfluës. On ne conçoit jamais nettement une vérité que l'on n'ait fait le discernement de ce qu'elle est d'avec ce qu'elle n'est pas, et qu'on ne s'en soit formé une idée nette qui se peut exprimer en peu de paroles [...]. Pour dire les choses nettement, il faut retrancher les paroles qui ne servent de rien et mener droit à la verité celui qu'on insère.[36]

Added to the third edition (1688), this passage shows distinct parallels with the ideas of Bouhours. The emphasis here on the need for the writer to trim his vocabulary, after meticulously delimiting the thought to be expressed, carries us far beyond the scope of Vaugelas's *Remarques*. These are comments which Lamy chose to add in 1688 to a text which he had originally published in 1675; again, we infer that the role of language in the expression of thought is being regarded with ever-increasing caution and suspicion.

Du Plaisir, also writing in the 1680s, states conventionally enough: 'Il me semble que rien n'est plus facile ni plus commun que de bien parler ou de bien écrire', but this seeming complacency towards the role of language is brusquely undercut in the next paragraph: 'Il me paraît même impossible d'écrire avec une entire exactitude. Souvent on manque d'adresse et plus souvent encore la vivacité de l'imagination' (71): hardly an argument which Vaugelas would have used.

As to how readers in this period reacted, we can only speculate. Mme de Grignan remarks in a letter to her mother, Mme de Sévigné, that she has difficulty making sense of one of La Rochefoucauld's maxims (Mme de Sévigné, I:435-36). A contemporary of Pascal's says that his view of 'l'éloquence' is that 'elle consiste donc dans une correspondance qu'on tâche d'établir entre l'esprit et le cœur de ceux à qui l'on parle d'un côté, et de l'autre les pensées et les expressions dont on se sert'[37] —there is no taking language for granted here either.

Among cartesian thinkers in the seventeenth century there persisted a deep concern about the ability of language to communicate thought adequately, and this concern seems if anything to grow more insistent after 1660. It is in this same period, that of the 'classical generation', moreover, that this current of thought surfaces in the writings of grammarians and rhetoricians: Bouhours, Bernard Lamy and Du Plaisir all focus on very different concerns from Vaugelas. Thus the movement which had begun as a reaction against poetic ornament and had then turned against poetry more broadly, extended finally into an attack on the very medium of communication: language itself. The classical rallying-cry of linguistic clarity comes to sound less and less like an exclamation of confidence and rather more like an expression of dismayed scepticism.

v. PROBLEMS OF MIMESIS

We have noted the emergence of the idea of the word as sign and the consequential growing mistrust in some quarters of poetry and rhetoric, and even of language. At the heart of these developments is a concern with the ever-problematic notion of imitation. The Horatian tag *ut pictura poesis* is repeated endlessly by critics of the period, and there is an understandably wearied note to Bernard Lamy's laconic lament in his *Nouvelles Réflexions* that 'dire que la poésie est une peinture parlante, n'est pas une nouvelle remarque' (1). The ubiquity of the concept did not mean, however, that it was perceived as unproblematic or uncontroversial.

Literary imitation in seventeenth-century France has customarily been divided into *imitation de la nature* and *imitation des anciens*, and Bray, for example, deals with these topics in two separate chapters. The notion that a writer could only fully assimilate his craft through selective imitation of certain models was of course not new: discussion of this question is found already in the rhetorical theory of classical antiquity and Longinus, for instance, recommends imitation of earlier writers as one means of achieving sublimity (*OS*, 475-76). The question of *imitatio* was much discussed during the Renaissance (see Cave, 35-77), but early in the seventeenth century a number of poets speak out strongly against servile imitation. Théophile de Viau, in his *Elégie à une dame*, declares his independence of the thousand poetasters who want to skin Malherbe alive (I:349): 'J'approuve que chacun escrive à sa façon.' Saint-Amant, in his *Avertissement* of 1629, claims that if he reads the work of others, it is only to *avoid* imitating them (I, 23). Deimier, in 1610, had ranked *imitation* below *invention* (209, 213); but in 1636, a rather different view is expressed by Guillaume Colletet when he read to the newly-formed Académie his 'Discours de l'éloquence, et de l'imitation des Anciens', in which he argues that imitation forms the mind, and is an author's best means of acquiring *gloire*; he opposes servile imitation, favouring the more liberal imitation of different writers' ideas without copying the style of any one individual. La Bruyère, a generation later, expresses similar sentiments more concisely: 'On ne saurait en écrivant rencontrer le parfait, et s'il se peut, surpasser les anciens que par leur imitation' (70). Belief in the importance of imitating the Ancients is asserted with even greater confidence and urgency in the second half of the century, when indeed it becomes an essential component of the definition of classicism.

The idea of literature as an imitation of nature equally gains wider currency as the century progresses. Burlesque authors had seemed more preoccupied with the imitation of other texts than with the imitation of nature, and again, it is Colletet's 'Discours de l'éloquence' which forcefully expounds the new orthodoxy:

> Qu'est-ce que le Poëme Epique, sinon une parfaite imitation des
> actions genereuses des grands Heros? La Comedie, qu'un miroir
> des mœurs du temps, qu'une image de la verité, et en un mot qu'une
> belle et excellente imitation de la vie? (18)

Although the notion of literature as an imitation of nature has its source in classical theory, Renaissance theorists like Sébillet or Du Bellay did not define poetry in these terms. It is only with Ronsard that we approach the Aristotelian notion of mimesis according to which the poet, by supplementing and improving his models, is able to pass beyond individual facts to the higher plane of generalities.[38] The Platonic view of mimesis had considered literature as a reflection of the world of the senses, which in turn was a reflection of the world of ideal forms; the corollary of this view was that literature, which found itself at the second remove from truth, was thought to depreciate its model—unlike the aristotelian understanding of mimesis, which saw literature as transcending an original model.[39]

One or two seventeenth-century theorists try optimistically to argue that imitation of nature should ideally be exact—whatever that means. Chapelain, for example, writes in his 'Lettre sur la règle des vingt-quatre heures' (1630): 'Je pose donc pour fondement, que l'imitation en tous poèmes doit être si parfaite qu'il ne paraisse aucune différence entre la chose imitée et celle qui imite' (115). Such a view is clearly problematic, and later theorists more typically argue that the poet must be selective in imitating only what is beautiful in nature; and to the extent that he thereby improves upon his model, this approach may be said to recall, albeit in a cruder version, the aristotelian notion of imitation. Le Moyne's view in his 'Discours de la poésie' (1641) is characteristic:

> Il faut que [le Poëte] corrige les defauts de la Nature, et qu'il acheve
> ce qu'elle n'a fait qu'ébaucher [...]; et que d'une Matiere commune
> et surannée, il tire des formes precieuses et nouvelles. (20)

Bray quotes this last view—we shall return to it below—as a satisfactory and coherent explanation of how classical writers understood and practised imitation (158). He concludes, tendentiously, by suggesting that the superiority of classicism over Renaissance humanism and 'l'idolâtrie grécomane de Ronsard' derives from its freer use of imitation (170), and by arguing that the principle of imitation is 'le ferment vital' of classicism because of the way in which it helped protect poetic beauty against the spirit of cartesian rationalism (190).

No one would dispute Bray's assertion of the centrality of the principle of imitation in classical poetics; but his analysis is inadequate because it fails to take account of the extent to which mimesis was perceived as a problematic concept—perhaps an increasingly problematic concept—for the theorists of classicism. Bray's conventional division between imitation of nature and imitation of the Ancients is not self-evident: on closer examination it seems that authors of the period do not themselves always make this distinction, and the 'nature' which they chose to imitate was often similar to the nature which the Ancients had opted to imitate. It is useful, on the other hand, to distinguish between an interest in the object of imitation, and an interest in the process of imitation. When Colletet in his 'Discours [...] de l'imitation des Anciens' comments that 'toutes les choses du Monde agissent par exemple et par imitation' (11), he seems to be envisaging mimesis not just as some kind of literary quality-control but as a metaphysical principle. We shall single out here three areas of discussion—art theory, platonist (or platonising) theories of imitation, and linguistic theory—where the discussion of mimesis is especially relevant to poetic theory.

Even for classical authors, imitation of the ancients was never quite as simple as they liked to pretend. La Bruyère 'imitates' Theophrastus, though his *Caractères* are really rather different from their Greek prototypes, as are the fables of La Fontaine, despite their author's ambivalent comments about his debt to Aesop (see Bray, 169). Racine uses the ancients (in the first preface of *Britannicus*) as a control to determine what it is permissible for him to write, yet we wonder to what extent this is simply a useful strategy rather than faithful imitation of classical practice. A translation might seem to be the simplest and least controversial form of imitation; but in the *Traité du sublime*, it often seems to be Boileau's voice that we hear behind Longinus's—again, a strategic use of imitation.

For the theorists of imitation, the process of copying nature is by no means as simple as Bray's summary implies; here is Rapin on the subject:

> La partie la plus importante et la plus nécessaire au poète pour réussir dans les grands sujets, est de sçavoir bien distinguer ce qu'il y a de beau et d'agréable dans la nature pour en faire des images. Car la poésie est un art où tout doit plaire. Ce n'est pas assez de s'attacher à la nature qui est rude et désagréable en certains endroits: il faut choisir ce qu'elle a de plus beau d'avec ce qui ne l'est pas: elle a des grâces cachées en des sujets qu'il faut découvrir. Quel discernement doit avoir le poète, pour faire ce choix et pour rebuter, sans s'y méprendre, l'objet qui ne plaira pas, et retenir celuy qui doit plaire? (*Réflexions sur la poétique*, 57)

Rapin's emphasis on the need for careful choice and discernment on the part of the poet, his admission that beauties are often hidden and need to be sought out, all this enhances the subjectivity and idiosyncrasy of the poet's imitation, and brings us a long way from Le Moyne's modest aim of 'correcting the faults of nature' quoted above.

Discussion of the way in which imitation operates is very often founded on the metaphor of painting, so it is hardly surprising that art theorists of this period discuss the concept of mimesis with fervour. 'On a beaucoup étudié la doctrine classique, sa formation et son rôle dans la littérature française,' writes Jacques Thuillier. 'Dans le domaine de l'art, qui méritait une étude parallèle, presque tout reste à faire.'[40] Predictably, perhaps, the problematic aspects of imitation theory emerge most clearly among art theorists. Contemporary poetic theorists were well acquainted with these discussions, yet the importance of the mutual influence of poetic and art theory in the classical period is still insufficiently recognised.

In the first half of the century, there had appeared a spate of French works concerned with optics and the problems of perspective (the most famous being Descartes's *Dioptrique*), and these had a decisive influence on discussions of how to achieve *vraisemblance* in the visual arts, in painting and in theatre design and theatre staging and décor. The discovery of the rules of perspective could be used, it was argued, to create the most compelling visual illusion.[41] However, the figure now considered the most important art theorist of the classical period, Roger de Piles (noted principally for his attempt to liberate painting from the vocabulary of literary criticism), explains illusion quite differently and thus marks a decisive shift away from the perspective-based aesthetic typical of the earlier years of the century. De Piles, writes Thomas Puttfarken, 'shares what seems to have been a fairly widely held view by the end of the seventeenth century, that geometrically correct perspective was not necessary to achieve pictorial illusion' (101).

The same dilemma surrounding the concept of imitation is also the object of a study by Thuillier, who discerns a tension between the ideal of *ars imitatio naturae* and what he terms the theory of *belles idées*—that is, one which valorises the personal contribution of the artist in magnifying his subject. These two approaches, though strictly incompatible, mostly coexist in pragmatic compromise, but Thuillier discusses three cases in which this underlying conflict surfaces. The engraver Bosse, for example, holds that, in the interests of the imitation of nature, the painter should observe the rules of optics in his use of perspective; but Le Brun, embarrassed by these rules, advocates a more flexible approach which relies on the painter's own instinct. Le Brun similarly defended Poussin's *Manne* from the criticism that it failed to reproduce literally the Biblical story by arguing that the painting is not history, but rather a commentary upon the event, and that the painter is entitled, within the limits of *vraisemblance*, to rearrange and reorganise his material as a dramatist recasts his within the framework of the three unities. Finally, Thuillier cites the example of the coloured wax sculptures of Antoine Benoist, which imitated nature in every detail and yet still did not escape the criticism that they lacked 'âme'. In every case in which the conflict between strict mimesis and *belles idées* breaks through the surface of compromise, the weight of critical opinion unfailingly favours the latter, and supports the right of the artist to shape his material, even at the expense of the ideal of imitation.

A different approach to this mercurial concept is provided by Roger Zuber ('La critique classique et l'idée d'imitation'). He pays due tribute to the work of Bray, but shows the shortcomings of his analysis of uniquely aristotelian-inspired imitation by pointing to a number of classical texts which imply a platonist understanding of mimesis. The following chapter will consider these ideas more closely; it will be sufficient here simply to consider Le Moyne's 'Discours de la poésie', which has already been quoted above, as abridged by Bray (151); here is the text as Le Moyne wrote it— the section omitted by Bray is italicised:

> Il faut que [le Poëte] corrige les defauts de la Nature, et qu'il acheve ce qu'elle n'a fait qu'ébaucher: *il faut qu'il se fasse luy-mesme un fonds d'Idées plus riches et plus belles que les siennes; il faut qu'il treuve des Estoiles où elle n'a mis que de l'obscurité; et* que d'une Matiere commune et surannée, il tire des formes precieuses et nouvelles. (20)

The full text reads rather differently from Bray's version of it: the suggestion that the poet metamorphoses nature's obscurity into stars, and the injunction to the poet to seek out 'Idées' richer and more beautiful than anything in nature, recall the ambivalences in the discussions of the art theorists and might be thought to imply a platonising view of imitation. They certainly do not imply any simple or unproblematic Aristotelian model of mimesis.

This deep-seated preoccupation with the concept of imitation also has important consequences for linguistic theory. Just as poetry is automatically conceived of as some form of imitation of nature, so the poetic word is automatically conceived of as the imitation of an object. In Molière's *Le Mariage forcé* (1664), Sganarelle sets out, like Panurge before him, to seek advice as to whether he should marry; he tries to ask Pancrace, a sage and 'docteur aristotélicien', who however seems more preoccupied with Sganarelle's linguistic than with his matrimonial intentions:

> La parole a été donnée à l'homme pour expliquer sa pensée; et tout ainsi que les pensées sont les portraits des choses, de même nos paroles sont-elles les portraits de nos pensées, mais ces portraits diffèrent des autres portraits en ce que les autres portraits sont distingués partout de leurs originaux, et que la parole enferme en soi son original, puisqu'elle n'est autre chose que la pensée expliquée par un signe extérieur: d'où vient que ceux qui pensent bien sont aussi ceux qui parlent le mieux. Expliquez-moi donc votre pensée par la parole, qui est le plus intelligible de tous les signes [...]. Oui, la parole est *animi index et speculum*; c'est le truchement du cœur, c'est l'image de l'âme. C'est un miroir qui nous représente naïvement les secrets les plus *arcanes de nos individus*. Et puisque

vous avez la faculté de ratiociner et de parler tout ensemble, à quoi
tient-il que vous ne vous serviez de la parole pour me faire entendre
votre pensée?[42]

Pancrace the pedant is clearly a stock figure of fun, but he is funny not because his
opinions are in any way exceptional, but because he is so long-winded in expressing
a view which is entirely obvious and self-evident. In substance, what he says is no
different from Lamy's description of language in his *Rhétorique*:

> Puisque les paroles sont des signes qui représentent les choses qui
> se passent dans l'esprit, on peut dire qu'elles sont comme une
> peinture de nos pensées, que la langue est le pinceau qui trace cette
> peinture, et que les mots dont le discours est composé en sont les
> couleurs. Ainsi, comme les peintres ne couchent leurs couleurs
> qu'après qu'ils ont fait dans leur esprit l'image de ce qu'ils veulent
> representer sur la toile, il faut, avant que de parler, former en nous-
> mêmes une image réglée des choses que nous pensons, et que nous
> voulons peindre par nos paroles. Ceux qui nous écoutent ne peuvent
> pas apercevoir nettement ce que nous voulons leur dire, si nous ne
> l'apercevons nous-mêmes fort nettement. Notre discours n'est
> qu'une copie de l'original qui est en notre tête: il n'y a point de
> bonne copie d'un méchant original.[43]

Mimesis and the metaphor of painting are thus pivotal to the classical understanding
of language; they provide the theoretical basis upon which nomenclaturism is founded.
This recently rediscovered idea of the word as sign, which we have already consid-
ered, has important consequences for poetic theory.

Firstly, nomenclaturism emphasises the priority of thought over language (thus
reversing the hierarchy established by Duret), since it assumes that the sign is only
meaningful when attached to a pre-existent thought. This in turn establishes clarity of
thought as the crucial prerequisite for clarity of language, and in the passage quoted
above, Lamy is quite explicit on this point. Providing that the subject of one's dis-
course is clearly thought through, then the nomenclature of language cannot fail to
attach the correct signs to the elaborated thoughts, and so communicate them lucidly.
The same idea is expressed by Boileau more epigrammatically in the *Art poétique*:

> Avant donc que d'écrire apprenez à penser.
> Selon que nostre idée est plus ou moins obscure,
> L'expression la suit, ou moins nette, ou plus pure.
> Ce que l'on conçoit bien s'énonce clairement,
> Et les mots pour le dire arrivent aisément. (85-86; I:150-54)

These lines are frequently cited as epitomising *la clarté classique*. They hinge on a linguistic theory, fully described by Bernard Lamy and by Pancrace, which is wholly dependent on the notion of imitation. But if, as we have seen, the idea of imitation is itself problematic for many classical theorists, where does that leave the status of language? More generally, any linguistic theory which accords priority to thought over language will be liable to pose a difficulty to the poetic theorist who is perhaps more concerned with words than with thoughts.

Secondly, the new insight into the 'separateness' of language which nomenclaturism betokens has been linked with the demands of scientists in a post-Galilean age for a medium which can represent objectively, 'from the outside', the world's phenomena. 'More and more,' writes T. J. Reiss, 'the *expression* of external 'reality' is received as representing reality as it is' (5). The rapid pace of scientific discovery in the seventeenth century puts particular demands and strains on language, as witness the burlesque style of Cyrano's *L'Autre monde*; it might have suited scientists to look upon language as an instrument able to assimilate and encompass reality without difficulty, but poets might understandably be less enthused by the idea.

So far we have considered the problems created by the attempt to achieve literary and linguistic imitation. The concept of mimesis poses another problem, too: why, even assuming imitation to be an attainable goal, is it a desirable one? In other words, why do we enjoy it?

In discussions of poetic style, critics will often remark on the power of a vivid image to impress us, as here, where Faret describes the poetry of his friend Saint-Amant: 'Lors qu'il descrit il imprime dans l'ame des images plus parfaittes que ne font les objets mesmes' ('Préface sur les œuvres de Mr. de Saint-Amant', Saint-Amant, I:16). The imitation in this case gives pleasure because it helps conjure up reality, and to great effect. The debate about the morality of the theatre which we noted above is similarly centred on the notions of imitation and illusion. In *La Pratique du théâtre*, d'Aubignac explains the didactic utility of theatre by pointing to the vividness of the illusion created:

> C'est là qu'un homme supposé les rend capables de penetrer dans les plus profonds sentimens de l'humanité, touchant au doigt et à l'œil, s'il faut ainsi dire, dans ces peintures vivantes des veritez qu'ils ne pourroient concevoir autrement. Mais ce qui est de remarquable, c'est que jamais ils ne sortent du Theatre, qu'ils ne remportent avec l'idée des personnes qu'on leur a representées, la connoissance des vertus et des vices, dont ils ont veu les exemples. Et leur memoire leur en fait des leçons continuelles, qui s'impriment d'autant plus avant dans leurs esprits qu'elles s'attachent à des objets sensibles, et presque toûjours presens. (9)

It would seem to follow from this that if the imitation were not adequately achieved, then the moral point of the drama would be lost. In this case, we enjoy the imitation firstly because it helps create a heightened sense of reality, but also secondly, because in the process it successfully imprints its moral lesson.

But it is precisely the vividness of the illusion and of the language that Nicole objects to. For him, plays and novels merely serve to teach us 'le langage des passions' and so prompt us to articulate evil intentions which would otherwise have been suppressed (50). Of modern dramatists he writes:

> Toutes leurs pieces ne sont que de vives representations de passions d'orgueil, d'ambition, de jalousie, de vengeance, et principalement de cette vertu Romaine, qui n'est autre chose qu'un furieux amour de soi-même. Plus ils colorent ces vices d'une image de grandeur et de generosité, plus ils les rendent dangereux, et capables d'entrer dans les ames les mieux nées, et l'imitation de ces passions ne nous plaît, que parce que le fond de notre corruption n'excite en même temps un mouvement tout semblable, qui nous transforme en quelque force, et nous fait entrer dans la passion qui nous est representée. (52)

Thus it is the very success of the imitation which, for Nicole, is pernicious. Pascal exhibits the same Jansenist mistrust of pleasure derived from imitations of the unpleasant: 'Quelle vanité que la peinture qui attire l'admiration par la ressemblance des choses, dont on n'admire point les originaux!' (L.40).

In the context of these views, the opening of the third canto of Boileau's *Art poétique* rings out defiantly:

> Il n'est point de Serpent, ni de Monstre odieux,
> Qui par l'art imité ne puisse plaire aux yeux.
> D'un pinceau delicat l'artifice agreable
> Du plus affreux objet fait un objet aimable. (96; III:1-4)

Not that Boileau is the first in his century to express such a view—Cotin had argued similarly in the course of his discussion of the *énigme* (1646):

> L'art en ce rencontre [...] est à certaines choses plus favorables que la Nature, et fait recevoir avec applaudissement dans les meilleures compagnies ce qu'auparavant on ne regardoit qu'avec frayeur, ou l'on ne souffroit au monde qu'avec peine; des comettes, des foudres, des torrents, des vers, des chenilles, et des moucherons. ('Lettre à Damis', *Œuvres meslées*, sig. i v)

The argument that art can improve upon the work of nature is not of course new; Boileau draws both argument and example directly from Aristotle (*Poetics*, 1448.b.9-12). But this seemingly innocent imitation of an Ancient masks the fact that the argument poses for Boileau's contemporaries a radical challenge. The principle of mimesis, strictly applied, leads the poetic theorist into difficulties; for, as we have seen, it has the effect of conflating the word and the object it represents so that language as the material of communication becomes virtually insignificant. What Boileau and Cotin do here is to underscore the artifice of art and so to reinstate the materiality of the communicative tool, language. The opposing views of d'Aubignac and Nicole are not so much resolved as transcended. By claiming that we enjoy imitation in its own right, Boileau and Cotin cleverly sidestep the contradictions involved in trying to explain how imitation functions.

This is a daring move, however, and Boileau's contemporaries mostly find Aristotle's remark that we derive pleasure from exact imitation hard to handle. Bernard Lamy discusses it in his *Nouvelles Réflexions*, only to become hopelessly tangled up in an explanation of his own: man instinctively prefers the spiritual to the material, and so necessarily prefers the poet's imitations to the base objects of reality (83); yet at the same time he argues that our pleasure depends on *vraisemblance* and the success of illusion (118). André Dacier, in his commentary on the *Poetics* (1692), flatly refuses to believe that Aristotle can have meant to say what every one assumes him to have said, that man's instinct to enjoy works of imitation is one of the original causes of poetry's development; and though a classical scholar of great repute, he deploys great ingenuity in order to misread Aristotle's text (36-37).

Happily it is Boileau who has the last word, for Brossette records in his 'Mémoires' the details of a conversation which he had with Boileau in 1702 on this very topic. Imitation of nature is pleasurable, Boileau insists, only when the imitation is to a degree inadequate. He quotes the example of Benoist's coloured wax bodies, which fail to convince because they are too life-like, and compares them to marble sculptures, which are more pleasing and more truthful, because they do not attempt to blur the distinction which necessarily exists between art and nature.[44] It is not even the exactness of the imitation which we enjoy, but rather the aesthetic function of representation in a given medium. The argument is a sophisticated one, and it leaves far behind the idea of art as the naïve imitation of nature.

The emergence of sign theory and the growing mistrust of poetry, rhetoric and language, are both developments which are grounded in the concept of imitation. But as we have seen, the concept of mimesis itself became increasingly contentious during the classical period, and this agonising over what we might term the poetics of imitation is an important component of contemporary discussions of language and poetry.

VI. CONCLUSION

This chapter has sought to identify some of the constraints which operated upon poetic theory in the classical period, at the moment when Boileau published his *Art poétique* and *Traité du sublime*. Seventeenth-century debate about the language of literature was prolific, and the first factor which we noted was the emergence of sign theory, and with it a new awareness of the 'separateness' of language. A second important factor is the growing mistrust of linguistic ornament, in part as a consequence precisely of this sense of separateness between language and reality. This develops into a broader mistrust of all poetic and rhetorical discourse; among some authors, there is even disquiet about the referential function of language itself. These various currents of debate are all grounded in the concept of mimesis: the notion of imitation lies at the heart of seventeenth-century poetic theory.

It is this which makes the burlesque writers (and theorists) so remarkable, for they alone seem wilfully to have run counter to the oncoming tide of Malherbian mimeticism. The tide proved irresistible, however, and among critics of the classical generation, Perrault alone sticks up for burlesque writing. Chapelain, Guez de Balzac, le Père Vavasseur and Sorel all write against the burlesque, their efforts culminating in the best-known critique of all, that of Boileau in the *Art poétique* (83-84).[45]

Burlesque writing pointedly and self-consciously gives emphasis to words over things; in this, it flies in the face of the newer wisdom that words should obediently and self-effacingly mirror things. This latter view, carried to an extreme, would allow words to be no more than the transparent tokens of thoughts, and literary style to be nothing more than the arrangement of ideas. The logical consequence of nomenclaturism is therefore to deny the materiality of language and to make discussion of poetic style an irrelevance. Boileau may not have liked burlesque writing (his main criticism was that it was tainted by popular speech); but he liked the nomenclaturist alternative even less. His views on narrowly mimetic, geometric writing are reported by Jean-Baptiste Rousseau in a letter to Brossette:

> J'ai souvent ouï dire à M. Despréaux que la philosophie de Descartes avait coupé la gorge à la poésie, et il est certain que ce qu'elle emprunte des mathématiques dessèche l'esprit et l'accoutume à une justesse matérielle qui n'a aucun rapport avec la justesse métaphysique, si cela se peut dire, des poètes et des orateurs. La géométrie et la poésie ont leur règles à part et celui qui s'avise de juger Homère par Euclide n'est pas moins impertinent que celui qui voudrait juger Euclide par Homère. (I: 15)

The first challenge, therefore, to anyone seeking to elaborate a theory of poetics in the classical period is to find a way of defending poetic values and even the fabric of language within the prevailing mimetic framework. Burlesque authors had tried to refute, or at least ignore, this framework and had been overtaken. By 1674, a return to the experiment of the burlesque was inconceivable. How, then, to frame a theory of poetry which could be reconciled with nomenclaturism?

The mimetic model contains unresolved tensions that challenge the poetic theorist from different directions. The criticisms of an overblown poetic style are well known, and they culminate in attacks on poetry and rhetoric more generally; less often discussed are the philosophical and literary problems deriving from the referentiality of language. It is vital to consider these two currents of thought together, since they pressurise the poet from opposite angles. On the one hand, concern about language's inadequacy or inefficiency leads to the idea that communication is best achieved when language imitates reality most closely, when words are closest to things. But if such is the ideal of the Cartesian philosopher, it is hardly the ideal of the Jansenist moralist. For, on the other hand, it is also argued by some that if poetic language imitates 'absolutely' and produces a vivid imitation of reality, it seduces us into viewing an invention, that is falsehood, as truth. For Foucault, the opposition between truth and falsehood is the most powerful constraint on discourse in Western culture,[46] and the seventeenth century fear of imagination's power over reason makes this constraint all the more acute.

The poetic theory of classicism is ensnared in a paradox deriving from the centrality it accords to mimesis. Within the nomenclaturist framework, poetic language finds itself in a double bind, where it is vulnerable to attack both for imitating too well (and obscuring truth) and for imitating too poorly (and falling short of the truth). Burlesque writing, by proclaiming the artifice of its own discourse, prompts no moral censure because it seems to pose no threat to truth; but of course it incurs criticism on other grounds, for failing to describe truth adequately.

Any account of poetic language in the 1670s will need therefore to address three specific issues:

i. *linguistic integrity*: the need to defend the materiality of poetic language (against the nomenclaturist drive to turn words into tokens);

ii. *linguistic force*: the need to achieve fullness of linguistic expression (to avoid criticism of language's representative function); and

iii. *moral worth*: the need to provide an ethical defence of poetry (to avoid the charge that it obfuscates truth).

These constraints underlie all the attempts to formulate a classical theory of poetic language. Conventional notions of French classicism have fostered the illusion of classical poetics as a closed, rule-bound system. The reality, of course, is rather different. Boileau, Bouhours and their contemporaries do not see themselves as constructing some grandiose and systematic doctrine; rather they feel themselves to be striving within narrow limits to reconcile conflicting demands and to elaborate a coherent explanation (and defence) of the power of poetry:

> Combien d'art pour rentrer dans la nature! combien de temps, de règles, d'attention et de travail pour danser avec la même liberté et la même grâce que l'on sait marcher; pour chanter comme on parle; parler et s'exprimer comme l'on pense; jeter autant de force, de vivacité, de passion et de persuasion dans un discours étudié et que l'on prononce dans le public, qu'on en a quelquefois naturellement et sans préparation dans les entretiens les plus familiers![47]

NOTES

[1.] Walter Benjamin, 'On language as such', p. 109.
[2.] Calvin, *Commentaire sur la Genèse* (1564), quoted by C.-G. Dubois, *Mythe et langage au seizième siècle*, p. 55.
[3.] C.-G. Dubois, p. 76.
[4.] *Cornucopian Text*, p. 6.

[5.] ibid., p. 19.

[6.] C.-G. Dubois, *Mythe et langage*, pp. 100-104.

[7.] *Ramus*, p. 129.

[8.] ibid., p. 203.

[9.] The word *nomenclaturism* is taken from the writings of Roy Harris, who describes the history of the concept (*The Language Makers*, pp. 33-78). De Mauro shows how nomenclaturism may be termed 'classical' in the true sense, tracing aspects of the theory back to Heraclitus, Plato (in the debate between Hermogenes and Cratylus) and, most influentially, Aristotle, who writes (*De interpretatione* 16a1): 'Words spoken are symbols or signs of affections or impressions of the soul; written words are the signs of words spoken' (quoted by De Mauro, *Introduzione alla semantica*, pp. 38-47). Harris derives the term *nomenclaturism* from Saussure's use of *nomenclature*: 'Pour certaines personnes la langue, ramenée à son principe essentiel, est une nomenclature, c'est-à-dire une liste de termes correspondant à autant de choses' (Saussure, *Cours de linguistique générale*, p. 97); Saussure was certainly acquainted with the Port-Royal *Grammaire* (*Cours*, p. 118).

[10.] See Donzé, *La Grammaire générale et raisonnée*, and Gniadek, 'La théorie sémantique de Port-Royal'.

[11.] See Rodis-Lewis, 'Un théoricien du langage au XVIIe siècle: Bernard Lamy'.

[12.] *Rhétorique*, p. 31; see also the opening of the second chapter (in all editions): 'Puisque les paroles sont des signes qui représentent les choses qui se passent dans notre esprit [...]' (p. 35).

[13.] *Rhétorique*, p. 32 (text of 1688 edition).

[14.] Foucault's conception of the classical episteme has been criticised on the grounds that the Port-Royal *Grammaire*, which is obviously central to that episteme, owes considerably more to such Renaissance grammarians as Scaliger and Sanctius than it does to Descartes (see Chevalier, 'La Grammaire générale de Port-Royal et la critique moderne'). While undoubtedly true in a strictly historical perspective, this fact does not necessarily invalidate Foucault's interpretation, which is concerned with identifying the broad structures of thought that determine understanding rather than with delineating the history of single 'ideas'. Whatever the historical antecedents of Port-Royal theory—and they include of course St Augustine—it does seem to be the case that the prominence of the linguistic sign in the discussions of the second half of the seventeenth century betokens a wholly new understanding of the nature of language.

[15.] Compare: 'The idea that the 'things' of the external world about us constitute the enduring reality from which words, as mere vocal labels, must ultimately derive their meanings is so entrenched in the Western tradition as to seem almost to stand in no serious need of substantiation' (Roy Harris, *Language Makers*, p. 47).

[16.] See Mornet, *Histoire de la clarté française*; and France, 'The language of literature'.

[17.] *Réflexions sur la poétique*, p. 47.

[18.] *Rhétorique*, p. 394.

[19.] Boileau's use of the phrase in the *Art poétique* is the best known formulation of a commonplace first found in a Latin letter, probably dating from the late 1630s, which Guez de Balzac addressed to Jean Silhon as a homage to the memory of Malherbe: 'Primus Franciscus Malherba aut in primis viam qua iretur ad carmen, atque, hanc inter erroris et inscitiae caliginem, ad veram lucem respexit primus' (*Œuvres*, II, 'Epistolae selectae', p. 65).

[20.] *Académie de l'art poétique* (1610), pp. 258-59.

[21.] *Elégie à une dame*, l.72; I, 349.

[22.] See France, *Racine's Rhetoric*, pp. 19-23; and Tocanne, *L'Idée de nature en France*, pp. 430-44.

[23.] See Phillips, *The Theatre and its Critics*; McBride, 'The evolution of the *Querelle du théâtre*'; and Fumaroli, 'La querelle de la moralité du théâtre'.

[24.] Foucault, *Les Mots et les choses*, pp. 92-93. Compare Barthes: 'Que signifie en effet l'économie rationnelle du langage classique sinon que la Nature est pleine, possédable, sans fuite et sans ombre, tout entière soumise aux rêts de la parole?' (*Le Degré zéro de l'écriture*, pp. 71-72).

[25.] Odette de Mourgues, *Quelques paradoxes sur le classicisme*, p. 4; Peter Bayley, 'Fixed form and varied function', p. 9.

[26.] 'Fixed form and varied function', p. 19.

[27.] See Knowlson, pp. 8, 86.

[28.] M. M. Slaughter, pp. 10, 11.

[29.] Slaughter, p. 10.

[30.] Slaughter, p. 218.

[31.] *Règle XIII*, I, pp. 161-62.

[32.] III, p. 143 (*Principia* I, 74).

[33.] See II, p. 389; I, pp. 452-53.

[34.] *Rhétorique trahie* (1704), p. 82; quoted by Gibert in his reply to Lamy (1705-07), pt. I, p. 68.

[35.] See Culler, 'Paradox and the language of morals'.

[36.] *Rhétorique*, pp. 109-10; text of the 1688 edition.

[37.] Quoted in Besoigne, *Histoire de l'abbaye de Port-Royal* (1752-53); the text was included by Brunschwig in the *Pensées* as fragment 16, and later as an appendix to fragment 15.

[38.] See Castor, *Pléiade Poetics*.

[39.] See Russell, *Criticism in Antiquity*, pp. 99-113.

[40.] Thuillier, 'Introduction' (1983), p. 4; see also Kibédi Varga, 'La rhétorique et la peinture à l'époque classique'.

[41.] See Siguret and Lyons.

[42.] I, pp. 726, 1313.

[43.] *Rhétorique*, p. 35, text of 1688 edition; in subsequent editions the last two sentences are softened: '[…] si nous ne l'apercevons nous-mêmes. Notre discours est la copie de l'original qui est en notre tête' (35).

[44.] 'M. Despréaux m'a encore parlé d'Aristote, qui dit que la force de l'imitation est telle sur l'esprit de l'homme, que les choses les plus horribles lui plaisent quand elles sont bien imitées.

M. Despréaux a ajouté, qu'il faut que cette imitation ne soit pas en tout semblable à la nature même: que trop de ressemblance feroit avoir autant d'horreur pour la chose faite par imitation, que pour la chose même qu'on auroit imitée. Par exemple: l'imitation parfaite d'un cadavre, représenté en cire avec toutes les couleurs, sans aucune différence sensible, cette imitation ne seroit pas supportable; de même d'un crapaut, d'une couleuvre etc.

Et c'est pourquoy les portraits que *Benoît* faisoit en cire, n'ont pas réussi; parce qu'ils étoient trop ressemblans. Mais que l'on fasse la même chose en marbre d'une seule couleur, ou en platte peinture: ces imitations plairont d'autant plus qu'elles approcheront de la verité parceque quelque ressemblance qu'on y trouve, les yeux et l'esprit ne laissent pas d'y apercevoir d'abord une différence telle qu'elle doit être nécessairement entre l'art et la nature' (Brossette, 'Mémoires', p. 537).

[45.] See Cronk, 'La défense du dialogisme'.

[46.] *L'Ordre du discours*, pp. 15-21.

[47.] La Bruyère, *Les Caractères*, p. 363 ('Des jugements', 34).

2: The Poetics of Platonism

> Poète proprement est celui-là qui, doué d'une excellence d'esprit
> et poussé d'une fureur divine, explique en beaux vers des pensées
> qui semblent ne pouvoir pas être produites du seul esprit humain.
> (Mairet)[1]

Platonism had played a central role in Renaissance poetic theory, and it was to reappear in a slightly modified guise as an equally crucial component of the aesthetic theory of Romanticism: thus the intervening period of the seventeenth and eighteenth centuries has seemed, almost by definition, to be anti-platonist. René Bray's *La Formation de la doctrine classique* draws on an extremely wide range of sources to argue for and exemplify the aristotelian (more strictly neo-aristotelian) basis of classical poetics. His study opens with a chapter on 'la rupture avec le xvie siècle', while a later chapter is devoted to 'le culte d'Aristote'. Plato, on the other hand, warrants scarcely a single mention. The sole seventeenth-century theorist who is mentioned as having even known Plato is Vossius, a Dutchman (93), and the very few other references to Plato that we do find are misleadingly selective: Bray speaks merely of Plato's belief in the moral utility of poetry (35-36). In an earlier study *French Classicism*, C. H. C. Wright (who is not cited by Bray) accords a significantly larger place to Plato: 'The French seventeenth-century thinkers were, in certain respects, quite in harmony with Plato who was closer to them than they themselves realized' (19). Wright's discussion, though it remains rather general, is certainly suggestive, and more recent research on particular aspects of the platonist tradition in the seventeenth century has demonstrated incontrovertibly the inadequacy of Bray's presentation. Borgerhoff's *The Freedom of French Classicism* is perhaps overall the most effective attack on Bray's excessively rule-bound conception of classicism, but it does not consider at all the sources or antecedent traditions of the ideas discussed, and so does not pick up on the hints dropped earlier by Wright. Thus there has been no overview of French classicism synthesising recent insights in a way which could challenge Bray's work, and the contribution of platonist thought to seventeenth-century poetic theory continues to be underestimated in consequence.

I. Plato and Platonism in the Seventeenth Century

How familiar with Plato were seventeenth-century readers? Certainly the evidence of publication shows little apparent enthusiasm: no single Greek edition of Plato appeared in France during this period;[2] and only a very small number of the dialogues were translated into French in the course of the century.[3]

Thérèse Goyet's survey of Plato editions in the seventeenth century does not, however, extend its coverage to include neoplatonist writers, and it is conceivable that they might have had a greater influence on aesthetic thought than Plato himself. Certainly Plotinus, to whom we would first turn as the source of a putative platonist aesthetic, appears to have been little known: no Latin translation appeared in France during the seventeenth century, and no translation into French before the nineteenth. There did however appear an important edition of the complete works of Ficino in Paris in 1641, so interest in neoplatonism was not entirely extinct. E. N. Tigerstedt has described how Ficinian neoplatonism was decisively rejected both by Claude Fleury in his *Discours sur Platon* (written 1670, published 1686), and by René Rapin in *La Comparaison de Platon et d'Aristote* (1671).[4] It is not perhaps entirely surprising that the Jesuit Rapin should have sought to distance himself from Ficinian 'platonic theology', and in all probability he read Plato only in the Latin translation; Fleury on the other hand was a highly competent Greek scholar, but he is equally dismissive of 'la pretendue theologie de Platon', and he proudly admits to not having read such neoplatonists as Plotinus, Porphyry, Iamblichus or Proclus. André Dacier, at the end of the century, is exceptional in his admiration of Plotinus and Proclus, and in the long prefatory essay 'La Vie de Platon, avec l'exposition des principaux dogmes de sa philosophie' which precedes his translation of ten of the dialogues (*Les Œuvres de Platon*, 1699) he comes closer than probably anyone else in his century to embracing the neoplatonist reading of Plato—though he, like Fleury, finds Ficino's philosophy too speculative and abstract. Munteano singles out only three names—those of Rapin, Fleury and Dacier—as particular admirers of Plato in this period,[5] and it seems reasonable to conclude that in general the seventeenth century knew little Plato and less neoplatonism.

Platonist ideas do none the less persist in the seventeenth century in certain areas. Ferdinand Gohin, in a pioneering study, distinguished two seventeenth-century currents of thought deriving from platonism: one concerned discussions of Platonic love, and the other centred around what he terms 'le platonisme théologique'.[6] The influence of neoplatonic theories of love in, for example, *L'Astreé* is well documented, but such influence is by no means confined to this one novel; and attention has recently been drawn to some five French treatises, all published between 1604 and 1622, that deal with neoplatonic ideas of ideal beauty and love.[7] The importance of neoplatonism for the theology of such authors as Bérulle, Camus and Bossuet has been thoroughly discussed by Jean Dagens, who has demonstrated their indebtedness to such leading Quattrocento figures as Ficino and Pico della Mirandola, while D. P. Walker has recently pointed to the existence in late seventeenth-century France of a group of Platonic and Hermetic Catholic theologians parallel with, but independent of, the Cambridge Platonists.[8] These various currents of thought, even if they do not impinge directly on aesthetic theory, do at least bear witness to continuing discussion of certain platonist ideas as they reached the seventeenth century through the filter of Florentine humanism or of St Augustine. (The term 'platonist' is used here in preference to 'neoplatonist', to refer generally to a cluster of ideas deriving directly or indirectly from Plato, and in order not to beg the question of the seventeenth century's indebtedness to any particular strand of neoplatonist thought.)

II. PLATO AND POETIC THEORY

If one obstacle to the definition of a platonist aesthetic is the fact that platonism was poorly known in this period, another is the diffuseness of what is generally understood by 'platonist aesthetics'. The influence of Aristotle, Horace or Longinus on poetic theory can be readily assessed by studying the reception of a specific text or texts; in the case of Plato's writings, however, no single work provides a synthesis of his aesthetic theory. Several modern writers have attempted descriptions of 'Plato's poetics', but such studies are inevitably obliged to synthesise a number of disparate (and sometimes apparently inconsistent) texts.[9] Thus the name of Plato can be invoked both to buttress the moral justification of poetry (using *Protagoras* 325-26) and to attack it (*Republic*, Book 10), the former strategy being common, for obvious reasons, in the Renaissance while the latter was more common in the seventeenth century. To complicate the issue still further, a text does not need to be by Plato to be considered platonist: both the *Epistles* and *Alcibiades II*, now thought spurious, were considered in the seventeenth century to be the authentic work of Plato. As for platonist aesthetics, as the term is most frequently employed nowadays, it derives from Plotinus and not from Plato at all. For these reasons, a 'platonist aesthetic' is likely to embrace a spectrum of attitudes to poetry rather than represent a specific list of precepts such as we might derive from Aristotle's *Poetics* or Horace's *Ars poetica*.

Contrary to what Bray suggests, Plato's name is certainly connected with poetic theory in the seventeenth century. Early in the century the Italian humanist Paolo Beni had produced a concise résumé (in a Latin paraphrase) of the texts dealing with poetry, entitled *Platonis poetica ex ejus dialogis* [...] *collecta*.[10] The work was noted by Baillet: 'On est encore redevable à son industrie de la Poétique de Platon, qu'il a recüeillie de divers Dialogues de ce Philosophe'.[11] The most extensive discussion of Plato's views on poetry in the classical period is to be found in two works dating from the 1680s, Louis Thomassin's *La Méthode d'étudier et d'enseigner chrétiennement et solidement les lettres humaines* (1681-82), and Adrien Baillet's *Jugemens des savans* (1685-86).[12] But in addition to these explicit discussions of Plato's ideas, we may expect to find other more covert references, in keeping with the spirit of platonist poetics. This contemporary discussion of platonist notions in poetic theory will be considered under four headings: the banishment of the poets; poetic fury; imitation; and hermetic symbolism.

A. THE BANISHMENT OF THE POETS

Plato's banishment of the poets from his ideal republic is certainly his best known pronouncement on poetry, and it is one with which the seventeenth century seems to have been entirely familiar. In his 'Préface' to the *Fables* (1668), La Fontaine notes with satisfaction that Plato banished Homer, but not Aesop, from his Republic: he evidently takes it for granted that his reader will understand the reference.[13] The banishment of the poets is not unproblematic, however, and Thomassin spends most of his half-chapter devoted to Plato seeking to explain how Plato is not at all hostile to poetry, notwithstanding the famous passage in the *Republic*. Baillet similarly regards the banishment of Homer as problematic, but quotes Scaliger in support of the view that it is not the dignity of the poet's role which is under attack, and then cites Vossius and Proclus to show that in any case, not all poets are intended to be excluded from the ideal republic.

B. POETIC FURY

In his *Iconologia* Ripa included a portrait of 'furor poetico', translated (slightly freely) by Baudoin as follows:

> Fureur Poétique: Cette sorte de fureur a pour tableau un jeune garçon, qui a le teint vermeil et plein de vivacité, des aisles à la teste, avec une couronne de Laurier, une ceinture de Lierre, le visage tourné vers le Ciel, et l'action d'une personne qui escrit.
>
> Les aisles demonstrent la promptitude de l'extreme vitesse du Genie Poétique, qui s'eslevant aux choses les plus hautes rend fameux à la posterité les faits memorables des grands hommes, et les maintient fleurissans durant plusieurs siecles; de mesme que le Laurier et le Lierre conservent leurs feuilles tousjours verdoyantes contre les efforts et les injures du temps.
>
> Il a le teint vif et vermeil, à cause que la Fureur Poétique est une surabondance de vivacité d'esprits, qui remplit l'ame de merveilleuses pensées, et luy enseigne à les deduire par nombres. A raison dequoy, comme il semble impossible que la Nature inspire des conceptions si hautes, on les tient pour des dons particuliers, qui procedent d'une singuliere grace du Ciel. Ce qui fait dire à Platon, que l'esprit des Poëtes est agité d'une divine Fureur. Aussi est-ce par elle mesme qu'ils se forment souvent dans l'idée diverses images de choses surnaturelles, qu'ils mettent sur le papier, et qui sont à peine entendus [*sic*], pource qu'elles contiennent je ne sçay quoy d'extraordinaire et de Prophetique. C'est la principale cause pour laquelle les Anciens appellent les Poëtes races du Ciel, fils de Jupiter, interpretes des Muses, et Prestres d'Apollon. J'adjouste cecy qu'il paroist evidemment par leurs escrits, que cette fureur ne s'engendre que par un long exercice, à quoy la Nature ne peut suffire si l'art ne l'assiste.[14]

What would a French classical writer have made of this image, so clearly indebted to the poetic theory of the Renaissance? The image, and the debt, are reinforced by the accompanying engraving of Jacques de Bie, derived from Ripa (see Figs. 1 and 2). The notion of poetic fury was certainly familiar to classical authors: the one feature of Plato's thought, besides the banishment of the poets, to which both

FVREVR.

FVREVR POETIQVE.

EVREVR EXTREME.

FVREVR INDOMPTABLE.

DIVERSES FVREVRS.

ET Homme, dont le visage & l'action ne respirent que rage; qui a les yeux bandez, qui semble lancer vn faisseau de diuerses armes, & qui n'est vestu qu'à demy, represente vray-semblablement la Fureur & les effects.

Les yeux bandez signifient, que la fureur n'estant autre chose qu'vn aueuglement d'esprit, lors qu'elle possede l'homme, il est priué tout à fait de la lumiere intellectuelle, & qu'il fait par consequent toutes choses hors de raison & sans les considerer.

Les armes diuerses dont il embrasse vn faisseau, nous enseignent que la fureur n'a besoin que de soy-mesme pour se satisfaire,

Figure 1. Jacques de Bie, 'Fureur poétique', engraving, from Ripa, trans. Baudoin, *Iconologie* (Paris, 1644).

ICONOLOGIA
FVROR POETICO.

GIouane viuace , & rubicondo con l'ali alla tefta , cotonato di lauro , & cinto d'edera , ftando in atto di fcriuere : ma con la faccia riuolta verfo il Cielo .

L'ali fignificano , la preftezza , & la velocità dell' intelletto Poetico , che non s'immerge : ma fi fublima , portando feco nobilmente la fama de gl'huomini , che poi fi mantiene verde , e bella per molti fecoli , come la fronde del lauro , & dell'edera fi mantengono.

Si fà viuace , & rubicondo, perche é il furor poetico vna foprabondanza di viuacità di fpirti , che arricchifce l'anima de numeri , & de'concetti merauigliofi , i quali parendo impoffibile che fi poffono hauere folo per dono della natura, fono ftimati doni particolari , & fingolar gratia del Cielo ,

Figure 2. 'Furor poetico', engraving, from Ripa, *Iconologia* (Roma, 1603).

Thomassin and Baillet draw attention is the description of poetic fury in the *Ion*. Here is how Thomassin presents the argument of that dialogue:

> [...] la fureur divine, dont il faut que non seulement les Poëtes, mais aussi ceux qui lisent leurs Ouvrages avec fruit soient animez, comme d'un esprit celeste, qui les ravit et les transporte hors d'eux-mesmes, en sorte que les lecteurs ou les auditeurs soient attachez aussi bien que les Poëtes à cet Esprit divin, comme plusieurs anneaux de fer s'attachent entr'eux, et se tiennent suspendus à un aimant. D'où il s'ensuit que les Poëtes ne sont que les organes et les interpretes de Dieu.[15]

Baillet quotes this passage verbatim. He remarks that Plato's views on poetry are not always consistent, but concludes his article by reaffirming the importance of the *Ion*; on this point, at least, Plato's opinions are consistent:

> Quoi qu'il en soit, on peut assurer que Platon n'a point laissé d'avoir une opinion avantageuse de la Poësie en général, et qu'il n'a jamais changé de sentiment à l'égard du génie ou de la *Fureur Poëtique*, qu'il a toujours prise pour une inspiration divine.[16]

But to what extent was the *Ion* known beyond the rather specialised volumes of Baillet and Thomassin? The fact that no French translation of the text appeared between that of Richard Le Blanc in 1546 and that of Jean-Nicolas Grou in 1770 may suggest that it was not among the most widely-read of the dialogues, and it is not mentioned in either Fleury's *Discours sur Platon* or in Rapin's *La Comparaison de Platon et d'Aristote*. The classical authors who do mention the *Ion* tend to be writers of the second rank—Gilles Boileau, for example, or the abbé Cotin.[17] Thomassin cites the *Ion* in Ficino's Latin translation, and Racine must be one of the very few writers of the period to have studied the dialogue in the original Greek.[18]

If knowledge of the *Ion* is not especially widespread in the classical period, nor is the related use of the term *fureur*. Earlier in the century the word had enjoyed common currency among authors, especially poets: d'Ablancourt speaks of himself as being 'pris d'une divine fureur' when reading novels; d'Aubigné, Régnier, Saint-Amant, Théophile de Viau all invoke the ideal of *fureur* in their poetry; and Gournay speaks of 'la vraye Poesie' as 'une fureur Apollinique'.[19] But the concept is evidently more consonant with the Renaissance conception of poetry than with Malherbe's. At the very beginning of the century Nicolas Richelet had written of Ronsard's *Ode à Michel de l'Hospital* that 'le poëte n'a besoin que de ce transport divin meslé du naturel sans autre science, car ceste inspiration luy fournit toute cognoissance' (132). Deimier, in 1610, is scathing about such a view, insisting that 'la nature a besoin aussi d'estre fortifiee et illustree de l'art, quoy qu'en dise Monsieur Richelet' (*Académie*, 16). And in the same vein, a supporter of Corneille was pleased to ridicule the remarks of Mairet quoted in the epigraph above: 'Je ne m'étonne plus s'il ne fait point conscience de manquer de jugement en toutes ses pièces: il croit la fureur de l'essence du poète, voilà un parfait raisonnement!'[20]

For Vaugelas, writing in 1647, *fureur* has not yet acquired the pejorative flavour which it will have later in the century (for example, in Bouhours's *Entretiens*): '*Fureur* se prend quelquefois en bonne part, comme *fureur poëtique, fureur divine*, [...] et *furie*, se prend ordinairement en mauvaise part'.[21] Yet although the term has negative connotations for Bouhours, the idea which it represents is not entirely absent from the *Entretiens*, where Bouhours speaks of 'cette flâme qui éclaire la raison, et qui échauffe l'imagination en mesme temps', an idea which he attributes to 'je ne sçay quel Philosophe Platonicien' (123).

Turning to the critical writings of Rapin, we again find the concept of *furor poeticus* rejected, yet still it hovers uneasily in the wings. In the *Réflexions sur la poétique d'Aristote* (1674), he attacks the idea head-on: 'Il n'est nullement vray, comme la pluspart du monde le croit, qu'il doive entrer de la fureur dans le caractère de la poésie.' A year later, in the edition retitled *Réflexions sur la poétique de ce temps*, this criticism is somewhat modified: 'Il y a quelque chose de divin dans le caractère du poète: mais il n'y a rien d'emporté et de furieux' (17). The 1674 edition had also contained a jibe at Plato, Rapin speaking of 'une vision de Platon, que cette fureur qu'il donne au poète dans le traité qu'il en fait: il avait entrepris de décrier la poésie n'ayant pu y réussir': this remark is omitted from the 1675 edition, only to be restored in that of 1684. For Rapin, poetry must 'ressembler au discours d'un homme inspiré', but this carefully cultivated appearance will be an artifice of the poet; genius, essential for poetic creation, must be reined in, hence the importance of the rules: 'Cette sérénité d'esprit, qui fait le sang froid et le jugement, est une des parties les plus essentielles du génie de la poésie, c'est par là qu'on se possède'.[22] Perhaps the most striking allusion to poetic fury—though avoiding the actual term—is that found at the beginning of Boileau's *Art poétique*:

C'est envain qu'au Parnasse un temeraire Auteur
Pense de l'Art des Vers atteindre la hauteur.
S'il ne sent point du Ciel l'influence secrete,
Si son Astre en naissant ne l'a formé Poëte,
Dans son genie étroit il est toûjours captif.
Pour lui Phébus est sourd, et Pégaze est retif. (p. 8, I, 1-6)

To speak of 'l'influence secrète du Ciel' is to come very close to the idea of *fureur*; and in choosing to place this image in the most prominent position possible—at the opening of his *Art poétique*—Boileau is going out of his way to accord the idea distinct importance.[23]

There are just one or two discussions of poetic fury in which the reference to Plato is overt. One of these, in the pre-classical period, is Le Moyne's 'Discours de la poésie' (1641), which appeared as the preface to four *Hymnes*. Le Moyne refers to the *Ion* in support of his contention that poetry's purpose is to turn our thoughts to God: 'Selon l'opinion de Platon, la Poesie doit estre l'Interprete et l'Imitatrice de la Divinité'

(15). There is no mention of *fureur*, but Le Moyne speaks repeatedly of 'le Feu', 'le Feu divin' (17, etc.), in an apparently similar sense. 'Ce Feu si pur et si actif' is 'la Nature de la Poësie', and with a reference to the *Ion* in a footnote, he goes on to describe it as follows:

> On dit que [la Nature de la Poësie] transporte l'Esprit, et qu'elle est
> venuë de la plus haute partie du Monde: on croit qu'elle est la
> Divination des Savans et des Sages: elle est prise pour une espece
> de Prophetie naturelle, et pour une Extase de la plus noble Partie
> de l'Ame: et en effet elle a quelque chose de pareil à l'inspiration
> qui fait les Prophetes, et ses elevations resemblent aux transports
> des Personnes extasiées. (6)

Le Moyne's references to Plato are crucial to the argument of the 'Discours', and on both occasions he quotes Plato, the point is underpinned by a footnote citing the *Ion* in the Greek original. Bouhours was intimately acquainted with the writings of the elder Jesuit Le Moyne, and he must have known this text; it is a striking reflection of the prevailing climate of classicism that his own allusive attempts to discuss poetic inspiration thirty years later in the *Entretiens* are so much more timid by comparison.

In the classical period proper there is however one author, just one, who discusses the idea of poetic fury at length.[24] Pierre Petit (1617?-1687) was known first of all as a physicist; he studied medicine, was tutor to the sons of the président de Lamoignon, and wrote a number of Latin scientific treatises in which he demonstrated his opposition to Descartes, notably on the question of animal-machines. In his *Liste de quelques gens de lettres* (1662), Chapelain writes that Petit 'est un jeune médecin très grand physicien, très savant en la langue grecque et qui écrit très bien en latin'.[25] Later he became known also as a Latin poet, and in 1683 he published a two-volume collection of his poetry, headed by an eighty-five-page essay 'De furore poetico'.

On the very first page Petit affirms as a generally accepted view that *furor* is essential to good poetry: 'Quod tamen nemo Poëta bonus sine furore esse possit in confesso est apud omnes' (1). He conceives of *furor* as something beyond human reason, a force which takes us beyond ourselves: 'Cum enim furor nihil aliud sit, qum vehementior animi concitatio et impetus, quo aliquis totus extra se rapitur, ut sit in eo quod cogitat et consequi studet' (4). Petit then proceeds in a quasi-scientific manner to analyse the causes and nature of poetic fury, citing in the process a list of authors including Aristotle, Cicero, Plutarch, Longinus, and Scaliger. But it is Plato who has pride of place among the acknowledged sources of this essay; and Petit, whose learning in the Greek language Chapelain had remarked upon, was well able to read Plato in the original. Petit begins by discussing the *Phaedrus*: he describes the four types of fury, and draws a distinction (which had been attributed to Plato by Proclus) between forceful poetry wrought by the craft of the poet, and forceful poetry that is the product of inspiration. Petit then passes on to the *Ion*, giving a lengthy résumé of the argument (27-30), and quoting the text in the original Greek.

Much of the detailed argument of 'De furore poetico' is rather tedious. But the importance accorded to Plato is certainly unexpected; and the mere fact of devoting so much space to the *Ion* is distinctly original for, as we have seen, the dialogue was little discussed or even known in the classical period. A particularity of Petit's platonism is that he draws directly on the writings of Plato and of neoplatonists such as Proclus who had written in Greek, rather than on Quattrocento neoplatonism; in this he is unlike the Pléiade theorists, notably Pontus de Tyard in his *Solitaire premier*, whose view of platonism is filtered through the commentaries of Ficino.

In line with Coleridge's dictum that 'Every man is born an Aristotelian or a Platonist', it is easy to think of aristotelianism and platonism as simple opposites, but this is not Petit's view. When, on the very first page of his treatise, he notes that Plato alone has spoken memorably about *furor poeticus*, and that even Aristotle in his *Poetics* does not touch on the issue, he seems to be trying to present certain platonist notions as complementary, and not antagonistic, to the prevailing—aristotelian—theory of poetry.[26] In describing the argument of the *Ion* at length, Petit is hoping to reaffirm the principle of poetic enthusiasm within the framework of classical doctrine: he is not setting himself up as an opponent of classicism. Indeed he could be seen as an exemplary classicist, in the sense that his concern as an accomplished reader of Latin and Greek is to make accessible to his own generation the wisdom of a neglected classical text.

'De furore poetico' was not translated into French, and never republished, so it is doubtful whether it exercised much direct influence. The treatise's importance was quickly noted by Baillet, however, three years after its publication, in his *Jugemens des savans*. Baillet's article on Plato's theory of poetry opens with a discussion of the *Ion* and of poetic fury, and a note directs the reader instantly to the essay of Petit.[27] When Baillet comes on to speak of contemporary poetic theorists, he devotes as much space to Petit as to Rapin or Boileau; his article on 'De furore poetico' stresses the originality of Petit's defence of poetic values:

> C'est un Traité fort singulier, et il contient des recherches savantes qui font connoître que l'Auteur est bien penetré de ce qu'il enseigne, et qu'il est également habile dans la Philosophie et dans la Poësie [...]. Ce qui me paroist d'autant plus important, que depuis l'*Ion* de Platon, c'est à dire depuis plus de deux mille ans, il me semble qu'il n'avoit presque point parû de Traité si singulier et si détaché sur ce sujet. Au reste, comme Monsieur Petit s'est consommé dans la lecture de Platon aussi bien que dans celle des autres anciens Philosophes, on doit estre moins surpris de voir une si grande conformité de sentimens et de connoissances entre Platon et luy. Mais loin de témoigner contre les Poëtes le chagrin que Platon a fait paroistre contre eux, il a bien voulu mesme augmenter leur nombre, et faire voir qu'il connoissoit les effets de cette *Fureur Poëtique*, autant par la propre experience que par les écrits des Anciens.[28]

Petit's 'De furore poetico' provides interesting testimony of how one classical poet and critic managed to embrace the platonist notion of enthusiasm within the prevailing system of poetic theory. 'L'aspect *jugement* retient beaucoup plus la critique du siècle Louis XIV, que l'aspect *inspiration*,'[29] writes Noémi Hepp: although true as a generalisation, the remark does underestimate the interest accorded to poetic enthusiasm. Admittedly, *fureur* has become a contaminated term for classicism; and Rapin's embarrassed hesitation in his handling of the concept exemplifies just how problematic classical critics found it. The idea of inspiration remains none the less a persistent undercurrent in classical poetic theory.

c. Imitation

In their discussions of Plato's views on poetry, Thomassin and Baillet confine their remarks to the two topics of the banishment of the poets and poetic fury, and they make no mention of Plato's theory of Ideas and its possible repercussions for aesthetic theory (the subject on which modern writers most readily focus when discussing platonist aesthetics). This is understandable, in so far as Thomassin and Baillet each base their remarks on specific (and non-controversial) passages. The subject of imitation is inevitably more problematic since it cannot be localised in any single work of Plato, nor even in the writings of Plato alone. Where Plato had conceived of poetry as a poor imitation at second remove from reality, the neoplatonists, beginning with Plotinus, argued that poetic imitation was the highest form of imitation because the successful poet copies a divine archetype or Idea rather than an already-existing model.

In his study *Idea*, Panofsky showed how from the second half of the sixteenth century neoplatonist theories 'were eagerly adopted and imbued the art-theoretical discussions of the problem of beauty with a unique character' (93), as notably in the case of the theorist Lomazzo, who maintained that ideal beauty had its source in God rather than in nature. Bellori's *L'Idea del pittore, dello scultore e del'architetto* (1664, published 1672) adopts a more aristotelian position, arguing that the Idea which an artist should imitate is an image of selected and embellished nature; while this marks a shift away from the neoplatonism of the previous century, the neoplatonist influence remains patent, noticeably in the opening chapter and in the critical vocabulary used throughout the work.[30] The work was well known in France (Panofsky, 105), and an obvious influence on the French classical doctrine of *la belle nature*. Art theorists of the period such as André Félibien and Roger de Piles express views with a distinctively platonist ring;[31] and the most striking evidence of 'pure' neoplatonism in French art theory at this time—striking because it is given a true metaphysical underpinning—is found in a fragment written by Poussin:

> L'idée de beauté ne descend dans la matière qu'elle n'y soit préparée
> le plus possible. Cette préparation consiste en trois choses: l'ordre,
> le mode et l'espèce ou forme. L'ordre signifie l'intervalle des parties,
> le mode est relatif à la quantité, la forme consiste dans les lignes et

couleurs. L'ordre ne suffit, ni l'intervalle des parties, ni ne suffit que tous les membres du corps aient leur place naturelle, si ne s'y joint le mode qui donne à chaque membre la grandeur qui lui est due, proportionnellement au corps, et si n'y concourt l'espèce, en telle sorte que les lignes soient faites avec grâce, et dans un suave accord de lumières et d'ombres s'avoisinant. Et de tout cela appert-il manifestement que la beauté est en tout éloignée de la matière du corps, de laquelle elle ne s'approche, si elle n'y est disposée par des préparations incorporelles. Et ainsi peut-on conclure que la peinture n'est autre qu'une idée des choses incorporelles, et que si elle montre les corps elle en représente seulement l'ordre, et le mode selon lequel les choses se composent, et qu'elle est plus attentive à l'idée du beau qu'à toute autre. Et de là quelques-uns ont voulu que cette idée fût la seule marque et, on peut dire, le but de tous les bons peintres, et que la peinture fût l'amante de la beauté et la reine de l'art.[32]

This passage, admittedly unparalleled in any of Poussin's other works, has close parallels in earlier neoplatonist writings, and testifies to their continuing presence in seventeenth-century France.[33]

Panofsky's study, first published in 1924, stimulated further research in the later history of neoplatonism, and made possible, for example, Louis Bredvold's 1934 article 'The tendency toward platonism in neo-classical esthetics', an essay dealing essentially with English neo-classicism. The first full-blooded assertion of the presence of neoplatonism in French classicism is made by Brody in his seminal 1961 essay 'Platonisme et classicisme', concerned exclusively with traces of a neoplatonist theory of imitation. Brody first points to the platonist colouring of much theological writing (and especially writing inspired by St Augustine), discussing examples from Bossuet, Pascal and Nicole. His great originality is to make a bridge between this theological tradition and aesthetic thought more generally. Classicism, argues Brody, is characterised by a search for absolute perfection: 'Dire qu'un bon esprit voit toutes choses comme elles doivent être vues, c'est dire d'un esprit qu'il sait se faire une idée de la chose en question qui correspond parfaitement à l'Idée de la chose telle qu'en elle-même' (12). The point is nicely made by La Fontaine, who conveniently links it to the name of Plato (though his reference to the *Phaedrus* is inaccurate): 'Platon, dans Phaedrus, fait dire à Socrate qu'il serait à souhaiter qu'on tournât en tant de manières ce qu'on exprime qu'à la fin *la bonne fût rencontrée*'.[34] For Brody, if we approach classicism not as a literary movement but as an attitude ('une mentalité particulière, une façon de voir, une manière de se représenter la nature essentielle de la vérité', 11), we may say that it is platonist in the very essence of its conception.

Brody's interpretation has been vindicated by more recent research into the notion of imitation, notably Roger Zuber's 'La critique classique et l'idée d'imitation', and Bernard Tocanne's *L'Idée de nature* (Pt. 3, Chap. 2). As we grow more sensitive to the importance of platonism and as we scrutinise the claims of classicism more closely, it becomes increasingly evident that many of the terms of Bray's *doctrine classique* can in certain contexts acquire a platonist tinge. The tension described above between strict imitation and *belles idées*, a tension invariably resolved in favour of the latter, is all the more significant in the light of platonist thinking. So too is Rapin's discussion of a well-worn classical term, *vraisemblance*:

> La verité ne fait les choses que comme elles sont; et la vray-semblance les fait comme elles doivent estre. La vérité est presque toujours défectueuse, par le mélange des conditions singulières, qui la composent. Il ne naist rien au monde qui ne s'éloigne de la perfection de son idée en y naissant. Il faut chercher des originaux et des modèles, dans la vray-semblance et dans les principes universels des choses: où il n'entre rien de matériel et de singulier qui les corrompe.[35]

In this passage, as Tocanne remarks, we find Rapin 'lisant Aristote à travers Platon' (317).

D. HERMETIC SYMBOLISM

Throughout his dialogues Plato employs myths and images to help communicate his ideas, and building upon this foundation, neoplatonist literature evolved all manner of allegorical and esoteric languages. Neoplatonist theories of inspiration and imitation inevitably emphasise this predilection for hermetic discourse, since they assume that reality cannot be captured in the inadequate language of uninspired rationality: the poet must resort to symbols in order to convey his vision of the divine Ideal. A further advantage commonly ascribed to hermetic discourse during the Renaissance was that it served to preserve precious knowledge from the vulgar herd: only the initiated would be able to penetrate the veil of allegory and symbol. This interest in hermetic symbolism is especially strong in the Renaissance, and it has obvious repercussions both for the language of religion and for the language of poetry (as witness the poetic theory of the Pléiade).

The generation of Malherbe and Deimier initiated the seventeenth-century rationalist reaction against such hermetic writing, and in Bray's account of classical doctrine, it appears that by the time of classicism all traces of Renaissance hermeticism had been expunged. This is demonstrably untrue. In his article 'Esoteric symbolism', D. P. Walker looks in detail at the various types of hermetic language which flourished in the sixteenth century, and it emerges at several points that these spill over into the following century; Walker notes, for example, that Leone Ebreo's extended discussion of the necessity for truth to be veiled is quoted in full by Mersenne in 1623 (225), and Walker concludes with a consideration of Pascal's indebtedness to the Renaissance tradition of hermetic symbolism (228-32). And although we habitually associate classicism with clarity, the literary criticism of, for example, Saint-Evremond has been characterised as concerned essentially with the perception of the *caché* or the *secret*.[36]

The salons were a rich breeding-ground for minor poetic genres, and these inspired a number of theorists; of these the best known is Guillaume Colletet, whose *Art poétique* (1658) consists principally of six treatises on such genres as the sonnet, the eclogue, and the *épigramme*. These theoretical writings have received little attention (even Colletet's *Art poétique* has still not been edited in its entirety), and Bray is dismissive of their possible importance: 'Cessons de glaner une si pauvre doctrine [...]', he writes, 'l'étude [des idées classiques] ne peut pas se faire dans ces minuscules miroirs' (354). In fact classical critics are more inclined to express themselves freely in treating seemingly trivial genres, when they do not feel the inhibiting presence of Aristotle. There are many seventeenth-century French theorists of the emblem, for example, who use the genre as a metaphor and as a pretext for discussing poetic discourse in general (we shall return to them in the next chapter). Among other genres which inspire similar interest are the *métamorphose* and the *énigme*.[37] The *métamorphose* attracted the attentions of two theorists, Charles Regnault ('Discours sur les métamorphoses françoises', 1641), and the abbé Charles Cotin ('Discours en général sur les métamorphoses', 1659), and both are evidently concerned with something more than trivial salon verse. Thinkers have been fascinated by transformations since the time of the 'Platoniciens', says Regnault, and he considers the importance of this idea for literature:

> Ovide en suitte a bien mieux estably les Métamorphoses, car en couvrant la vérité d'un voile fabuleux, il a rendu, s'il faut dire ainsi, le mensonge agréable, aussi bien qu'Apulée qui par un dessein contraire a fait sortir adroitement le jour et la vérité du sein mesme de l'ombre, et de la fable. (Vol. 2, p. 11)

Cotin, declaring that he does not wish to write a long preface, playfully sets out the problems which he does not have time to discuss:

> Quelle liaison il y a du sens physique & du moral, par quel art ce genre de poësie se rend merveilleux & divin; & quel mysterieux rapport se doit rencontrer entre la fable qu'on raconte & les veritables qualitez des personnes illustres, en faveur de qui on les a faites. (4)

Thus both writers are concerned with the use of fable as a hermetic language: Regnault's suggestion that Ovid had used poetry as 'un voile fabuleux' to cloak truth is paralleled by Cotin's juxtaposition of 'le sens physique' and 'le sens moral' co-existing in a 'mysterieux rapport'.

Cotin—now best remembered for having been ridiculed by Boileau and Molière—is described by Adam as 'l'un des théoriciens les plus en vue',[38] and in addition to this essay on the *métamorphose*, he wrote on such other genres as the madrigal, the *épigramme* and the *énigme*. The enigma perpetuates the Renaissance concern with neoplatonist hermetic disourse, and the *Recueil des énigmes de ce temps*

(1646) contains two theoretical prefaces, 'Discours sur les Enigmes' and 'Lettre à Damis', both bearing Cotin's signature. Then, in 1665, Nicolas Fardoil, a lawyer and minor poet, published a brief essay 'Sur le style des énigmes', and as a fitting culmination at the end of the century Menestrier's *La Philosophie des images énigmatiques* (1694) provided a compendious study of a whole range of symbolic forms, including the enigma, the emblem, the oracle and the hieroglyph. Though there are some differences of approach between these theorists of the enigma, all three relish the linguistic opacity that is its hallmark. Moreover the principle is evidently applicable to literary texts of all kinds; Cotin is emphatic in the concluding lines of his 'Discours' that the enjoyment of poetry is enhanced by a—partially—hermetic style:

> Ces rares allusions, ce langage surnaturel, ces tromperies innocentes, et ces continuelles allegories, cét [*sic*] artifice de representer si adroitement un sujet sous la forme d'un autre, que tout ce qui le represente nous enseigne que ce ne l'est pas; et cette finesse d'equivoques qui le couvrent en le découvrant, cette invention de faire la fortune des petites choses, et de les dérober à la veuë à force de les faire paroistre grandes, cette abondance et richesse de rimes; et ce qui est le plus difficile, cette heureuse et apparente facilité, soit à bien penser, soit à exprimer ses pensées: Enfin ces traits de moralité qui donnent quelquefois en passant un coup à l'ame endormie; chaque beauté separément, et toutes ensemble font le veritable office de la poësie, qui est de plaire et de profiter.[39]

Nothing could demonstrate more vividly an awareness of the inadequacy of the contemporary doctrine of *clarté*; Cotin, through the pretext of the enigma, defends the value of hermetic symbolism as a crucial ingredient of literary style. The three theorists do not properly discuss the sources of their ideas, but it is evident that the enigma, like the device, is a genre with roots which run deep into Renaissance neoplatonism; and while Cotin alone actually quotes Plato, it is significant that both Fardoil and Menestrier cite St Augustine.

The abbé de Villars's *Le Comte de Gabalis, ou Entretiens sur les sciences secrètes* (1670) enjoyed an immediate and enduring success and provides an interesting instance of the classical ambivalence towards hermeticism. The book, a set of five *entretiens*, presents itself as a satire on the occult sciences, but the sophisticated use of the dialogue form combined with the constant recourse to irony make this a far more subtle and challenging text than *De la délicatesse* (to which we shall return in the next chapter). The writing is frequently and deliberately ambiguous, opposing the prevailing rationalism with flights of extraordinary fancy; uncritical acceptance of the Count's cabalistic beliefs is ridiculed, but so too, it seems, is uncritical acceptance of any creed, orthodox religion included. Thus when the reader comes upon a defence of oracular and hermetic speech, it is not immediately evident what his proper response should be. Is oracular discourse being advocated, or satirised? The argument and indeed the vocabulary certainly recall some of the poetic theorists cited above:

> Quand à l'obscurité de quelques Oracles (poursuivit-il
> serieusement) que vous appellés friponnerie, les tenebres ne sont-
> elles pas l'habit ordinaire de la verité. Dieu ne se plaist-il pas à se
> cacher de leur voile sombre, et l'Oracle continuel qu'il a laissé à
> ses enfans, la divine Escriture n'est-elle pas envelopée d'une
> adorable obscurité, qui confond et fait égarer les superbes autant
> que sa lumiere guide les humbles. (104)

In the end, the possibility of irony in this passage generates an uncertainty which is more intriguing than any simple statement, favourable or hostile, about hermetic discourse. The text obviously testifies to a continued interest in a platonist aesthetic; and in posing an interpretative challenge to the reader, it exemplifies the hermetic symbolism which it playfully presents.

It is useful in conclusion to quote at length Baudoin's 'Préface' to his translation (1644) of Ripa's *Iconologia*, which provides extraordinary testimony of the continuing seventeenth-century fascination with hermetic discourse:

> Car bien qu'il n'y ait celuy qui ne sçache, que de la proposition des
> traits, de l'esclat, du teint, et de ce qu'on appelle, *le je ne sçay quoi*,
> se forme une parfaite Beauté; il y auroit de la faute neantmoins à la
> representer par l'Image d'une personne extrémément belle et bien
> proportionnée. La raison est, à cause que ce seroit expliquer le
> mesme par le mesme, et vouloir, par maniere de dire, faire voir
> distinctement le Soleil à la clarté d'un flambeau: d'où il s'ensuivroit
> qu'à faute de ressemblance, qui est l'Ame de la Figure, celle-cy se
> trouveroit imparfaite, et ne pourroit jamais plaire, pour n'avoir pas
> la diversité requise à l'agrement: A raison dequoy, en la peinture
> de cette mesme Beauté dont nous parlons, nous luy avons caché le
> visage dans les nüs, sans oublier les autres particularitez, qui nous
> ont semblé luy estre convenables.
>
> Or pour avoir moins de peine à treuver des ressemblances
> et des rapports qui soient propres au sujet que l'on imagine, il est
> bon de remarquer avecque les Maistres de l'Eloquence, que par les
> choses connoissables on cherche les hautes, par les loüables les
> splendides, et par les recommendables les magnifiques. Que si
> l'esprit s'accoustume à ces observations, elles luy fourniront à la
> fin une si grande quantité de pensées, s'il n'est entierement sterile,
> qu'il ne luy sera pas dificile de contenter autruy sur tous les sujets
> qui luy seront proposez pour en former des Images. Ceux qui nous
> en ont donné des Regles, disent que l'invention en est deüe aux
> Egyptiens, et la font passer pour un veritable effet de l'abondance
> de leur doctrine. Tellement qu'il est de cette Connoissance, comme
> d'une personne sçavante, qui a vescu long-temps toute nüe dans le
> desert, d'où elle se resout de sortir enfin, pour voir les compagnies,

et s'habille pour cét effet le mieux qu'elle peut, afin que ceux qui l'aborderont, attirez par l'ornement exterieur du Corps, qui en est comme l'Image, ayent envie d'apprendre ponctuellement quelles sont les qualitez qui donnent du lustre à l'Ame, qu'on peut appeller la chose signifiée.

Ce ne fut aussi que le seul desir de s'esclaircir des obscuritez qui estoient cachées dans ces mysterieuses Images, qui fit aller Pythagore au fonds de l'Egypte; d'où estant retourné plein de science et d'années, il merita que de sa maison se fist un Temple, qui fut consacré solemnellement à son admirable Genie. J'obmets que Platon tira de ces Figures Hyeroglifiques la meilleure partie de sa doctrine, que les saincts Prophetes enveloperent de nuages leurs veritables Oracles; et que Jesus-Christ mesme, qui fut l'accomplissement des Propheties, cacha sous des Paraboles la pluspart de ses divins secrets.

Ces Images, si la disposition en est bonne, et la maniere ingenieuse, ont je ne sçay quoy de si agreable, qu'elles arrestent la veuë, et font aussi-tost desirer l'esprit de sçavoir ce qu'elles signifient. (sigs e iii r-v)

Such sentiments had been commonplace in the Renaissance; and perhaps even in the mid-seventeenth century they were more widespread than we might have supposed.[40]

III. Conclusion

Looking back in 1989 to his article 'Platonisme et classicisme' published nearly thirty years earlier, Brody remarks simply that 'this is an idea [...] whose time has come'.[41] In that earlier article, he convincingly argues that platonism provides classicism with its essential metaphysical underpinning: 'The major values and tenets of French 'classicism'—its preoccupation with form, universality, perfection, etc.—should be regarded as coded variants in the Platonic-Platonistic paradigm of the Good.'[42] Classicism without this metaphysical basis would be unrecognisable; or rather, Racine's tragedies would become undistinguishable from Voltaire's: 'En l'absence d'une telle métaphysique', writes Brody, 'le classicisme se réduit à une doctrine, à un système de procédés et de règles, à une rhétorique; il se réduit précisément à ce qu'il devint au dix-huitième siècle: un académisme décadent et moribond.'[43]

It is worth noting that Brody comes to this conclusion exclusively on the basis of a study of imitation. But, as we have seen, a platonist aesthetic can go beyond a concern with imitating the Ideal, and can also embrace the concepts of divine inspiration and hermetic discourse. A 1988 number of *XVIIe Siècle* devoted to 'Hiéroglyphes, langages chiffres, sens mystérieux'[44] and a 1989 exhibition catalogue in which Fumaroli explores the platonist resonances of Poussin's *L'Inspiration du poète* (see Fig. 3; compare Figs. 1 and 2) are two examples of how recent scholarship has reappraised the significance of both these topics. Though separate, the notions of divine inspiration and hermetic discourse are clearly connected: only the oracular speech of

Figure 3. Poussin, *L'Inspiration du poète*, c.1630 (Paris, Louvre).

a divinely-inspired poet can hope to communicate a sense of the Idea. Moreover, these notions are connected in the minds of contemporaries: Cotin, for example, discusses 'la Fureur Poëtique' and quotes from the *Ion* in a text dealing with the *énigme*.[45] Brody's argument that platonism is a necessary part of classicism (when properly defined) is therefore further reinforced by the evidence of classical interest in the ideas of poetic fury and enigmatic discourse.

That there is a platonist current in classicism is undeniable; but the definition of its precise nature and form remains problematic. This is in part because the various currents of thought which have been described here are partially submerged, with the result that their influence is easily underestimated.[46] In a manoeuvre entirely consonant with the platonist aesthetic, classical theorists show considerable deftness in discussing Plato's ideas without appearing to affront rational, aristotelian appearances. Thus the *Ion* is discussed explicitly by a number of critics and poets (Le Moyne, Petit, Cotin, Gilles Boileau), but almost always in apparently minor and innocuous works. The idea of poetic fury is quite widely discussed, even though the term *fureur* is mostly avoided by classical theorists. Classical platonism is an idea in search of an appropriate language.

NOTES

1. Mairet, *La Silvanire*, 'Préface' (1631), in *Théâtre du xviie siècle*, Pléiade, I, p. 479.

2. The complete works were of course easily available, complete with Latin translation, in two rival editions, that of Ficino, and that of Henri Estienne with the translation of Jean de Serres.

3. See Thérèse Goyet, 'Présence de Platon dans le classicisme français'.

4. *Decline and Fall*, pp. 42-45.

5. *Constantes dialectiques*, p. 175.

6. 'La Fontaine et Platon', *La Fontaine*, especially pp. 20-37.

7. See A. Adam, 'La théorie mystique de l'amour dans *L'Astreé*'; A. H. T. Levi, 'The early seventeenth century: the significance of the *Astreé*'; and L. W. Johnson, 'Literary neoplatonism in five French treatises of the early seventeenth century'.

8. See J. Dagens, *Bérulle et les origines de la restauration catholique*, and 'Hermétisme et cabale en France de Lefèvre d'Etaples à Bossuet'; and D. P. Walker, *The Ancient Theology*, Chap. 6, 'The survival of the ancient theology in late seventeenth-century France, and French Jesuit missionaries in China'.

9. See P. Vicaire, *Platon: critique littéraire*, and M. H. Partee, *Plato's Poetics: the authority of beauty*.

10. The earliest edition in the BnF is Venice, 1622.

11. *Jugemens*, Vol. 4, Pt. 1, art. 1063.

12. Thomassin, *La Méthode d'étudier*, I, pp. 102-14; and Baillet, *Jugemens des savans*, 1685-86 (Vol. 4, Pt. 1, art. 1047).

13. I, pp. 9-10.

14. Pt. 2, p. 69.

15. I, p. 103.

16. Baillet, *Jugemens des savans*, Vol. 4, Pt. 1, art. 1047.

17. Gilles Boileau, *Advis à Monsieur Ménage* (1656), p. 19; Charles Cotin, 'Lettre à Damis', *Œuvres meslées* (1659), sig. iii r.

18. See F. Gohin, 'La Fontaine et Platon', *La Fontaine*, pp. 38-39, 47.

19. Perrot d'Ablancourt, *Lettres et préfaces critiques*, p. 66; J. T. Nothnagle, 'Poet or hierophant' (on d'Aubigné); E. T. Dubois, '*Ingenium* et *iudicium*'; and Gournay, p. 152.

20. Quoted by Bray, p. 87.

21. *Remarques*, pp. 446-47.

22. *Réflexions*, p. 17.

23. See the important article of D. C. Potts, '"Une carrière épineuse"'.

24. See Cronk, 'Une poétique platonicienne à l'époque classique'.

25. *Opuscules critiques*, p. 350.

26. Similarly, Beni, who produced the précis of Plato's writings on poetry mentioned above, can hardly be described as anti-aristotelian, as he was also the author of a long commentary on the *Poetics* of Aristotle. The same supportive coexistence between aristotelianism and platonism is found in a quite different area: in describing physics teaching in the faculties, L. W. B. Brockliss remarks that the strong emphasis on aristotelianism did not preclude a deep interest in Plato on the part of some teachers, a tradition which survived 'at least till the mid-seventeenth century', and was perpetuated by the Oratorians (whose founder was Pierre Bérulle). 'Not that these supporters of Platonism had any intention of replacing Aristotle by Plato,' writes Brockliss. 'On the contrary, they were simply interested in showing how much Aristotle himself had relied on his predecessor, and stressing areas where the latter had something extra to offer, as in the study of the soul's faculties' (*French Higher Education*, p. 339).

27. Vol. 4, Pt. 1, art. 1047.

28. Vol. 4, Pt. 1, art. 1085.

29. 'Esquisse du vocabulaire', p. 367.

30. These ideas are discussed in more detail by R. W. Lee, *Ut Pictura Poesis*, pp. 13-16. Since Panofsky and Lee, D. Mahon has discovered a fragment of a manuscript treatise on painting

(1607-15) by Giovanni Battista Agucchi which anticipates Bellori's ideas by half a century, and which shows that Bellori was summarising and codifying ideas which were already current (*Studies in Seicento Art and Theory*).

[31.] André Félibien, *Entretiens sur les vies des peintres* (1685-88) (see the passage quoted by Brody, 'Platonisme et classicisme', pp. 194-95); and Roger de Piles, *L'Idée du peintre parfait* (1699) (see the passage quoted by Tocanne, *L'Idée de nature*, p. 339).

[32.] *Lettres*, pp. 171-72. (The fragment is one of a series of fragments first published when Bellori appended them to his life of the artist.)

[33.] Panofsky demonstrates the similarities between this fragment of Poussin and texts of Ficino and Lomazzo (*Idea*, pp. 242-43); Blunt has since suggested that Poussin's direct source is the Italian translation of a treatise by Dürer, and adds: 'Ce fragment représente un aspect exceptionnel de la pensée de Poussin; c'est en effet, à notre connaissance, l'unique cas où il ait noté une idée néo-platonicienne' (Poussin, *Lettres*, p. 172).

[34.] La Fontaine, *Œuvres diverses*, p. 770.

[35.] *Réflexions*, XXIV, p. 41.

[36.] Quentin Hope assesses Saint-Evremond's critical principles in this way: 'What delicacy, penetration, and finesse perceive is usually something hidden—*caché* or *secret*. They would offer little delight if they revealed only observations accessible to all; to unveil a secret, to discover what is hidden, is an exquisite pleasure. Such revelations are the mark of a great author: Corneille discovers "ce qu'il y a de plus caché dans nos cœurs"' (*Saint-Evremond*, pp. 96-97; the quotation is from 'un Auteur qui me demandoit mon sentiment d'une Piece où l'Héroïne ne faisoit que se lamenter'). Hope also quotes (p. 102) a passage from 'De la Comédie Angloise' which shows Saint-Evremond's belief that simplicity must be artful; *le naturel* and *le caché* are not mutually exclusive: 'Le facile et le naturel conviennent assez, dans leur opposition à ce qui est dur ou forcé; mais quand il s'agit de bien entrer dans la nature des choses, ou dans le naturel des personnes, on n'avouera que ce n'est pas toûjours avec facilité qu'on y réussit. Il y a je ne sais quoi d'intérieur, je ne sais quoi de caché qui se découvriroit à nous, si nous savions approfondir les matieres davantage.'

[37.] On the *métamorphose* and the *énigme*, see my articles 'Metaphor and metamorphosis' and 'The enigma of French classicism'.

[38.] *Histoire*, III, p. 164.

[39.] *Œuvres*, 'Discours', sig. ev r.

[40.] In later editions of the translation, Baudoin makes modest changes to the 'Préface'; it seems as if by the end of the century, it had become more necessary to insist on the utility of the image: 'Aprés cela il ne faut pas douter, que l'Invention des Images ne soit, non-seulement trés-ingénieuse et trés-agréable, mais encore fort-avantageuse et fort-utile et trés digne de la curiosité de toutes les Personnes spirituelles et qui aiment les belles choses' (1698 edition, I, sigs. *3r-v).

[41.] 'What *was* French classicism?', p. 75, note 30.

[42.] 'What *was* French classicism?', p. 75, note 30.

[43.] 'Platonisme et classicisme', p. 14:

[44.] 40/1, No. 158.

[45.] 'Lettre à Damis', *Œuvres*, sig. iii r.

[46.] There is perhaps a remote parallel in the results of recent research into Newton's alchemical studies, which show surprising connections between the seventeenth-century scientific revolution and Renaissance neoplatonism (see B. J. T. Dobbs, *The Foundations of Newton's Alchemy*).

3: Inventing *LE JE NE SAIS QUOI*: Bouhours's *Entretiens d'Ariste et d'Eugène*

L'art de deviner, qui est deffendu pour tant de choses, a tousjours esté permis pour les Enigmes. (Cotin)[1]

'Nous avons vû peu de Livres de nos jours qui ayent été reçus plus favorablement parmi ce qu'on appelle le beau monde, et qui ayent été lus avec plus d'avidité et de plaisir.'[2] So wrote Baillet of the *Entretiens d'Ariste et d'Eugène*. Dominique Bouhours (1628-1702) taught at the Jesuit Collège de Clermont in Paris, and acquired a considerable reputation in the capital as an arbiter of literary taste—it is to Bouhours that Racine apparently submitted *Phèdre* for his grammatical approval[3] —and as a polemicist against the Jansenists. The *Entretiens*, his first work of poetic theory, provoked much debate on first publication in 1671, and there were immediate responses from Jansenists (notably Barbier d'Aucour) and from the grammarian Ménage.[4] Published just three years before Boileau's *Art poétique* and *Traité du sublime*, Bouhours's work is one of the most sophisticated statements of French classical poetic theory: yet it has received scant attention from modern commentators, and a critical edition is badly needed. Influenced perhaps by the model of Méré's six *Conversations*, published only a couple of years earlier (1668-69), the *Entretiens* are constructed as a series of six dialogues on seemingly diverse yet obviously interlocking topics; the work has a much more complex structure than, say, Rapin's *Réflexions sur la poétique*, and it poses a deliberate interpretative challenge to the reader. The work has regularly been plundered for quotations on a variety of topics, but the six dialogues have rarely if ever been considered as an integrated whole.

I. Speaking of language: 'La Langue françoise'

The second entretien, on 'La Langue françoise', provides us with the simplest entry into the work. A large part of this dialogue is taken up with an enumeration of words whose precise meanings had recently been extended or had shifted. Thus: '*Habile*, a presque changé de signification. On ne le dit plus gueres, pour dire docte et sçavant: et on entend par un homme *habile*, un homme adroit et qui a de la conduite' (63). Such remarks mark Bouhours as a successor to Vaugelas, as Saint-Evremond remarked: 'Il n'y a pas d'Ecrivain que j'estime plus que lui: nôtre Langue lui doit plus qu'à aucun Auteur, sans en excepter Vaugelas.'[5]

Bouhours does not confine himself to lexical issues, however, and he is also concerned with poetry and the nature of poetic expression. This whole discussion rests explicitly on a mimetic model whereby language is the instrument which we use to mirror our thought: 'Les langues n'ont été inventées que pour exprimer les conceptions de nôtre esprit: et [...] chaque langue est un art particulier de rendre ces conceptions sensibles, de les faire voir, et de les peindre' (32). The theory acquires here a chauvinistic slant, for he argues that each language possesses its individual imitative genius, with French, not surprisingly, as the only modern language which is a worthy successor to Latin. Spanish, like some fairground distorting-mirror, enlarges grotesquely the objects it reflects, 'elle fait pour l'ordinaire les objets plus grands qu'ils ne sont, et va plus loin que la nature: car elle ne garde nulle mesure en ses metaphores' (33). Italian, on the other hand, falls prey to the opposite vice of prettifying its subjects, at the expense of truth: 'Elle n'enfle peut-estre pas tant les choses; mais elle les embellit davantage. Elle songe plus à faire de belles peintures que de bons portraits; et pourveu que ses tableaux plaisent, elle ne se soucie pas trop qu'ils ressemblent' (33-34). Bouhours's strategy is clear: he is attempting to describe contemporary stylistic norms as the inevitable and unchanging product of the 'genius' of the French language. The criticisms directed at ornate style, and at poetry and rhetoric more generally, arise in the first instance from moral scruples (elaborately metaphorical language distorts truth, while simple, unadorned language runs the risk of obscuring the distinction between actual reality and the lie of fiction), and these tensions resurface here, now disguised in the attributes of other—inferior—languages. When the Jesuit Bouhours describes the Spanish language as grandiloquent, overblown and stilted, 'monté sur des échasses' (29), this is a ringing pronouncement of moral disapprobation: to indulge in Spanish hyperbole is not merely absurd but sinful. Italian preoccupation with pretty artifice is no less inimical to truthful imitation—that is, to truth. Like the painter who, failing to capture a good likeness in his portrait, compensated by plastering it with gold, so Italian rhetoric is concerned more to please than to tell the truth (34). French, now sole master of the field, is left as the only remaining viable repository of truth:

> [La langue Françoise] n'aime point les exagerations, parce qu'elles alterent *la verité* [...]. Nôtre langue n'use aussi que fort sobrement des hyperboles, parce que ce sont des figures ennemies de *la verité*: en quoy elle tient de nôtre humeur franche et sincere, qui ne peut souffrir la fausseté et le mensonge. (34, my emphasis)

The French language rejects excessive ornament, and would ideally like its words to be entirely naked (37), hence the repeated emphasis on the quality of *naïveté*.[6] Bouhours thus sidesteps the obstacle of rhetoric and presents the French language as the golden mean, the instrument of truthful simplicity, in Ariste's words 'le langage des hommes raisonnables' (42).

The dilemma facing the seventeenth-century critic lies of course in trying to elaborate a theory of poetic discourse which can reconcile this ideal of a language unrhetorical enough to be morally acceptable with another, apparently incongruous ideal, of a language forceful enough to be linguistically acceptable. In other words, how to be limpid but not limp? This tension is felt in Bouhours's revealing comment that 'le beau langage ressemble à une eau pure et nette qui n'a point de goust' (37). Bouhours claims that French, and French alone, enshrines 'l'ordre naturel' of thought, expressing ideas in a like sequence to that in which the mind conceives them, an advantage to which not even Latin or Greek could lay claim (38). This explains how untutored Frenchwomen speak so well, 'naturellement et sans nulle étude' (39), for they need merely to allow their thoughts to be formulated spontaneously, and the French language will do the rest:

> Il est vray, reprit Ariste, qu'il n'y a rien de plus juste, de plus propre,
> et de plus naturel, que le langage de la pluspart des femmes
> Françoises. Les mots dont elles se servent, semblent tout neufs, et
> faits exprés pour ce qu'elles disent, quoy-qu'ils soient communs:
> et si la nature elle mesme vouloit parler, je croy qu'elle emprunteroit
> leur langue pour parler naïvement.[7]

The attraction of this explanation is evident: the postulation of an 'ordre naturel' helps Bouhours to explain how language that is 'simple' can simultaneously be 'noble'. The mere unadorned expression of thought, in its 'natural' order, will possess intrinsic persuasive force, without the author needing to have recourse to the armoury of rhetorical figures and tropes. The French language has attained a point of perfection, as is shown by the best modern translations, which are in no way inferior to the originals (65). He who knows the language well can express anything in French, and though Ariste notes some lacunae in the vocabulary of French, Eugène counters with the observation that even classical Latin lacked the capacity to express in one word numerous concepts for which modern French has a term (47-49).

II. SPEAKING AROUND LANGUAGE: 'LA MER' AND 'LE SECRET'

The long *entretien* on 'La langue françoise' is flanked on either side by two much shorter *entretiens* on apparently quite different topics. 'La Mer', one of the earliest of all Bouhours's works, provides a pleasing and easy way into the book. Two friends, reunited after a period of separation, resolve to talk together during daily walks along the sea's edge. The location has been carefully chosen:

> Car outre que le sable est ferme et uni en cét endroit-là, ce qui rend
> la promenade aisée, on voit d'un costé une citadelle fort bien bastie;
> et de l'autre, des dunes d'une figure fort bizarre, qui regnent le
> long de la coste, et qui representent dans la perspective quelque
> chose de semblable à de vieux palais tombez en ruine. (5)

Already in this, the fourth sentence of the book, the metaphorical value of this description of the natural world seems predominant. Ariste and Eugène will tread a firm line in their discussions—'ferme et uni' might describe their tread, even their language, as well as the sand—between the rival distractions of the regular and the irregular.

The opposition between force and simplicity which we saw to be pivotal to the second *entretien* is thus already in evidence at the start of the book. It recurs only a couple of pages later in a discussion of the relative merits of the sea, calm or rough: Ariste admires calmness, which he finds 'doux' and 'beau'; Eugène, predictably, dismisses these qualities as 'bien fade', preferring the excitement of roughness: 'La mer n'est jamais plus belle, que quand elle est irritée: c'est alors qu'elle frappe les yeux, et qu'elle se fait regarder avec admiration' (8). Again, it is hardly the literal description of the natural world that is of primary importance here.[8] The application of this dichotomy to contrasting prose styles (attic/asiatic, Italian/Spanish, etc.) is obvious, especially in the light of the discussion that will follow in the second *entretien*. And yet to introduce the argument here in connection with nature alters the argument, for an additional tension is added, that between art and nature.

Admiring the ever-changing colours of the sea, Ariste comments that this is something beyond the power of art to imitate: 'Ce mélange fait une peinture naturelle, que l'art ne peut imiter' (7). They return to the theme when they are contemplating shells on the beach; these are so varied in colour and form, and so carefully shaped, that they resemble works of art, says Ariste. 'Je dirois presque [...], répondit Eugène, que la nature pour se divertir, imite quelquefois celuy qui fait toûjours gloire de l'imiter' (10). Thus art cannot always adequately imitate nature (the sea); and even when it can, the result is not necessarily more beautiful or more regular than the objects which nature herself produces (the shell). The first dialogue concludes with a discussion concerning the characteristics of pearls. The beauty of most precious stones emerges only after man has worked on them: 'La nature ne fait que les ébaucher; il faut que l'art les acheve en les polissant'. Pearls are exceptional, 'des chef d'œuvres de la nature, où l'art n'a rien à ajoûter', because they come from the sea already perfectly round, white and polished: 'La nature y met la derniere main, avant qu'on les arrache de leurs nacres' (24). Art may sometimes improve upon nature, but not always. Nature sometimes has the last word.

The sea-shore setting thus provides the ideal backdrop for a debate about the relationship between art and nature, since all the necessary metaphorical props—sea, shells, pearls—are conveniently and naturally at hand. Commentators have remarked on Bouhours's sensitivity to nature in this inaugural dialogue;[9] much more remarkable, however, is Bouhours's sensitivity to nature's metaphorical potential.

If the discussion is in the final resort inconclusive, it serves at least to raise the question of imitation: what does it mean to speak of art imitating nature? Already in the first *entretien*, Bouhours addresses the question which Boileau will confront in the third canto of the *Art poétique* ('Il n'est point de Serpent, ni de Monstre odieux, / Qui par l'art imité ne puisse plaire aux yeux', III, 1-2). Ariste favours calmness; he has himself experienced a storm at sea, and points out to Eugène that if he too had had this experience, he would not be so admiring of the angry sea, 'ou du moins vous en trouveriez le portrait plus beau que l'original' (8). Eugène does not however dissent from this last view. The fear of a genuine storm would distract one from admiring its beauty, he says; but more importantly, he suggests that the view of the storm from an outside vantage point is more beautiful than viewing it from the centre: 'Peut-estre

Elle l'appaise & l'emeut.

E gouuerne d'icy le calme & la tem-
   peste.
Sous moy s'emeut le trouble, & le trouble
   s'arreste;
A mon illustre frein la Mer soufmet ses flots:
Et selon que le vent le besoin du bas Monde,
   Mon puissant esprit fait de l'onde
   Le mouuement & le repos.

B iij

ON a cent fois comparé les Peuples auec les va-
gues de la Mer: mais ie ne sçay si l'Eloquence
qui gouuerne les Peuples, auoit encor esté compa-
rée à cette Vertu superieure, à qui les Mers obeis-
sent. C'est la pensée de cette Deuise, où le Croissant
& les Ondes asurées des Armes de M. le President de
Mesmes, representent cette Magistrature d'esprit, &
cette Souueraineté d'Eloquence . par laquelle il re-
gne dans les Assemblées. Aussi a-t'on dit de luy qu'il
estoit l'agreable Tyran des opinions, & que la vio-
lence de ses ars maintenoit le Droit & appuyoit la
Iustice. On l'a veu sous le regne passé & sous le pre-
sent, conseruer l'authorité du Prince par l'authorité
de sa parole; on l'a veu emouuoir ou appaiser les Es-
prits selon les diuers besoins de l'Estat; & par là il a
fait voir que les Particuliers ont leur empire aussi bien
que les Souuerains, & que la Souueraineté la plus ab-
soluë n'est pas tousiours celle de la Pourpre.

Figure 4. A *devise* on the subject of eloquence, from Le Moyne,
Devises heroiques et morales (Paris, 1649).

que la mer courroucée sera encore plus belle dans l'éloignement et en perspective' (8). He thus acknowledges the crucial importance of the aesthetic process; the object itself, Bouhours's storm or Boileau's serpent, may be frightening, but its artistic representation can evoke a quite different response. Bouhours is clearly sensitive to the difficulties underlying any poetic theory grounded on the principle of mimesis.

These problems surface most revealingly in the shifting metaphorical patterns of the first dialogue. The example of the changing colours of the sea is first used to demonstrate art's inability to imitate nature (7); but only a page later, the example of a storm at sea is used to show the qualitative difference between object and artefact, and the aesthetic superiority of art over nature (8). And from being in different ways a metaphor of literary discourse, the sea is later produced both as an image of God, combining both his 'grandeur' and his 'pureté' (though this takes us back by a different route to the idea of literary discourse), and also as an image of the world and of the vanity of man: 'Mais ne remarquez-vous pas, poursuivit Ariste, que la mer a plusieurs faces' (18).

The title and subject of the opening dialogue is a cleverly chosen one, for it provides a multi-faceted metaphor which allows Bouhours to suggest a number of problem areas without necessarily delineating a solution. The simplicity/strength dichotomy which is central to the second dialogue is also present here, but we can sense Bouhours straining to go beyond it when he introduces the art/nature dichotomy and the consequent reflections on imitation. In addition there are moments in the text when Bouhours alludes to at least the possibility of a non-mimetic poetic theory, and so to something distinctly different from the theory assumed in 'La Langue françoise'.

The first of these is when he hints at what we might now label the 'aesthetic' of the Romantic sublime. Near the start of the first dialogue, Eugène describes the excitement of the angry sea:

> Il me semble que la mer n'est jamais si belle que dans sa colere, lorsqu'elle s'enfle, qu'elle s'agite, qu'elle mugit d'une manière effroyable, et qu'il se fait une espece de guerre entre les vents et les flots. Ces vagues qui s'entrechoquent avec tant d'impetuosite; ces montagnes d'eau et d'écume qui s'élevent et qui s'abaissent tout d'un coup; ce bruit, ce desordre, ce fracas, tout cela inspire je ne sçay quelle horreur accompagnée de plaisir, et fait un spectacle également terrible et agreable. (7)

This is a far cry from the notion that 'la principale règle est de plaire et de toucher'.[10] The pre-romantic topos of the tempest and the description of an aesthetic response in which pleasure and horror are intermingled seem almost to anticipate the Burkeian sublime; it is crucial to note, therefore, that the word *sublime* is not used here (though it is used elsewhere in the book, always in a different sense).

There is an echo of this theme in the third dialogue, 'Le Secret'. Eugène is describing his admiration for men who are able to keep secrets, a mark, he thinks, of a noble soul:

> Pour moy je regarde les personnes secretes comme ces grandes
> rivieres, dont on ne voit point le fond, et qui ne font point de bruit;
> ou comme ces grandes forests, dont le silence remplit l'ame de je
> ne sçay quelle horreur religieuse. (97-98)

Again, the emotion described is one in which admiration is tinged with horror. It is significant that in both these passages Bouhours employs the phrase 'je ne sçay quelle horreur' which prepares us for the fifth dialogue. But more important than the tentative anticipation of Burke is the deliberate rejection of Horace. The line 'Omne tulit punctum, qui miscuit utile dulci' is echoed throughout the classical period:[11] for Bouhours to juxtapose 'plaisir' with 'horreur', 'agreable' with 'terrible' is to flout the Horatian precept—and to suggest a signal shortcoming in prevailing poetic theory.

A second distinctly dissident element in Bouhours's approach is his recurrent interest in the mysterious and the secretive. This is apparent in the first dialogue when Ariste and Eugène discuss the cause of the tides and later the cause of the sea-water's saltiness. The views of a whole series of 'Philosophes', from Aristotle and Plato onwards, are recounted; their various theories about the tides are juxtaposed in a way which recalls the technique of Montaigne in the 'Apologie de Raymond Sebond', where the spiralling accumulation of mutually inconsistent explanations leads to ultimate scepticism. Bouhours is evidently closer to the Ancients than to the Moderns: although the Ancient philosophers were unable to find a solution, it is clear that their seventeenth-century successors have fared no better. We must accept, Bouhours concludes, that some aspects of nature are inaccessible to human reason—not a view that cartesians would have shared.

> Il y a des mysteres dans la nature, comme dans la grace,
> incomprehensibles à l'esprit humain: la sagesse ne consiste pas à
> en avoir l'intelligence; mais à sçavoir que les plus intelligens ne
> sont pas capables de les comprendre. Ainsi le meilleur parti pour
> nous est de confesser nôtre ignorance, et d'adorer humblement la
> sagesse de Dieu, qui a voulu que ce secret fust caché aux hommes.
> (18)

After trying in vain to make sense of the various theories put forward to explain the saltiness of the sea, the two friends conclude in similar fashion: 'Ce sont des secrets, qu'il faut adorer, et qu'il ne faut point aprofondir. Disons-le encore une fois; c'est proprement dans la mer, que Dieu est admirable, et incomprehensible' (21).

This reference to 'secrets' prepares us for the third dialogue. The subject of 'Le Secret' might seem an unexpected one, but it was something of a literary topos, and Bouhours draws on a wide range of literary sources.[12] Discussion ranges from the personal morality of keeping secrets and to the necessity of secrecy in public life; nowhere, in either 'La Mer' or 'Le Secret', is the subject of language explicitly mentioned, yet it seems always present. Any number of remarks in the third dialogue could easily be turned to apply to literary discourse: Ariste suggests that the 'grandeur' of a Prince depends on 'le secret' (98); and Eugène comments on the difficulty of being secret:

> Tout le monde est persuadé [...] qu'il faut estre secret; mais peu de gens sçavent comment il faut l'estre. On connoist assez la necessité et l'excellence de cette vertu; mais on ignore fort la methode et la maniere de la pratiquer. (105)

Bouhours's strategy is clear. In discussing 'La Langue françoise' explicitly, he cautiously alludes to the problems posed by the prevailing mimetic poetic theory. He then innocently surrounds this dialogue with two other shorter discussions on apparently different topics, in both of which he is able to underpin the importance of the secretive and the mysterious, qualities which are not adequately accounted for by any simple mimetic explanation. It is left for the reader to apply the lessons of the first and third dialogues to the second. The total absence of discussion of literary language in 'La Mer' and 'Le Secret' becomes a device which allows Bouhours to carry forward the debate from the safe ground of 'La Langue françoise' into more daring waters. The first three dialogues of the work constitute a triptych, in which the large central panel sets the theme, and in which the two side panels reflect upon it and obliquely expand upon it.

III. 'LE BEL ESPRIT' AND THE BEGINNINGS OF NEOPLATONISM

With the fourth dialogue, 'Le Bel Esprit', Bouhours returns openly to a consideration of literary language. Themes from earlier dialogues are taken up once more; the discussion of secrecy and mystery in the first and third dialogues is echoed and extended in a passage which deals with certain writers who express themselves in enigmas and mysteries (120). More importantly, the extended sketch of the history of the French language in the second dialogue is here continued with a discussion of why certain periods produce greater works of art than others ('le siecle present est pour la France', 135), and a more detailed account of how the ideal of linguistic perfection had emerged. In the first edition, Bouhours writes of Ronsard's crucial influence: 'Ronsard fut le premier, qui chassa la barbarie de la France, en inspirant à nos peres l'amour et le goust des lettres' (133). Two years later, in the fourth edition, this sentence undergoes an interesting change, with Malherbe ousting Ronsard as the godfather (or midwife?) of modern French: linguistic history is thus rewritten, and a contemporary commonplace reaffirmed: 'Malherbe a reformé en France l'idée de la poésie, et nous a donné le goust des bons vers'.[13] The dialogue concludes with a consideration of the various factors which have helped purify the language in recent times, notably the influence of women, and the impact of religious polemics (135-38).

Less discursive than the earlier dialogues, however, the fourth *entretien* is more expository and more assertive in tone. The starting-point of the discussion is the already familiar tension between 'delicatesse' and 'force' in literary discourse, between what is 'agreable et fleuri' and what is 'solide et fort' (117). Twice in the space of a few pages Bouhours juxtaposes the terms 'delicatesse' and 'force':

> Je vois bien à cette heure, dit Eugene, pourquoy les veritables beaux esprits sont si rares: des qualitez aussi opposées, que la vivacité et le bon sens, la delicatesse et la force, sans parler des autres, ne se rencontrent pas toûjours ensemble. Mais je voudrois bien sçavoir, ajoûta-t-il, d'où viennent toutes ces qualitez qui font le bel esprit. (123)

It is this crucial question which the fourth dialogue will address.

Dismissing what passes for wit in society, Bouhours produces a definition of 'bel esprit' which is centred on the individual's ability to discern objects at their proper value:

> Car la veritable beauté de l'esprit consiste dans un discernement juste et delicat [...]. Ce discernement fait connoistre les choses telles qu'elles sont en elles-mesmes, sans qu'on demeure court, comme le peuple, qui s'arreste à la superficie: ni aussi sans qu'on aille trop loin, comme ces esprits rafinez, qui à force de subtiliser, s'évaporent en des imaginations vaines et chimeriques. (115)

Here again is Bouhours's characteristic feel for compromise as he treads a path between two extremes. But now the emphasis shifts away from the object of imitation (the sturdy citadel versus the irregular dunes, in the first dialogue) and towards the perceiving subject, the spectator.

This train of thought leads on naturally to the idea of genius. '[La beauté de l'esprit] demande un genie capable de toutes les belles connoissances; une intelligence élevée et étenduë, que rien ne surpasse, et que rien ne borne' (120). Nature alone does not make a 'bel esprit', asserts Eugène (125), but he nonetheless acknowledges the important role of genius:

> Le genie est une habileté particuliere, et un talent que la nature donne à quelques hommes pour de certaines choses. Les uns ont du genie pour la peinture; les autres en ont pour les vers: il ne suffit pas d'avoir de l'esprit et de l'imagination pour exceller dans la poësie; il faut estre né poëte, et avoir ce naturel qui ne dépend ni de l'art, ni de l'étude, et qui tient quelque chose de l'inspiration. (130)

The word 'inspiration', although tentative ('qui tient *quelque chose de*'), is daring, and Bouhours underscores the idea when he goes on to speak of 'le genie' as 'un don du ciel où la terre n'a point de part; c'est je ne sçay quoy de divin' (130).

With such a choice of vocabulary, Bouhours seems to be edging gently towards a platonist account of poetic creation. Plato's name has already been mentioned twice in the work: in 'La Mer', there is an innocuous reference to his views on the tides (11), and in 'Le Secret', perhaps not totally innocuously, Plato is cited on the need for secrecy: 'ce qui a fait juger à Platon, que le devoir de l'homme prudent est de connoistre quelles sont précisément les choses qu'il faut taire, et qu'il faut dire' (111). Plato or platonism recurs twice more in this fourth dialogue. First Eugène quotes Plato's view that beauty depends on goodness: 'Souvenez vous de ce que dit Platon, que la beauté est comme la fleur de la bonté' (117). For the first time Bouhours refers to Plato in a discussion of poetic language, though it is neither the best known nor, for Bouhours's generation, the most contentious aspect of his poetic theory. The closest Bouhours comes to mentioning poetic fury is the account Ariste gives of the views of 'je ne sçay quel Philosophe Platonicien', who maintains that genius is a product of the humours combining to produce 'une exhalaison chaude':

> C'est cette flâme qui éclaire la raison, et qui échauffe l'imagination
> en mesme temps; que c'est elle qui rend visibles à l'ame les especes
> des choses, et qui luy fait voir tous les objets dans leur jour: en un
> mot, que c'est à la lueur de ce beau feu, que l'entendement découvre
> et contemple les veritez les plus obscures. (123)

Though attributed to an unnamed platonist rather than to Plato himself, this sounds remarkably similar to Plato's idea of divine fury. But the all-important word 'fureur' is studiously avoided. Indeed, on the only occasion that the term does appear in the work, in the second dialogue, it is used with a distinctively pejorative flavour:

> [Nos Muses] sont si sages, et si retenuës, qu'elles ne se permettent
> aucun excès. Elles n'ont garde de s'abandonner à cette fureur, qui
> toute divine qu'elle est, fait dire aux autres assez souvent bien des
> folies. (35-36)

The fourth dialogue has poetic language as its central concern, but the emphasis on 'le bel esprit' and 'le génie' takes the discussion beyond the mimetic framework of the earlier part of the work in two ways. First, consideration of the writer's 'inspiration' and the tentative hints of a neoplatonist poetic theory suggest that the writer is more than a simple imitator through words of an external reality. Secondly, Bouhours appears to be making the radical suggestion that 'le bel esprit' and 'le discernement' are active qualities required in the reader of a literary work. His explanations of 'le bel esprit' are not entirely coherent. What is significant, however, is the attempt, however rudimentary, to give a 'reader-oriented' dimension to his poetic theory, an attempt which by implication demonstrates the inadequacy of the narrow mimetic literary model according to which the reader/spectator looks on passively at the author's imitation of reality. To stress the reader's active participation in the text is to make partially redundant the passive mimetic relationship between reality and artefact.[14] And perhaps, too, it is a timely invitation to Bouhours's present readers to read between the lines of the text before them.

The discussion of 'le bel esprit' further provides an answer to those who criticised the moral function and status of literature. If the writer is possessed of 'un don du ciel, [...] je ne sçay quoi de divin', and if readers are equipped with 'bel esprit' and 'discernement' to help them interpret the writer's inspired pronouncements, it is hard to argue that poetry obfuscates truth. On the contrary, it is 'discernement' which allows the reader to see 'les choses telles qu'elles sont en elles-mesmes' (115); it is the writer's inspiration which reveals 'tous les objets dans leur jour', 'les veritez les plus obscures' (123). The Jesuit Bouhours is adamant that poetic language has the power to reveal higher truths; by implication, therefore, it can be a force for moral good. The problem which he still faces is how to set that conviction on a theoretical footing.

IV. THE CREATION OF A NEW CONCEPT: 'LE JE NE SÇAY QUOY'

'Le je ne sçay quoy a beaucoup de vogue parmi nous, et [...] nous sommes en cela aussi mysterieux que nos voisins' (145): the phrase was much used in French, and Bouhours is also aware of the Spanish, Italian (and indeed Latin) equivalents.[15] The two interlocutors discuss the *je ne sais quoi* in relation to a range of topics, from friendship to kingship, but moving methodically, despite appearances, from nature, via art, to theology (grace). By its very nature the *je ne sais quoi* is indefinable, a point which Bouhours makes repeatedly: 'Ce ne seroit plus un je ne sçay quoy, si l'on savoit ce que c'est; sa nature est d'estre incomprehensible, et inexplicable' (140); 'on n'en peut mieux parler à mon gré, qu'en disant qu'on ne peut ni l'expliquer, ni le concevoir' (142); 'le pinceau et la langue ne peuvent exprimer le je ne sçay quoi qui fait tout' (145). As this last quotation makes clear, the *je ne sais quoi* transcends the received mimetic model; unable to be depicted in either words or pictures, it is something that defies imitation in the usual sense. 'En effet c'est quelque chose de si delicat, et de si imperceptible, qu'il échappe à l'intelligence la plus penetrante, et la plus subtile' (142).[16] If the *je ne sais quoi* is beyond imitation, it is also beyond rational explanation (147); we admire the machine, but without being able to see the spring which works it (142-43). And because it is not a rational phenomenon, different individuals may sometimes perceive it differently: taste is perhaps not an absolute value (146).

The *je ne sais quoi* is most obviously seen in the effect which it produces (143), and Bouhours repeatedly emphasises its affective force with a series of emotive verbs. Without the *je ne sais quoi* even the finest qualities 'n'ont rien qui frappe, ni qui touche' (141); Bouhours speaks of 'ce je ne sçay quoy qui surprend, et qui emporte le cœur à une premiere veûë' (145); and again, 'c'est je ne sçay quoy qui nous surprend, qui nous éblouït, et qui nous enchante' (149): this is to anticipate Boileau's description of the impact of the sublime. But this view of the *je ne sais quoi* as something which sweeps over us seems to fit uneasily with Bouhours's other suggestion that it attains it effect by stimulating our imaginations: 'Il est du je ne sçay quoy comme de ces beautez couvertes d'un voile, qui sont d'autant plus estimées, qu'elles sont moins exposées à la veuë, et auxquelles l'imagination ajoûte toûjours quelque chose' (145).

The theme of mystery has already been anticipated, and the fifth *entretien* has echoes both of 'La Mer'—the mystery of the tides (147)—and of 'Le Secret'—cer-

tain things are best admired in silence (150). The significant innovation of this dia-
logue is to apply the *je ne sais quoi* specifically, though not exclusively, to literary
discourse. Eugène suggests that it is found only in natural objects, 'car pour les ouvrages
de l'art toutes les beautez y sont marquez, et l'on sait bien pourquoy ils plaisent'
(148). Ariste, predictably, disagrees, arguing that the *je ne sais quoi* is just as vital to
art as to nature, instancing the charm of paintings, of statues, and of 'les pieces delicates
en prose et en vers' (148). He contrasts the works of Balzac, whose beauties are
regular (and obvious), with those of Voiture, 'qui ont ces charmes secrets, ces graces
fines et cachées' (148), and which are far more pleasing.

In the final pages of the dialogue, Bouhours moves on to the subject of grace,
building on an earlier suggestion (144) that the *je ne sais quoi* is unknown and un-
knowable in the same way as God: 'Cette grace, dis-je, qu'est-ce autre chose qu'un je
ne sçay quoy surnaturel, qu'on ne peut ni expliquer, ni comprendre?' (149). We may
see this as a fitting climax to the discussion, which began with nature and then art, and
now culminates with theology. But what do we make of the conclusion, if we choose
to see the text as being essentially centred on problems of poetic theory? From this
standpoint, the 'theological' conclusion is even more interesting, for the reference to
a 'je ne sçay quoy surnaturel' seems to take on a neoplatonist tinge. At the very begin-
ning of the dialogue, in discussing the nature of close friendships, Eugène had spoken
of the influence of the stars: 'Mais ne peut-on pas dire [...] que c'est une influence des
astres, et une impression secrete de l'ascendant sous lequel nous sommes nez?' (140).[17]
Later the two interlocutors speak of 'un je ne sçay quoy dans les maladies'; in some
illnesses there is 'quelque chose de divin', while others are accompanied by fever,
and even this possesses a certain mystery: 'Ces accés si reglez, ces frissons et ces
chaleurs, ces intervalles dans un mal qui dure des années entieres, ne sont-ce pas
autant de je ne sçay quoy?' (147). Again, out of context, the remark might just be
taken to apply to *furor poeticus*—except of course that the earlier use of *fureur* was
pejorative. As in the fourth dialogue, these sporadic and tentative allusions to
neoplatonist poetic theory (both cast in the interrogative form) seem too frequent to
be altogether coincidental; yet they never occur as part of a discussion angled specifi-
cally on poetic theory. The seed of an idea is no more than planted.

Critics have not been generous about this fifth dialogue; Borgerhoff, for ex-
ample, finds it 'not very profound'. True, if we look to Bouhours for precise defini-
tions, then we will be disappointed; but we ought at least to recognise that Bouhours
is attempting to create a new literary concept. The term was of course already in
existence, but not as a literary critical term. There is no earlier theoretical discussion
of the *je ne sais quoi*: Pascal speaks of the idea, but in the context of an ethical discus-
sion, while Vaugelas's discussion is in the context of social behaviour.[18] For Méré,
the term is closely connected to the 'art de plaire' cultivated by the *honnête homme*, as
he describes it in *Des Agrémens* (1676):

> Ce que j'aime le mieux, et qu'on doit selon mon sens le plus
> souhaiter en tout ce qu'on fait pour plaire, c'est je ne sçay quoi qui
> se sent bien, mais qui ne s'explique pas si aisément, et je ne sçay de

quelle façon me faire entendre si je ne me sers du mot de gentillesse.[19]

Méré had earlier made frequent use of the phrase *je ne sçay quoi* in *Les Conversations*, and this may well have caught Bouhours's attention.[20] Thus Bouhours adopted a current phrase and turned it into a noun, reinventing it as a substantival literary critical term, *le je ne sais quoi*. His striking success can be gauged by contemporary dictionary-makers: no French dictionary before 1671, with the sole exception of Oudin (1640), contains the expression *je ne sais quoi*; after the *Entretiens*, every seventeenth-century dictionary except one includes the phrase. Richelet (1680) repeats Bouhours's quotation from Persius ('C'est une inflüence des astres'), and Furetière (1690) refers explicitly to Bouhours; only Ménage (1694) omits the phrase—and given his well-known hostility to Bouhours, the omission is surely calculated.[21]

Bouhours set out to launch a new critical term, and he succeeded. Rather than cavil at the imprecision of his definition, it is more instructive to consider how Bouhours uses the term and why he needs it. And while it is difficult—as Bouhours himself is the first to admit—to explain the nature of the *je ne sais quoi*, it is not difficult to explain its function within Bouhours's critical system. One of the criteria identified above as being essential to any innovative theory of poetic discourse was the need to achieve fullness of linguistic expression: Bouhours's concept of the *je ne sais quoi* does exactly that. The emphasis on its affective impact is designed to fulfil just that function. 'Toucher', 'frapper', 'surprendre', 'emporter', 'éblouir', 'enchanter'—Bouhours uses all these verbs in the course of the fifth dialogue to describe the effect of the *je ne sais quoi*; it is hard to object that language exhibiting this quality is failing altogether in its representative function.

If we consider the first five dialogues as a whole, the problematic nature of poetic language emerges strongly as a central concern. Bouhours is moreover evidently ill at ease with the prevailing mimetic model available to him, and he discreetly attempts a number of different 'secretive' strategies to overcome this. The idea of the 'bel esprit' is a clear attempt to introduce a morally positive concept and to draw attention away from the imitative word-object relationship and to focus it instead on the response of the perceiver. The introduction of the concept of the *je ne sais quoi* is similarly an attempt to produce a more reader-oriented theory of poetic discourse that can account for the idea of full expressivity. Together the *bel esprit* and the *je ne sais quoi* are designed to counter the twin objections that literary language is both over-imitative (therefore immoral) and under-imitative (therefore weak).

But two obvious problems remain for Bouhours. Firstly, it is not clear how the two concepts of the *bel esprit* and the *je ne sais quoi* relate to each other. Secondly, Bouhours has still not tackled the crucial dilemma posed by mimetic poetic theory, that is its tendency to turn language into a nomenclaturist instrument. In these first five dialogues, Bouhours has employed various strategies to hint at the hidden secrets of poetic language above and beyond the rational explanations of contemporary theorists. But neither the *bel esprit* nor the *je ne sais quoi* help us to understand the material structure of the poetic word: it is that problem which Bouhours reserves for the final dialogue.

v. 'Des Devises': the poetics of the emblem

The sixth and final *entretien*, occupying almost half the book, is not necessarily the 'conclusion' we might have expected. The subject of the 'device' is technical and rather rebarbative, and Bouhours deals with it at extraordinary length. The problem for the reader is evident: is this a free-standing essay, or does it relate in any significant way to the preceding discussion of poetic language? It is necessary, in order to answer this question, to situate Bouhours's discussion in the broader context of a debate about the *devise* and other related forms of symbolic representation which has its origins in the Renaissance.

One conspicuous instance of the Renaissance's new attitude towards symbolic representation is shown by the interest in the hieroglyph following the rediscovery in 1419 of Horapollo's *Hieroglyphica*.[22] The hieroglyph, absorbed into the prevailing structure of neoplatonist thought, was seen to provide a prototype for the perfect expression of an idea: 'If one could only decipher hieroglyphs,' writes Wittkower, 'one would have access not only to many ancient mysteries, but above all to the secret of how to express the essence of an idea, its platonic form, as it were, perfect and complete in itself, by means of an image.'[23] The extent to which these Renaissance concerns with hieroglyphics survive and prosper in the so-called scientific age of the seventeenth century has not always been understood. Horapollo was still considered interesting enough in 1618 for the Jesuit Nicolas Caussin (also the author of a work on sacred and secular rhetoric) to publish *De symbolica Ægyptiorum sapientia*, containing the Greek original together with a Latin translation, and followed by various other compilations of hieroglyphic and symbolic material.[24] Pierio Valeriano's *Hieroglyphica* (1556), the great summa of Renaissance hieroglyphical thought and material which draws on classical sources, the Kabbala and the Bible, as well as on Horapollo, continued to be republished in the original Latin,[25] and in 1615 even appeared in a French translation.[26] In the same period, Pierre Dinet published his *Cinq Livres des hieroglyphiques, où sont contenus les [...] secrets de la nature* (1614). In the preface he writes that the greatest gift of grace which God gave man, and which separates him from animals, is the use of reason and language, and he goes on to describe two types of language:

> Cette escriture pareillement se considere en deux façons: en la commune, dont on use ordinairement: et l'occulte secrette, qu'on déguise d'infinies sortes, chacun selon sa fantaisie, pour ne la rendre intelligible qu'entre soy, et ses consçachans, inventee aù surplus ja dés les premiers, et plus heureux siecles, souz l'ombre et nuage des plantes, animaux, et autres telles choses, par les Prestres et Sages des Hebrieux, Chaldees, Egyptiens, Ethiopiens, Indiens, pour voiler les sacrez secrets de leur Theologie et Philosophie: afin de

les garentir et soustraire du prophanement de la multitude et en
laisser la cognoissance aux gens dignes: Pour autant que les yeux
de l'ame du commun peuple, ne sçauroient bonnement supporter
les lumineux estincellemens de la Divinité. (sigs iii r-v)

This advocacy of an occult and secret language for initiates, to coexist with the
common language of everyday usage, is all the more remarkable when we recall that
in the very same period Pierre de Deimier was arguing for a poetic language grounded
narrowly on the criterion of reason:

Le mesme rang d'excellence et de vertu que le Soleil tient au monde,
et l'ame au corps, la raison se l'atribuë en toutes les actions des
hommes, et mesmes en la Poësie où la raison est estroictement
necessaire.[27]

The Malherbian plea for reason and clarity in poetry is well known, but it acquires a
different significance when we recall that the years immediately following the ap-
pearance of Deimier's *Académie de l'art poétique* saw the publication of works by
Caussin, Valeriano and Dinet, whose common interest in the hieroglyph was wholly
inimical to the spirit of Deimier's ideal of rational poetic discourse. Neoplatonist
notions of language survive openly at least into the early part of the seventeenth cen-
tury, and form part of the context in which Malherbe and others argue for a clear and
reasonable poetic language.[28] The ideas of Horapollo and Valeriano are also perpetu-
ated in the seventeenth century through Cesare Ripa's *Iconologia*, first published in
1593, and soon an established classic. A French version of Ripa by Jean Baudoin was
published in the 1630s and reprinted all through the century, an essential text for the
understanding of French allegorical painting and sculpture in the seventeenth and
eighteenth centuries.[29]

This interest in symbolic expression extended still further, however. The redis-
covery of hieroglyphical and other allegorical languages stimulated the invention of
original symbols or picture-images and a new genre, the emblem, was born. The
founding text of this tradition is Andrea Alciati's *Emblemata* (1531), and thereafter
emblem books poured forth from the presses in countless number. The term *emblem*
seems to have been used initially to describe a purely verbal artefact, and in the 1560s
it became confused with another term, *devise*;[30] by the 1640s, however, the form of
the emblem had become conventionalised as a trio of caption, figure and epigram.

For the Renaissance the emblem had the virtue of exploiting the combined
advantages of the image and the word so as to permit the inculcation of a truth which
could not be as effectively communicated in any other form. The hermetic, neoplatonist
nature of the genre evidently held much appeal for Renaissance humanists, who saw
it as helping to safeguard the integrity and intensity of the message. And it is striking
that the emblem retained all its popularity in the seventeenth century, even at a time
when the neoplatonist philosophy that underpinned it was no longer prevalent. Somaize
describes the personal devices adopted by many of the *précieuses* who figure in his

Dictionnaire, and the genre had an important pedagogic function for Jesuit teachers. A collection such as Pierre Le Moyne's *Devises heroiques et morales* (1649),[31] containing many emblems specially created for society ladies, or his *De l'art de regner* (1665), with its emblems describing the qualities of the ideal ruler, suggest that there was a reading public beyond the pupils of Jesuit colleges which appreciated the genre. Poetry of the period was also influenced by the genre; Menestrier, discussing poems by La Fontaine and Benserade, draws an explicit link between the fable and the emblem: 'Les Apologues d'Esope sont aussi d'eux-mêmes des Emblèmes.'[32]

The emblem typifies the view that truth cannot be conveyed simply or openly, but that it must be communicated in an encoded or hermetic form; the reader or spectator must tease out the truth for himself. This view, a topos of Renaissance thought, takes on a different complexion in the 'scientific' age of cartesian clear and distinct ideas, and not surprisingly, therefore, there grew up a considerable body of seventeenth-century theoretical writing about the emblem.

There were no fewer than ten French theorists of the emblem and device between the years 1620 and 1686, so Bouhours's dialogue contributes to a lively contemporary debate; there is no such comparable theorising activity in seventeenth-century Italy or Spain.[33] The term *emblem* has hitherto been employed to embrace all the various manifestations of the genre, but the object of the French theorists' special interest is the *devise*, sometimes known by its Italian name *impresa*, and which I shall here label *device*. Strictly speaking, the device constitutes a sub-category of the emblem, but the distinction between the two terms was very often blurred. Bouhours addresses this question, in an article 'Explication de divers termes françois', written thirty years after the *Entretiens*. He follows earlier theorists in suggesting that the emblem differs from the device in being less restricted by rules and in having as its primary aim the inculcation of moral truths. But the point to which Bouhours accords greatest emphasis is the distinction (first drawn by Ruscelli) between the emblem, whose words do no more than supplement the figure, and the device, in which they are conjoined with the figure to constitute an integral part of the meaning. Bouhours gives the following example:

> Ainsi pour marquer le caractere de Louis le Grand, on a peint le Soleil, qui tout lumineux qu'il est a encore plus de vertu que d'éclat: et pour mieux déterminer le sens de la peinture à cette signification particuliere, on y ajoûte ce mot Castillan, *Mas virtud que luz*.[34]

The sun, standing alone, could be used to symbolise a whole range of meanings, and so it is the role of the motto to sharpen the sense ('mieux déterminer le sens') by limiting the spectrum of connotations. The words and the figure exist in a symbiotic relationship in which neither element is individually meaningful, but the expressive value of the total is greater than the aggregate of its two or three constituent parts (three, because sometimes a short poem was added to the figure and motto).

One idea common to many of the theorists is that the device is a form of poem;[35] and they emphasise the characteristically cryptic, semi-hermetic nature of the genre.

Le Moyne is perhaps the most explicit of all the theorists in underscoring the hermetic quality of the device:

> De plus, la Devise est le langage d'une passion mysterieuse; qui fait secret de tout; qui se plaist aux couvertures et aux enveloppes; qui ne voudroit parler que des yeux, et ne se faire entendre que par signes. Les Periphrases et les Circonlocutions ne sont donc pas à son usage: il ne luy faut que des mots coupez, des dictions imparfaites, des expressions qui signifient beaucoup et disent peu, qui s'expliquent plus à l'intelligence qu'à l'oreille. Ce stile concis et Laconique est le stile des Secrets et des Mysteres. (194)

The model which Le Moyne proposes here, in which most cogent expression is achieved through 'imperfect' grammatical language ('des dictions imparfaites'), and in which mystification is cultivated as something pleasurable ('la Devise se plaist aux couvertures'), is remote indeed from the contemporary poetic orthodoxy of unchallenging simplicity. The humble emblem hardly seems to warrant theoretical treatment on such an ambitious scale: as with the other salon genres examined in the previous chapter, the French theorists of the seventeenth century seem to be attracted to these minor genres as a cover for the discussion of poetic discourse *tout court*.

Bouhours consciously places himself within this tradition, citing both earlier theorists like Tesauro and contemporaries such as Menestrier and Le Moyne. Like these predecessors, he is in part concerned with the establishment of rules for the *devise*, and he reiterates many of the arguments of earlier theorists, distinguishing the device from the emblem (169), comparing 'figure' and 'parole' to 'corps' and 'ame' (154, 166), and so forth. All this is conventional enough, and at one level it is quite possible to regard this sixth dialogue as a résumé of rules concerning the device. Many contemporaries did regard the dialogue in this way, and the unsigned *Encyclopédie* article 'Devise' (IV, 1754) quotes no authority other than Bouhours and draws exclusively on this final dialogue for its description of the rules governing the genre.

Like his French predecessors, Bouhours too makes great claims for the *devise*: he explains why it was unknown to classical antiquity (220-21); he claims that the device is the most complete form of symbol (154), and that there is nothing which it cannot express (235). Its aim should be to express a noble thought (184); it is, in short, one of the most complete manifestations of the human spirit: '[La devise] est de plus de toutes les productions de l'esprit la plus jolie, et la plus spirituelle. C'est un genre d'ouvrage extraordinaire qui a toutes les perfections des autres, sans en avoir les defauts' (220).

Bouhours shows particular interest in the device as a signifying structure: the *devise* is 'une similitude metaphorique' (152). Metaphor is the essence of the device, and it is on account of this metaphoric structure, which gives the viewer two things for the price of one, that the device is a source of pleasure (220). The metaphorical construction of the device obliges us to draw out the connection between two apparently quite separate objects (157), placing the subject of the device in a new light: 'Le secret de l'art consiste à découvrir ces nouveaux jours' (188); and again, '[la metaphore] plaist encore parce qu'elle nous fait voir les objets sous un habit étranger, et si je l'ose dire, sous un masque qui nous surprend' (220). Bouhours thus insists on the idea of the device as a form of metaphor, and in making this connection so explicit, he establishes a clear parallel between the device and literary language more generally.

This is not all: to insist on the metaphorical structure of the device is also to underline the fact that the genre depends upon the interplay of two levels of meaning. Firstly, the motto of the device must not be fully comprehensible on its own, but must rather be complementary to the picture; the full meaning of the device is the product of the conjunction of these two elements: 'La signification du Corps prise separément est imparfaite; celle des Paroles l'est aussi: mais la signification qui resulte de l'une et de l'autre, est entiere' (169). Secondly, in piecing together the two elements of a successful device, the reader will become aware of a further meaning beyond the literal one: 'D'un mesme regard [l'esprit] voit la Figure, et la chose figurée' (174). Bouhours speaks of the device as having both 'le sens propre et literal' (174) and 'le sens mystique' (174), 'un sens profond et caché' (186).

If the device is thus understood to function at two levels of meaning, it evidently cannot be explained according to any simple mimetic model, for it is apparently imitating more than one concept at once, and Bouhours makes a number of remarks which suggest his unease with the prevailing theory of imitation. The motto of a device should be brief, but must contain more than one word (171)—this already ensures a certain degree of complexity in the production of the device's overall meaning. In the best devices, the words of the motto are taken from an ancient author and then reapplied to the figure in a different sense, so that the author—Virgil for example—is made to utter something he had not intended (172); the successful reader of the device will recognise both the original sense of Virgil's words and their misappropriated sense in the context of the device. The device thus thrives on the distortion of language and on the disruption of the normal mimetic process. Bouhours uses Pliny's example of Timanthes to emphasise the point that a successful device seems to transcend usual mimetic expectations:

> [La devise] cache cependant à la façon des mysteres beaucoup plus de choses qu'elle n'en découvre; et l'on y conçoit je ne sçay quoy d'admirable que l'on ne voit point, comme dans les tableaux de ce fameux peintre, dont parle Pline. Quoy-que l'Art y fust dans sa perfection, et qu'il n'y eust rien à ajoûter à la peinture, les connoisseurs y remarquoient toûjours quelque chose de plus beau et de plus parfait que la peinture mesme. (220)[36]

Thus the device is constructed as a metaphor operating on two levels of meaning and so casting doubt upon the received imitative model of language. How does a sign so constructed affect the reader? If a word is understood simply to reflect an object, then the reading of a word is in theory entirely unproblematic. But in the case of the device, the reader is challenged to sort out for himself the metaphorical sense. Thus 'équivoque'—which for most classical critics would be a term of abuse—now becomes for Bouhours an entirely positive term. Of the motto of one device he writes: 'Toutes les Paroles en sont heureuses et equivoques' (176), and he goes on to explain the sort of ambiguous terms best suited to this genre (177). The most satisfactory devices produce a form of fractured meaning which the reader has then to complete: 'Les Paroles pour estre fort justes doivent avoir un sens suspendu, et laisser quelque chose à deviner' (169). And this effect is heightened by the use of a language other than the native one: 'Il faut que le Mot soit en une langue etrangere, afin qu'il soit plus mysterieux, et que le peuple ne l'entende pas' (182).[37] The aim, however, is fractured meaning and certainly not total obscurity, a point which Bouhours reiterates with the help of Aristotle and Cicero.[38] The device is a sign conveying a particular meaning: but that meaning is not transparently obvious, and it requires the reader's active participation in order for it to be made manifest.

This is not to imply, however, that the interpretation of a device should be an arduous process. On the contrary, the effective device is one which communicates its meaning quickly, and paradoxically the ambiguity of the motto is a complexity designed not to slow down the process of interpretation but rather to speed it up, by conveying both levels of meaning simultaneously: 'Un Mot equivoque épargneroit à l'esprit cette fatigue, et luy donneroit du plaisir: car nous aimons les voyes abregées, et les Paroles les plus agreables sont celles qui nous instruisent promptement' (174). Brevity is held up as an essential characteristic of the device: the shorter the motto, the more graceful it will be (170). This is because brevity is essential to the metaphor, and since it requires more wit to express a great thought through a single object, the most concise device will be the most perfect and beautiful, and therefore the most expressive (165).

This notion of a concisely constructed metaphor which communicates its meaning instantly underlines the affective impact which the device is intended to have. The device is 'une metaphore peinte et visible qui frappe les yeux' (153), 'elle frappe les sens, et particulierement la veüë qui est de tout les sens le plus vif, et le plus subtil' (220). Aristotle's *Poetics* are invoked, not for the first time, to buttress the argument:

> La metaphore étant inventée pour mettre les choses devant les yeux, elle est d'autant plus parfaite, qu'elle les marque plus vivement, et qu'elle les fait voir en action: car, comme dit Aristote, lorsqu'il parle de la metaphore, on met les objets devant les yeux, quand on les represente agissans. (162)

The ultimate aim of the device is thus to create astonishment, to arouse a sense of *le merveilleux*: 'Les devises ne sont point parfaites, si le merveilleux ne s'y rencontre' (186). This *merveilleux* is founded not merely on *vraisemblance* but on truth itself: 'il faut que ce qui cause de l'admiration, soit vray et réel de tous les costez qu'on le regarde' (187). Bouhours goes far beyond the usual classical aim of 'plaire et instruire': the author of the *devise* aims to 'plaire, instruire *et étonner*' (my emphasis): 'Le merveilleux resulte [...] d'une Figure, qui cause de l'étonnement, et du plaisir tout ensemble' (188).

In several respects this consideration of the device can be seen to relate to earlier subjects of discussion. The need for the motto to be 'mysterieux' (182) recalls 'Le Secret', while the *entretien* on 'Le Je Ne Sçay Quoi' is brought to mind by the requirement that the motto have 'je ne sçay quoy qui pique, ou dans le sens, ou dans les paroles' (182), 'quelque chose de piquant' (189). Above all, 'Le Bel Esprit' is invoked in order to make sense of the device: Bouhours's reader must have 'subtilité' (157), 'un discernement fin, et beaucoup de delicatesse dans l'esprit' (188), 'une veûë éclairée et penetrante' (259).

Thus the discussion of the device is not altogether unprepared by what has preceded. But what does this long final dialogue add to the preceding five? The *devise* is no trivial subject, especially in the eyes of 'le beau monde' who—as Baillet tells us—read the book so avidly. But it is clear that the dialogue is about something more and that, like the *devise* itself, it operates on two levels:

> En verité, dit Eugene, on apprend dans la Devise beaucoup plus que je ne pensois. J'avois presque creû jusqu'à cette heure que ce n'étoit qu'une bagatelle: mais mon Dieu que de beautez! que de choses dans cette sorte de bagatelle! (257)

It is evident that the *devise* can be read as a symbol, indeed a meta-symbol, for (among other things) poetic language in general.

Aspects of Bouhours's commentary on the *devise* underline the fact that it is morally improving (e.g. 184) and that it attains fullness of linguistic expression (e.g. 220), the two problems which had been resolved in the previous two dialogues with the notions of *bel esprit* and the *je ne sais quoi*. But the device goes further in asserting the full materiality of the poetic symbol. If nomenclaturism, pushed to its logical conclusion, has the effect of turning words into mere tokens, thereby making impossible any account of language's poetic function, the *devise*, with its roots in Renaissance neoplatonism, provides Bouhours with the perfect counter-example. It imitates reality, but not simply; it depends crucially for its effect on a double level of meaning, a point which Bouhours emphasises. Consequently it is a sign which can never be simplistically clear, since it will inevitably make demands upon its reader, who has to tease out its metaphorical sense. Although at the level of theory Bouhours is unable to argue against the prevailing mimetic model in language and art, he does produce in practice a poetic model which manages to subvert totally the principle of linguistic mimesis. The *devise* obviously does not reflect one simple single object, as in the Port-Royal's ideal world every linguistic token should. Yet, as Bouhours's description makes clear, it is precisely because it does not that the device is so expressive, so intriguing, so affecting.[39] Bouhours thus hints at a poetic theory entirely at odds with the prevailing view; and the reader, having been schooled in the technique of 'reading' the device, is thereby enabled to read the totality of Bouhours's work. The *devise* becomes a metaphor for the book in which it is discussed; beyond that, it stands as a metaphor for a theory of literary discourse that it dare not discuss.

The *Entretiens* provoked an instant response from Barbier d'Aucour, followed by an instant counter-response from Villars. For the most part this debate is a trivial Jansenist–Jesuit exchange, but one revealing difference of opinion concerns discussion of the device. In his *Sentimens de Cléante sur les Entretiens d'Ariste et d'Eugène* (1671), Barbier d'Aucour is dismissive of Bouhours's treatment both of *bel esprit*, which he claims to find unclear and contradictory, and of the *je ne sais quoi*, which he finds verbose; so it is hardly surprising that he expresses gross scepticism about Bouhours's final dialogue. He mocks Bouhours's enthusiasm for the device, a genre which he regards as 'un jeu d'esprit' (136), and which he refuses to take seriously:

> [Notre Auteur] est trop attaché à la Devise; c'est un principe qu'il
> ne quitte point, et duquel il fait à peu près ce que les Chimistes font
> de leur soufre, de leur sel et de leur Mercure. Il la trouve par tout, et
> il y reduit tout. (140-41)

The device, as a metaphor which represents one thing by means of another, can teach us only what we know already (143); it is therefore decorative, but not intellectually serious. And Barbier d'Aucour specifically criticises the ambiguity of certain devices: 'L'Auteur devoit donc prendre soin d'éviter l'Equivoque, et d'autant plus que, par je ne sçay quelle pente d'Esprit, il y tombe fort souvent' (145-46). This is surely a deliberate misunderstanding, and when he remarks that in the field of philosophy or politics, the device has only very limited powers of expression (142), he is clearly missing the point: it is the hermeneutic problems posed by the device which matter for Bouhours, more than the content as such. Just as he professes himself unable to understand Bouhours's arguments concerning *bel esprit* and the *je ne sais quoi*, Barbier d'Aucour deliberately ignores the symbolic interest of the device.

Villars attempts to defend Bouhours's arguments, but clearly he has not understood them. His defence of the device against Barbier d'Aucour in *De la délicatesse* (1671) is feeble: 'Les Devises sont propres à aider la memoire; et en second lieu [...] ce sont des jeux d'esprit' (121)—hardly what Bouhours would have wanted to hear. Villars seems to be impervious to the originality of Bouhours's aesthetic argument and he misunderstands utterly the importance which Bouhours attributes to ambiguity ('Il seroit juste, ce me semble, de mettre cette difference dans les equivoques, qu'elles peuvent estre affectées, quand en tous les deux visages elles portent un beau sens', 126)—just as later Villars will attack Pascal for having composed detached fragments (172). His position is one of impeccable poetic orthodoxy, and it only reinforces the wholly radical nature of Bouhours's argument. Bouhours's use of the device to shape a particular aesthetic argument is highly innovative—so innovative, in fact, that his daring was not apparent even to some of his Jesuit colleagues.

VI. CONCLUSION: AN AESTHETIC OF SUGGESTION

All six dialogues of the *Entretiens* bear, directly or indirectly, on issues relating to the nature of poetic discourse. It is possible moreover to discern a certain progression in the sequence of the dialogues. The subject of poetic expression is dealt with, explicitly but cautiously, in the second dialogue, and this is flanked by two more speculative pieces which approach the same topic obliquely but more daringly. The fourth, fifth and sixth dialogues build upon these foundations; and each can be seen as an attempted response to one of the problems outlined in Chapter One. 'Le Bel Esprit' introduces a reader-oriented dimension designed to make manifest the moral value of reading literature (as against those who argue that literature imitates too well and is therefore immoral); 'Le Je Ne Sçay Quoy' is an attempt to establish a new literary concept which can defend forcefulness of expression (as against those who believe that literary discourse, as a second-degree imitation, is inherently flawed). The argument is brought to a fitting climax in the final and longest dialogue, 'Des Devises', which brings together the themes of the previous two and goes beyond them to address the most crucial problem posed by a mimetic theory of language and art: how to explain and justify the nature of the poetic sign.

The *Entretiens d'Ariste et d'Eugène* reveal clearly the various tensions underlying poetic theory in the 1670s. Bouhours is evidently sensitive to the dilemmas posed for poetry by a nomenclaturist theory of language. But how successful is he in his attempt to resolve them? The drift of discussion in the *Entretiens*, with its emphasis on *le je ne sais quoi*, *le bel esprit* and *la devise*, points towards an aesthetic of suggestion—an aesthetic which stands in inevitable opposition to the prevailing poetic theory of unproblematic clarity. Bouhours will seek to elaborate upon this notion further in *La Manière de bien penser* (1687), where he tries out a new term for this ineffable literary quality, *la délicatesse* (an echo of Villars's defence of the *Entretiens*).[40] This 'alternative' classical aesthetic of suggestion brings to mind La Fontaine, and John Lapp's 'esthetics of negligence';[41] and Jean Lafond speaks of 'cette esthétique de la grâce, dernier écho de l'influence du néo-platonisme au xviiᵉ siècle'.[42] Bouhours's aesthetic of suggestion similarly has its roots in neoplatonism. There is no extensive or overt discussion of platonist thought—that would be inconceivable, given the contemporary status of 'aristotelian' poetics; but the first, third, fourth and fifth dialogues contain a series of references to Plato and to the neoplatonist idea of poetic fury. This undercurrent of discussion finds a fitting culmination in the extended discussion of the device in the final dialogue: interest in the device is a direct product of Renaissance neoplatonist thought, and there is no need in this final dialogue to discuss neoplatonism overtly since it is implied by the very discussion of the device. The bid to perpetuate a neoplatonist aesthetic is surely one of the most significant features of the *Entretiens*. Bouhours perceives very clearly the problems in contemporary poetic theory, and his response is to go back to the neoplatonist tradition, in the form of the device, and to use this to underpin an aesthetic of suggestion.

Such a response, however suggestive, is at best tentative and piecemeal. Tentative, because Bouhours's approach is timid, his angle of attack almost always oblique; the idea of the *devise* seems a clever solution to a number of problems, but it is never anything more than a symbol, and he does not help us to see how it can be applied practically to create a coherent theory of poetic discourse. And piecemeal, because he proposes in separate dialogues a number of different solutions—*le bel esprit, le je ne sais quoi, la devise*—to the various problems confronting him, but does not finally attempt to explain how they might be synthesised to form a coherent overall theory. In the final analysis we are left with the impression of a book more absorbing for its insight into the essential problems than for the clarity and coherence of the solutions which it proposes.

It has been assumed here that Ariste and Eugène may both be taken to speak for Bouhours, so it is appropriate finally to consider Bouhours's use of the dialogue form. Later, in *La Manière de bien penser* (1687), Bouhours will write a 'dialogic' dialogue in which Philanthe and Eudoxe adopt obviously contrasted positions which they proceed to debate; of course there are plenty of examples of didactic *entretiens* in this period, in the manner of Fontenelle's *Entretiens sur la pluralité des mondes*.[43] But Bouhours's *Entretiens* differ from Fontenelle's in one crucial respect. Fontenelle's work is explicitly didactic and has a clear argument at its core; Bouhours, on the other hand, has written a set of dialogues which are much more challenging to the reader, and more fundamentally ambiguous. If it is true that there is no dialogic interaction between Ariste and Eugène, there are certainly dialogic tensions between the individual dialogues. Bouhours does not seek to set up his two characters in a dialectical relationship, but he surely intends to establish some form of dialectical argument, in which the reader is left—as in the best emblems—to piece together and make sense of the different elements of the work before him, and so to embody an aesthetic of suggestion.[44] It is also the case that the dialogue form helps shield what might otherwise appear as a fundamental incoherence in Bouhours's critical thought, for it helps Bouhours to deal allusively with the difficulties which he clearly perceives in contemporary poetic theory but which he feels unable to address more directly. It is clear in any event that the impact of the six dialogues taken together, read as an interlocking whole, is incomparably greater than the impact of the six constituent parts considered separately. The argument which the *Entretiens* propound, even if not coherent in all respects, is one argument and not six.

NOTES

1. Cotin, *Œuvres meslées*, sig. a ii r.
2. Baillet, *Jugemens des savans*, III, p. 265.
3. See Racine, *Œuvres complètes*, II, p. 462.
4. Baillet describes the critical reception in some detail (III, pp. 267-79).
5. Saint-Evremond, *Lettres*, II, pp. 263-64.
6. See pp. 32, 36, 39.
7. p. 39; Méré had spoken of women possessing 'une délicatesse d'esprit' (*Œuvres complètes*, I, p. 17).
8. Le Moyne in one of his *devises* had already used the contrasting moods of the sea as a metaphor for eloquence; see Fig. 4.
9. R. G. Maber links the choice of subject of this dialogue with Bouhours's stay at Dunkirk in the early 1660s, though he also points out that the description of the sea was something of a literary topos; he finds that some of the strikingly beautiful descriptions are inspired by Le Moyne ('Bouhours and the Sea', pp. 76-77).
10. Racine, I, p. 467.
11. See R. Bray, pp. 64-74; and, for example, Boileau, *Art poétique*, canto IV, vv.87-88 (p. 112),

and La Fontaine, I, 5.

[12.] Jean-Pierre Camus, for example, has a chapter entitled 'Du secret' in his *Diversitez* (Book IX, Chap. 2, first published 1609), and several classical anecdotes (the anti-feminist jibes, the tale of the Roman boy and his indiscreet mother, the story of Alexander sealing the lips of his friend) are common both to Camus and to Bouhours; La Mothe Le Vayer has an essay 'Du secret et de la fidelité' (*Œuvres*, II, 54-58); and Le Moyne, in his *De l'art de régner*, includes a chapter 'Du secret et de la confiance qu'il faut apporter [...]' (489-91). Other contemporary writers who treat the theme of secrecy include La Rochefoucauld, La Fontaine and La Bruyère. As in the other dialogues, the sources on which Bouhours draws are numerous and varied: it has been shown that in 'Le Secret' alone, there are some 80 borrowings, 53 from classical authors and the Scriptures, 27 from contemporary sources (mainly French, of course, but also Spanish, Italian, and even in one case, English—Bacon). Very many such borrowings remain unacknowledged—Plutarch's *De garrula* is quoted frequently in the course of this dialogue, but it is mentioned only once; some are quoted from the original source, some gleaned at second hand, either from contemporary authors, or quarried from the anthology, *polyanthea*, of Lange (1512, sixth edition 1624), which is a possible source for some 16 of the 80 borrowings (see M. Le Boulengé, unpublished dissertation, pp. 12-40).

[13.] *Entretiens*, 4th ed. (1673), p. 275. Compare Boileau's use of 'Enfin Malherbe vint': see Chap. 1, note 19.

[14.] See N. Cronk, 'Aristotle, Horace, and Longinus: the conception of reader-response'.

[15.] The principal discussions of *le je ne sais quoi*, in order of publication, are: B. Croce, *Estetica*, pp. 219-20 (1902); H. Jacoubet, '*Le je ne sais quoi*' (1928), reprinted in *Variétés d'histoire littéraire*; S. H. Monk, 'A grace beyond the reach of art' (1944); E. B. O. Borgerhoff, *The Freedom of French Classicism*, pp. 186-200 (1950); H. Sommer and P. Zumthor, 'A propos du mot génie' (1950); G. Natali, 'Storia del "non so che"' (1951); E. Köhler, '*Je ne sais quoi*' (1953-54); E. Haase, 'Zur Bedeutung von je ne sais quoi im 17. Jahrhundert' (1956); V. Jankélévitch, *Le je-ne-sais-quoi et le presque-rien* (1957); P.-H. Simon, 'Le "je ne sais quoi" devant la raison classique' (1959); S. Guellouz, 'Le P. Bouhours et le *je ne sais quoi*' (1971); F. Schalk, 'Nochmals zum *je ne sais quoi*' (1974); and J.-P. Dens, *L'Honnête Homme et la critique du goût* (1981), pp. 52-56. See also the forthcoming study on this subject by Richard Scholar.

[16.] Later in the century Nicole was to speak of 'pensées imperceptibles' (see G. Chinard, *En lisant Pascal*, 'Nicole et les *pensées imperceptibles*', pp. 119-30).

[17.] Richelet underlines the importance of this quotation by singling it out in his dictionary definition of the *je ne sais quoi*. The remark seems to have its immediate source in a text of Persius (*Fifth Satire*, vv.45-51) where friendship is also the subject of discussion.

[18.] Pascal, fragment L. 413; Vaugelas, *Remarques*, pp. 476-77. There was one earlier literary treatment of the *je ne sais quoi*, but this was already lost in Bouhours's time. One of the first decisions of the Académie was that each of the academicians in turn should deliver a speech on a topic of his own choosing. The sixth of these weekly lectures was delivered in March 1635 by Gombauld, and he chose to speak about *le je ne sais quoi*. This lecture, now lost, seems to have been the first attempt to discuss *le je ne sais quoi* as a literary concept, and in so doing Gombauld was paving the way for Bouhours's fifth *entretien* nearly forty years later. Bouhours alludes to the reference to the lecture in Pellisson's history of the Académie française (I, 75), though he does not mention Gombauld by name and he evidently has no first-hand knowledge of the lecture (150).

[19.] Méré, *Œuvres complètes*, II, p. 12.

[20.] In the 'Première conversation' alone, we find 'je ne sçay quoy de modeste', 'je ne sçay quoy de libre ou d'aisé', 'je ne sçay quoy de naïf', 'je ne sçai quoi de brillant', 'je ne sçai quoi de piquant', and 'je ne sçai quoi de plus retenu' (*Œuvres complètes*, I, pp. 8, 9, 11, 18, 20, 21).

[21.] On seventeenth-century dictionary definitions of the *je ne sais quoi*, see Haase, pp. 50-51.

[22.] On Renaissance interest in the hieroglyph, see Iversen, *The Myth of Egypt*; Seznec, *La*

Survivance des dieux antiques, pp. 93-94; and Wittkower, 'Hieroglyphics in the early Renaissance'.

23. Rudolf Wittkower, *Allegory*, p. 116. Wittkower quotes some apposite texts from Plotinus and Ficino which illustrate the point well: 'In what visual form is ultimate truth revealed? Plotinus, whom Ficino himself had translated, had given the answer. In a passage in the Fifth Book of the *Enneads*, Plotinus had said, "The Egyptian sages [...] drew pictures and carved one picture for each thing in their temples, thus making manifest the description of that thing. Thus each picture was a kind of understanding and wisdom and substance and given all at once, and not discursive reasoning and deliberation," to which Ficino added the following gloss, "The Egyptian Priests did not use individual letters to signify mysteries, but whole images of plants, trees and animals; because God has knowledge of things *not* through a multiplicity of thought processes, but rather as a simple and firm form of the thing." And he gives as an example the image of Time, painted as a winged serpent biting its tail, and concludes, "The Egyptians presented the whole of the discursive argument as it were in one complete image." In other words, in Ficino's exposition the image does not simply represent the concept—it embodies it' (*Allegory*, pp. 115-16).

24. The work was reprinted several times during the century (Paris, 1634; Paris, 1647; Cologne, 1654; etc.).

25. Lyon, 1602, 1610, 1626, etc.

26. *Les Hieroglyphiques de Jean Pierre Valerian* (Lyon, 1615).

27. *Académie*, p. 488.

28. Interest in the hieroglyph extends beyond the early decades of the seventeenth century in certain respects; Anthony Blunt, for example, in 'The Hypnertomachia Poliphili in seventeenth-century France', has discussed the influence of Colonna's *Songe de Poliphile*, both on the visual arts in the seventeenth century, and also on literature (La Fontaine, among others, borrowed from it); the *Songe de Poliphile* was known in particular to the *précieux*, partly through pastoral novels of the period, and partly on account of its hieroglyphics, on which they drew for their devices and emblems.

29. The first part of the book appeared in Paris, 1636 and 1637, both parts in Paris, 1644, with the title *Iconologie, ou Explication nouvelle de plusieurs images, emblemes, et autres figures hyerogliphiques des Vertus, des Vices, des Arts, des Sciences, des Causes naturelles, des Humeurs differentes, et des Passions humaines. Œuvre [...] necessaire a toute sorte d'esprits, et particulierement a ceux qui aspirent a estre, ou qui sont en effet Orateurs, Poetes, Sculpteurs, Peintres, Ingenieurs, Autheurs de Medailles, de Devises, de Ballets, et de Poëmes Dramatiques [...]*—as the title shows, Baudoin envisaged poets as part of his potential readership; the work was reprinted in 1677, 1681, 1698; and again in 1759.

30. See Hessel Miedema, 'The term "Emblema" in Alciati'.

31. As an example of this work, see Fig. 4.

32. *L'Art des emblemes* (1684) p. 27. See also Georges Couton, who first drew attention to certain formal parallels between emblems and the fables of La Fontaine ('La Fontaine'); and Margaret McGowan, who develops these suggestions, showing that the similarities between the two genres go beyond external form and exist also at the level of interpretation: both genres have an overt moral or didactic function ('Moral intention').

33. They are, in chronological order: Amboise, *Discours ou Traicté des devises* (1620); Estienne, *L'Art de faire des devises* (1645); de Boissière, *Un Traicté des règles de la devise* (1654); Menestrier, *L'Art des emblèmes* (1662); Labbé, 'De symbolis', *Elogia sacra [...]* (1664); Le Moyne, *De l'Art des devises* (1666); Bouhours, 'Des Devises', *Entretiens* (1671); Gardien, 'Discours sur les devises, emblesmes, et revers de medailles' (*Mercure galant*, 1678); Menestrier, *La Philosophie des images* (1682); Menestrier, *L'Art des emblemes* (1684; illustrated and greatly augmented); Menestrier, *La Science et l'art des devises* (1686); Clément, 'Règles pour la connoissance des Devises' (MS); and 'Discours sur l'art des devises' (MS).

34. 'Explication', p. 177.

[35.] Menestrier declares that 'La Devise est un argument poëtique' (1686, p. 43), and states that the emblem must both please and instruct, quoting the relevant line from Horace, 'Omne tulit punctum, qui miscuit utile dulci' (1662, p. 90). Estienne similarly requires the device to procure 'le ravissement de l'esprit' and 'le profit et l'utilité' (pp. 46-47); and Amboise recalls Horace's parallel between poetry and painting, 'ut pictura poësis erit' (p. 116).

[36.] 'Indeed Timanthes is the only artist in whose works more is always implied than is depicted, and whose execution, though consummate, is always surpassed by his genius' (Pliny, *Natural History*, Loeb Classical Library, Vol. 9 (Cambridge, Mass. and London, 1952), p. 317; Book 35, 36.74).

[37.] Significantly, this is one of the few rules which is invented by French theorists and has no Italian precedent or prototype.

[38.] See pp. 162, 180, 189.

[39.] In the *Lettre sur les sourds et muets* (1751), Diderot famously uses the emblem/hieroglyph as a symbol for the poetic word, stating explicitly and vigorously the idea implicitly and more cautiously expressed in this *entretien* by Bouhours: 'Il passe alors dans le discours du poète un esprit qui en meut et vivifie toutes les syllabes. Qu'est-ce que cet esprit? J'en ai quelquefois senti la présence; mais tout ce que j'en sais, c'est que c'est lui qui fait que les choses sont dites et représentées tout à la fois; que dans le même temps que l'entendement les saisit, l'âme en est émue, l'imagination les voit, et l'oreille les entend; et que le discours n'est plus seulement un enchaînement de termes énergiques qui exposent la pensée avec force et noblesse, mais que c'est encore un tissu d'hiéroglyphes entassés les uns sur les autres qui la peignent. Je pourrais dire en ce sens que toute poésie est emblématique. Mais l'intelligence de l'emblème poétique n'est pas donnée à tout le monde' (*Œuvres*, II, p. 549). Could Bouhours's sixth dialogue possibly be a distant source of this passage? Paul H. Meyer, in his critical edition of Diderot's *Lettre*, makes no mention of Bouhours, and traces the idea of the hieroglyph back through Condillac to Warburton (p. 17). This certainly explains Diderot's use of 'hiéroglyphe'; but what of the terms 'emblématique' and 'emblème poétique'? A possible source has been noted in Bacon (*Lettre*, eds. M. Hobson and S. Harvey, p. 191); but another possible source is Bouhours's sixth *entretien*; see also K. Tunstall, 'Hieroglyph and device'. Diderot is likely to have known the *Entretiens*, which were frequently reprinted in the eighteenth century (e.g.: Amsterdam 1703, 1708; Paris 1711, 1721, 1734, 1768); the author of the unsigned article 'Devises' in the *Encyclopédie* (the chevalier de Jaucourt?), which appeared three years after the *Lettre sur les sourds et muets*, names Bouhours and draws on him as the sole source of the article. The image of the hieroglyph reappears in the aesthetic writings of Baudelaire: 'Tout, forme, mouvement, nombre, couleur, parfum, dans le *spirituel* comme dans le *naturel*, est significatif, réciproque, converse, *correspondant*. [...] Tout est hiéroglyphique, et nous savons que les symboles ne sont obscurs que d'une manière relative, c'est-à-dire selon la pureté, la bonne volonté ou la clairvoyance native des âmes. Or qu'est-ce qu'un poète [...], si ce n'est un traducteur, un déchiffreur?' (*Œuvres complètes*, II, p. 133).

[40.] *La délicatesse* is also a term much used by Saint-Evremond; Quentin Hope, who translates it as 'discrimination', describes it as 'the most important' key word in Saint-Evremond's critical vocabulary (see *Saint-Evremond*, pp. 87-93).

[41.] *Contes*, pp. 30-43.

[42.] 'La beauté et la grâce', p. 488.

[43.] According to B. Beugnot, this is the most typical form of literary dialogue in the classical period (*L'Entretien au xviie siècle*).

[44.] The first (quarto) edition of the *Entretiens* contains a 29-page 'Table des matières' which confers at least some sense of structure on the work and allows the reader to focus on certain key themes and preoccupations ('Platon', for example, earns three references). The alphabetical index is omitted from later editions, however, leaving readers with no pointers at all to help guide them through the text. Perhaps Bouhours chose to excise the 'Table' precisely because it detracted from the allusive quality which he was aiming to describe.

4: INVENTING *LE SUBLIME*: BOILEAU'S *TRAITÉ DU SUBLIME*

Je ne dis les autres, sinon pour d'autant plus me dire. (Montaigne)[1]

'Longinus has been pursued by misfortune,' laments E. R. Curtius. 'It seems grotesque that a schoolmaster like Boileau made his name known.'[2] The Romantic, post-Burkeian, notion of the sublime as something vast, overwhelming, ineffable, hardly accords with the conventional view of French neoclassical poetic theory with its cartesian preoccupation with clear and distinct ideas. Hence the considerable embarrassment of commentators that the term 'sublime' gained critical currency as a result of Boileau's translation of Longinus, and the view (still widespread) that Boileau was somehow muddled and did not really understand the text he was translating.[3] Thus for Monk, '[Boileau's] credo has the dual physiognomy of Janus'.[4] Brody's is virtually a lone voice in suggesting that the argument of the *Traité du sublime* is consonant with that of the *Art poétique*.

I. THE *TRAITÉ DU SUBLIME*: PROBLEMS OF ORIGIN

It is an extraordinary fact that Boileau should have undertaken a translation of Longinus. Before considering its significance, it is important to consider Boileau's motivations in undertaking the translation of a relatively obscure text, and his intentions in then including it, so prominently, in his *Œuvres diverses*.

How would the French reading public of 1674 have reacted to the name of 'Longin'? The *editio princeps* of *Peri hupsous* was published by Robortello in 1554, when it appeared with the Latin title *De grandi sive sublimi orationis genere*, thereby helping to establish *sublimis* as the translation of the Greek *hupsos* (literally 'height'). The treatise was already known in France, however, for Muret, in his commentary on Catullus (also 1554) makes reference to his Latin translation of Longinus, though this remains undiscovered; the first printed Latin translation was published in 1566. Longinus was known and cited by numerous critics of the Italian Renaissance;[5] not surprisingly the earliest extant vernacular translation, in manuscript, is into Italian (1575), as is the first printed vernacular translation, by Niccolò Pinelli (1639). An English version followed in 1652, by John Hall, who translates the title as *Of the Height of Eloquence*, avoiding the word 'sublime'.[6]

The writings of Italian Renaissance authors helped establish Longinus's fame in France. Boileau's translation is not, as used to be thought, the first into French: there is a manuscript version dating from the 1640s, and attributed tentatively by Weinberg to Mazarin.[7] This is not surprising, for there was clearly quite extensive knowledge of Longinus's treatise among French scholars from the early seventeenth century onwards.[8] To take just one example, le Père Louis de Cressolles's *Vacationes autumnales* (1620), a work dealing with the role of gesture in oratory, makes frequent reference to Longinus to support his argument that supreme eloquence is an expression of nobility of soul.[9] The group surrounding Patru and La Mothe Le Vayer is known to have been interested in Longinus, but they may have been attracted primarily by the political possibilities of the final section of his treatise which links the decline of literature to the shift from republican to monarchical government.[10] One French literary critic before Boileau to show significant interest in Longinus is Guez de Balzac, who draws on *Peri hupsous* in a description of Demosthenes's eloquence in the 'Avant-Propos' to his *Socrate chrétien*.[11] More far-reaching is an allusion to Longinus in Le Grand's 'Discours sur la rhetorique françoise', which appeared as a preface to Bary's *La Rhetorique françoise* (1659).[12] Le Grand devotes three pages to a discussion of Longinus and the idea of sublimity, and he quotes at length the 'fiat lux' example:

> Quelle pompe et quelle grandeur n'apperçoit-on pas dans la pureté de ces mots? que Moïse dit beaucoup, et que Moïse parle peu! que sa sublimité est divine! que son Eloquence est celeste! qu'elle remplit l'esprit et qu'elle communique de secrets! elle ne tient rien de l'homme; et elle est tout de Dieu. (sig. i r)

Such references reveal knowledge of *Peri hupsous*, but do not suggest that scholars of the period were especially aware of the particular qualities of Longinus's treatise as a work of literary criticism or were keen to make it better known.

Brody has convincingly dismissed the suggestion that Gilles Boileau might have begun work on a translation of Longinus and that after his death in 1669 the unfinished manuscript could have passed into the hands of his younger brother.[13] One crucial stimulus, however, to Nicolas Boileau's decision to translate Longinus was the publication in 1663 of a critical edition of *Peri hupsous* by Tanneguy Le Fèvre, one of the most eminent French Hellenists of the period.

In the absence of any full-scale study of the fortunes of Longinus in France before Boileau, any conclusion on this subject is necessarily tentative; recent research has tended to suggest that Longinus was more widely known to scholars in seventeenth-century France than was previously thought, but even so his name was not familiar to a wider audience. Aristotle, Cicero and Quintilian were all much better known, and even they had only recently been translated into the vernacular when the *Traité du sublime* appeared in 1674.[14] It may also be significant that in a work of 1665, Le Fèvre employs indiscriminately the forms 'Longin' and 'Longinus', suggesting that the French version of the name had not become fixed as late as the 1660s.[15] Boileau certainly assumes no prior knowledge on the part of his readers, for he takes the precaution of specifying in the sub-title of his translation that the original had been composed in Greek ('traduit du grec de Longin'), and he goes on in his 'Préface' to speak about the (presumed) author. A scholar in 1674 would have been quite familiar with the name of Longinus and could have read him in any one of several Greek editions or Latin translations. There was no 'need' for a French translation of Longinus, indeed many far more celebrated classical authors still remained untranslated into French at this date.

A further peculiarity of the *Traité du sublime* which should not be overlooked arises from the prestige of its translator. The translators of works of classical rhetoric in this period are invariably rather minor *hommes de lettres*: the abbé François Cassandre, who spent twenty years revising his much-praised translation of Aristotle's *Rhetoric* (1654); the abbé Jacques Cassagnes, a founder member of the Académie des Inscriptions et des Belles-Lettres, translator of Cicero's *De oratore* (1673); or the obscure 'sieur Jacob', a lawyer in the Paris *parlement*, who produced the first French version of the *Rhetorica ad Herennium* (1652). Boileau stands out rather conspicuously in such company. An ambitious poet in his late thirties, well known as the author of some highly successful *Satires*, he did not seemingly have much to gain by translating what in the eyes of his contemporaries might appear to be a rhetorical textbook.

A final puzzle concerns the manner in which the *Traité du sublime* was published. It did not appear as a separate volume, like other rhetorical texts, but as part of the 1674 two-volume *Œuvres diverses*. Before 1674, Boileau had been known essentially as a satirist; thereafter, his reputation was also as a critic, and in particular in connection with the term *sublime*. The title-page gives exclusive prominence to the translation of Longinus, moreover, with no mention of the *Art poétique* or of the other texts included (the first four cantos of *Le Lutrin*, the first four *Epîtres*, and the first nine *Satires*): *Œuvres diverses du sieur D***, avec le Traité du sublime ou du merveilleux dans le discours, traduit du grec de Longin* (see Fig. 5). Thus from the first the *Art poétique* and the *Traité du sublime* were, quite literally, bound together. During Boileau's lifetime, the *Œuvres diverses* were frequently reprinted;[16] there was never an edition of the *Art poétique* without the *Traité du sublime*,[17] and only on a couple of occasions did Boileau publish the *Traité du sublime* without the *Art poétique*.[18] The bibliographical evidence is unambiguous: Boileau conceived of the *Traité du sublime* and *Art poétique* as a critical diptych, and it is clear that we ought to interpret the two texts in this light. The modern tendency to concentrate almost exclusively on the *Art poétique* in assessing Boileau's contribution to poetic theory flies in the face of the facts.[19]

II. *LE SUBLIME*: PROBLEMS OF INTERPRETATION

A. THE 'PRÉFACE'

Boileau introduces his translation of Longinus in the *Œuvres diverses* with a 'Préface'. This short text is of pivotal importance, as it constitutes our sole explicit guide to Boileau's intentions in undertaking the translation, though its apparent simplicity turns out, on closer scrutiny, to be somewhat deceptive. (Boileau extends his discussion in later editions of the 'Préface', and in the 'Réflexions critiques'; these subsequent definitions and arguments will be considered in the next chapter, together with the various criticisms which had provoked them.)

ŒUVRES
DIVERSES
Du Sieur D * * *

A V E C

LE TRAITÉ
DU
SUBLIME
OU
DU MERVEILLEUX
DANS LE DISCOURS.

Traduit du Grec de Longin.

A PARIS,
Chez LOUIS BILLAINE, au deuxiéme Pillier de
la grand'-Salle du Palais, au grand Cefar.

M. DC. LXXIV.

AVEC PRIVILEGE DU ROI.

Figure 5. Title-page of Boileau, *Œuvres diverses* (Paris, 1674).

The key passage in the 'Préface' concerning the meaning of the *sublime* is the following:

> Il ne reste plus, pour finir cette Preface, que de dire ce que Longin entend par Sublime. Car comme il ecrit de cette matiere après Cecilius, qui avoit presque employé tout son livre à montrer ce que c'est que Sublime; il n'a pas crû devoir rebattre une chose qui n'avoit esté déjà que trop discutée par un autre. Il faut donc sçavoir que par Sublime, Longin n'entend pas ce que les Orateurs appellent le stile sublime: mais cet extraordinaire et ce merveilleux qui frape dans le discours, et qui fait qu'un ouvrage enleve, ravit, transporte. Le stile sublime veut toujours de grands mots; mais le Sublime se peut trouver dans une seule pensée, dans une seule figure, dans un seul tour de paroles. Une chose peut estre dans le stile Sublime, et n'estre pourtant pas Sublime, c'est-à-dire n'avoir rien d'extraordinaire ni de surprenant. Par exemple, *Le souverain Arbitre de la nature d'une seule parole forma la lumiere.* Voilà qui est dans le stile sublime: cela n'est pas neanmoins Sublime; parce qu'il n'y a rien là de fort merveilleux, et qu'on ne put aisément trouver. Mais, *Dieu dit: Que la lumière se fasse; et la lumière se fit.* Ce tour extraordinaire d'expression qui marque si bien l'obeissance de la Creature aux ordres du Createur, est veritablement sublime, et a quelque chose de divin. Il faut donc entendre par Sublime dans Longin, l'Extraordinaire, le Surprenant, et comme je l'ai traduit, le Merveilleux dans le discours. (*TS*, 45-46)

Two major ambiguities are immediately apparent in this passage. First, in distinguishing between the sublime and the sublime style, Boileau does not explain whether the latter is intended to preclude entirely the former. Something in the sublime style need not be sublime, claims Boileau; but is it none the less possible for something to be both sublime *and* in the sublime style? The precise distinction between the two is not explained, and the position is clearly more complex in Longinus's treatise, where he gives as two of his five sources of the sublime (in Boileau's translation) 'les Figures tournées d'une certaine maniere' and 'la noblesse de l'expression' (*TS*, 59). Moreover the sentence which Boileau invents to exemplify the sublime style ('Le souverain Arbitre…') seems a poor example: the vocabulary is not obviously of the 'high style', and there are no noteworthy rhetorical devices, except for the initial periphrasis ('le souverain Arbitre de la nature'); it appears that it is really the Biblical subject-matter which is responsible for the sublimity of the style here—but that is not the point which Boileau is trying to argue.

Secondly, Boileau's suggestion that the sublime may be found in a thought, a single figure, or a phrase, is confusing in the extreme. Does this mean that the sublime is founded either in thought or in language? Or perhaps in both simultaneously? This crucial ambiguity hovers over the example drawn from Genesis, in which, Boileau seems to be saying, it is the form of the expression which makes it so powerful. One might plausibly argue that the sentence 'Dieu dit...' achieves its poetic impact by means of the grammatical parallelism 'se fasse'/'se fit', in which the curtailed vowel sound and the reduction by one (half-) syllable of the second verb form seem to underscore the decisiveness and even brusqueness of the act described. But if the alleged sublimity of this sentence is located uniquely in a feature peculiar to the sound and syntax of the French translation, how does this help us explain the literary quality of the Greek passage discussed by Longinus—unless, by chance, Greek possesses a parallel syntactical construction, and, by still greater chance, Boileau has been able to reproduce a parallel phonetic effect in his translation?[20]

One obvious conclusion which Boileau might have drawn from his example is that the sublime is untranslatable, but he chooses to ignore this possibility. If the sublime truly is translatable, then it will seem more likely that the sublimity of the sentence from Genesis arises from the thought which it expresses—Boileau's counter-example, 'Le souverain Arbitre...', notwithstanding—, and we are left in effect with a 'moral' view of the sublime: certain ideas possess this quality intrinsically. Boileau notes that his example has 'quelque chose de divin'; and the very fact that his sole example is the one and only Biblical quotation in Longinus's treatise (and in ancient literary criticism *tout court*) also begs comment: the elevated nature of the subject-matter tends inevitably to blur the argument.

In the passage quoted above, Boileau begins with the ingenuous claim that his intention is merely to make explicit Longinus's own understanding of the sublime: in the event, he predictably privileges certain aspects of that theory. The centrepiece of Boileau's 'Préface' is the distinction, presented as his own, between the sublime and the sublime style. The basic notion that powerful language need not be pompous language is clearly attractive to a classical critic; but it leaves many questions unresolved. If the sublime is grounded in language, to what extent may it be equated to a simple or non-figurative style? If the sublime is conceived of as a moral concept, to what extent is this linguistic dimension relevant? And are these two views of the sublime compatible, or mutually exclusive? The distinction between 'le Sublime' and 'le stile Sublime' conceals more problems than it solves.

B. RHETORIC VERSUS AESTHETICS

In his pioneering study of the history of the sublime, first published in 1935, S. H. Monk characterises Boileau's achievement as having been to initiate a process propelling the sublime towards the realm of aesthetics, so ultimately severing it from its rhetorical origins (35-36).

Although this interpretation of the distinction between the sublime and the sublime style has been widely accepted, Monk's distinction between rhetoric and aesthetics in itself raises numerous problems. It has been argued that certain of the ambiguities surrounding the concept of *hupsos* in Longinus's treatise arise from the fact that the author was shackled by an outmoded rhetorical vocabulary,[21] and it is tempting to see a parallel here between Longinus's situation and that of Boileau: perhaps both writers are engaged in a struggle to break free from an inherited rhetorical tradition and to forge a new aesthetic doctrine. But it is also important for an understanding of Boileau's purpose to consider the literary tradition within which he was working.

In this regard Monk's critical terminology ('rhetoric', 'aesthetics') is deeply ambivalent, for to speak of a shift from rhetoric to aesthetics could be said to be a tautology in the context of seventeenth-century critical thought. The term 'rhetoric' seems appropriate to the period; but how is it to be understood? Monk's implied notion of rhetoric as a 'theory of ornate form' has distinctly Crocean overtones, and it is indeed true that such a view of seventeenth-century eloquence has found favour among some critics who have claimed that in the wake of Ramist reforms, when *inventio* and *dispositio* were hived off from rhetoric into the domain of logic, rhetoric came to be equated with *elocutio* alone.[22] More detailed studies of French classical rhetoric have refuted this view, however, and have argued that, though *elocutio* was becoming increasingly prominent, the discussions of *inventio* and *dispositio* remained vital parts of the rhetorics of the period.[23] Furthermore, poetics was not at this time considered separately from rhetoric, but rather as a part of that wider discipline; manuals of rhetoric frequently drew on poets for their examples. 'La poétique classique a perdu toute autonomie,' writes Kibédi Varga, 'elle est profondément rhétorisée'.[24] The vocabulary of literary criticism remains therefore inescapably bound to that of rhetoric: as Claude Fleury remarks, 'il ne faudrait pas beaucoup de préceptes de poétique à un homme qui saurait ceux de l'éloquence'.[25] Therefore to speak of severing a literary-critical term from its rhetorical origins is not meaningful in the context of French neoclassicism. It would make perhaps more sense to think of Boileau attempting to redefine a given critical term within the overall domain of rhetoric and poetics.

Boileau is at great pains in the passage from the 'Préface' quoted above to emphasise the affective qualities of the *sublime*, and the accumulation of verbs and adjectives is particularly forceful: 'frape', 'enleve', 'ravit', 'transporte'; 'extraordinaire', 'surprenant', 'merveilleux'. Whatever the other ambiguities of the 'Préface', it is abundantly clear that one measure of the sublime for Boileau is calculable in terms of its impact on the reader. In the terminology of M. H. Abrams, he adopts a *pragmatic* approach to literary criticism in according primary importance to the relationship between a work of literature and its audience.[26] If we redefine rhetoric in its broadest sense as 'the art of persuasion', then Boileau's emphasis on a pragmatic critical approach, far from severing the sublime from rhetoric, could be seen as doing precisely the opposite and instead reaffirming the sublime as a rhetorical concept (albeit as a somewhat different one). The engraving chosen to accompany the title-page of the *Traité du sublime* in the *Œuvres diverses* seems designed to encourage a rhetorical view of sublimity (see frontispiece). It depicts an orator, in full rhetorical flight, brandishing a thunderbolt in his right hand; the members of the audience bear expressions registering various degrees of amazement, all apparently held spellbound by the force of his rhetoric. The choice of frontispiece was in no way accidental, for Brossette relates how Boileau intended the orator in question to represent Demosthenes, whom Longinus describes as possessing brilliant rhetorical powers.[27]

But what of Monk's assumption that the *sublime* originates in the domain of rhetoric? He apparently has in mind here the idea of the sublime as the highest (most ornamented, most forceful) of the three styles of classical rhetorical theory. But was this (as Monk implies) the only way in which the *sublime* would have been comprehended before 1674? Before studying Boileau's own use of the term, it is necessary to consider how the term *sublime* might have been understood by his contemporaries.

The concept of a high style appropriate to poetry is first established in France during the Renaissance. The desire for 'un plus hault style' in poetry was evident from around 1520: Marot showed particular awareness of different poetic levels, and Scève was perhaps the first poet to exemplify this heroic style.[28] With the poets and theorists of the Pléiade, the notion of a heightened style for poetry becomes a commonplace: Du Bellay speaks of 'cette grandeur de style' and of the potential of the French language for 'quelque plus hault et meilleur style que celuy dont nous sommes si longuement contentez', while Ronsard speaks of the necessity in a heroic poem for 'un style nombreux, plein d'une venerable Majesté' and for 'les paroles plus rehaussées et recherchées.'[29] But neither Du Bellay in the *Deffence* nor Ronsard in his preface to *La Franciade* employs the term *sublime*, even though they are both clearly describing what has in other periods been termed the sublime poetic style. Sixteenth-century writers similarly recommend the high style in tragedy, but again they do not use the term *sublime* to describe it: Jean de La Taille, in 1572, talks of 'un genre de Poésie [...] elegant, beau, et excellent'; and Pierre Matthieu in 1589 of 'les vers [...] haults, grands et plains de majesté'.[30] The sixteenth century (re-)establishes the idea of the high style in epic and dramatic poetry, but does not call it *sublime*.

The doctrine of the three levels of style—or, as it was sometimes called, the theory of characters—is not known to Aristotle, and it finds its first full exposition in the *Rhetorica ad Herennium* (1st century BC); the most notable subsequent discussions of the theory are to be found in Cicero and Quintilian.[31] These texts were all widely known in seventeenth-century France and all, with the exception of Cicero's *Orator*, were translated into French before 1674. If it is correct that the *sublime* was considered at this time a purely rhetorical term, then we might reasonably expect to find the word used in the translations of the classical rhetoricians. Jacob's translation of the *Ad Herennium* (1652, reprinted 1670) does indeed use 'sublime' for Latin 'gravis', in contrast to 'mediocre' and 'bas et simple' (233). The abbé de Pure, however, in his translation of Quintilian's *Institutes* (1663), renders 'genus grande atque robustum' as 'le [genre d'Oraison] plus abondant et plus fort' (II, 404), and not by 'sublime', which would have been a perfectly plausible translation of 'grandis'. Again, in Cassagnes's version of Cicero's *De oratore* (1673), the Latin 'gravis' is translated not by 'sublime' but by 'magnifique' (521). Thus in only one of the three seminal texts dealing with the theory of characters is the French word 'sublime' used to translate the idea of the sublime style of rhetoric or 'genus grande'.

The French rhetorics of this period also discuss the three characters.[32] Jean Salabert, for example, labels the high style 'excellent, sublime', though he usually prefers the phrase 'style excellent', which, he says, is characterised by sententiousness, high-flown vocabulary and frequent use of figures of speech.[33] René Bary similarly uses 'sublime' and 'excellent' interchangeably, though in his remarks on style he opts for 'sublime'; again, like Salabert, his view of the sublime style is centred on the high-flown nature of the language employed: 'Le style sublime doit estre pur, net, articulé, lié, orné, bruyant et pompeux';[34] he differs from Salabert only in attributing to the three characters specific forms of discourse (letters in the simple style, for instance, and harangues in the high style).

Pierre de Bremond d'Ars composed a rhetoric in French during the early 1650s, when he was in his late teens, as an exercise for his Jesuit tutor.[35] This work, ignoring such contemporary French rhetorics as those of Salabert and Bary, draws exclusively on the classical sources of Aristotle, Cicero and Quintilian, which were the mainstay of Jesuit instruction at this time (Longinus is not mentioned). It makes no use of the term *sublime*, and refers to the three orders of style as 'le plus bas', 'le moyen', and 'le suprême', each of which it links with a particular genre, respectively conversation and letters, serious or philosophical discussions, and legal speeches or sermons (216). The complete unoriginality of this work gives it its own particular interest as a guide to the commonplaces of the period. The word *sublime* is not used at all, though it is striking that this 'amateur' work's treatment of the theory of characters is essentially similar to that of the 'professional' rhetorics of Salabert and Bary, in that each character is defined by a given linguistic level and by specific genres appropriate to it.

Moving forward to the time of the *Traité du sublime*, Le Gras distinguishes the three characters as 'Bas', 'Moyen', and 'Sublime'.[36] But whereas his predecessors quoted above describe the various levels of style in terms of the appropriate linguistic features (such as the frequency of figures of speech), with Bary and Bremond d'Ars further attributing to each style certain forms of discourse, Le Gras goes beyond an insistence that the style should match the subject-matter, and further links each of the characters with a precise rhetorical strategy: 'instruire', 'plaire', and 'mouvoir' (250). This notion, absent from the *Ad Herennium*, is considered to be the contribution of Cicero: Pierre du Ryer's version of Cicero's *Du meilleur genre d'orateurs* (1654, reprinted 1670) describes the three duties of the orator in similar terms—'enseigner', 'delecter', 'esmouvoir' (7), though in this text there is no specific discussion of the three characters. It is clearly questionable whether this addition to the theory is altogether compatible with the earlier ideas of given levels of style as the preserve of particular literary forms. This new slant on the theory of characters shifts the emphasis significantly away from the orator's subject, and towards his relationship with the audience, anticipating perhaps the shift in Boileau's critical theory already noted, from a mimetic to a pragmatic approach:

> Et comme il a esté cy-devant parlé de toutes ces choses, il ne reste plus icy que de faire voir que l'Eloquence consiste à diriger ces trois Genres, selon la qualité de la matiere et du sujet, *ou* selon le dessein de l'Orateur, qui est, ou d'instruire, ou de plaire, ou d'emouvoir, selon la qualité de la matiere. (250; my emphasis)

Le Gras evidently senses the potential incompatibility between the mimetic and the pragmatic definitions of character theory, as the all-important 'ou' here shows, and this represents a significant development of the theory. The linking of the high or sublime style with the rhetorical strategy of moving one's audience brings us markedly nearer to Boileau's interpretation of the Longinian sublime.

Lamy also distinguishes between three levels of style, which he labels 'simple', 'mediocre', and 'sublime', though unlike Le Gras he focuses attention on the relationship between subject-matter and level of style: 'C'est la matière qui doit déterminer dans le choix du style'.[37] And unlike both Salabert and Le Gras, who had effectively equated the sublime style with inflated diction, Lamy attempts to tread a middle path, arguing that the sublime style must be sufficiently enriched with figures of speech to convey the emotion aroused by the subject under discussion. Too few figures, and the discourse will be inadequately animated; too many, however, and the style will be overblown. This is a rather more sophisticated notion of the sublime style, and again, we may detect here certain parallels with Boileau's 'Préface'.

The fact that these latter two rhetorics both label the high style 'sublime', whereas two of the earlier works had hesitated between 'sublime' and 'excellent' and the other had not used the term 'sublime' at all, might tend to suggest that 'sublime' was gradually establishing itself as the habitual description of high style. But the brief *Abrégé de Rhétorique*, which appeared anonymously in the same year as the *Traité du sublime*, prefers to speak of 'le stile heroïque et levé' and of 'le stile levé' (147, 148), though the brevity of the work excludes any specific discussion of the characters under the heading of 'Elocution'.

It is not uniquely in rhetorics, of course, that we may find references to the theory of characters; for example, Vaux's *Tombeau de l'orateur français* (1628) refers to the three levels of style as 'sublime', 'delicat' and 'moyen' (120). The term *sublime* occurs notably in discussions of the epic or heroic poem: thus Georges de Scudéry, considering the question of style in the preface to *Alaric* (1654), notes that 'Il en est [du Style] de trois especes: le sublime; le mediocre; & le bas', although he also employs the term *magnifique*, adding that 'Le magnifique est donc le propre de l'Epopée [...]. Le magnifique, degenere aysément en bouffy & en enflé.' Similarly, Michel de Marolles states: 'J'appele Poëme Heroïque, un Ouvrage Poëtique, écrit d'un stile sublime & pur pour un sujet grave & serieux'.[38] Thus in the seventeenth century, the 'stile sublime' seems to be invoked systematically with reference to the epic poem. This is hardly surprising, for it was a truism of the period that the epic represented the highest pinnacle of achievement in poetry, a view deriving from the Italian Renaissance—though as we have already seen, Ronsard, while sharing the same view, had not used the term *sublime*.

To conclude these remarks about the theory of characters, we may say that while the word *sublime* was often used to describe the *genus grande* (and more frequently in French rhetorics than in the French translations of classical works of rhetoric), it was by no means the only, or even habitual, translation. There is also evidence in the rhetorics which we have considered that the notion of the high style itself was undergoing something of a development: whereas the earlier French rhetoricians (Salabert, Bary) view it simply as the most elaborate and decorated style, later writers like Lamy warn against redundant *enflure* and argue for moderation in the use of figurative speech while Le Gras places a distinctly new emphasis on the role of the sublime style in expressing emotion. Indeed, Lamy and Le Gras between them seem to have stolen much of Boileau's thunder.

Méré too speaks interestingly about the power of simple diction in *Les Conversations*, and although he is discussing eloquence rather than the theory of characters, his views on *cette haute éloquence* foreshadow Boileau on the *sublime*:

> Qu'est-ce qu'on entend par cette haute éloquence qui fait tout ce qu'elle veut, à ce que disent tant de gens? [...]
>
> Il me semble que cette haute éloquence n'est pas comme on se l'imagine. On veut qu'elle éblouïsse, et qu'elle soit toûjours sur le haut ton. Car comme on est persuadé, que le stile simple et familier est bas; on croit aussi qu'elle n'y sçauroit paroistre en son naturel. C'est que l'on a plus d'égard à la parure qu'à l'excellence de la chose, et que l'on ne songe pas qu'il en faudroit juger comme de l'or, qui est estimé selon qu'il est plus fin et plus pur. Je croirois tout au contraire de ceux qui la veulent toûjours orageuse, qu'elle aime naturellement à se montrer sans fracas et sans bruit.[39]

Clearly the plea of Boileau's 'Preface' for a simpler style with greater affective and emotional impact is anticipated in a number of contemporary writings, so that even Boileau's attempt to redefine the *sublime* within the overall domain of rhetoric which we discussed above no longer appears an innovation. How then are we to account for the enthusiam with which contemporaries greeted the appearance of the *Traité du sublime*?

We have seen that prior to 1674, *le sublime* was by no means the sole rhetorical term used to describe the high style, as Monk apparently assumed. The corollary of Monk's assumption that *le sublime* was a rhetorical term is that it was not employed in other, non-rhetorical contexts (since otherwise it would make no sense to speak of a shift from rhetoric to aesthetics); this second idea must also be examined.

In her survey of the critical vocabulary of this period, Noémi Hepp suggests that *le sublime* was current even before Boileau's translation had brought it to the forefront of critical debate, but she produces in support of her contention only two examples from Chapelain: in his *Sentiments de l'Académie*, he writes of modern works that 'la plupart [ne sont] colorés ni par la sublimité des pensées, ni par la pureté de l'élocution'; and in his discussion of the epic in general in the preface to the first part of *La Pucelle*, Chapelain describes 'ces puissants génies d'Homère et de Virgile [qui ont] porté ce genre de poésie à une très sublime hauteur'.[40]

An interesting use of the Latin *sublimis* in a poetic context occurs in Descartes's *Olympica* (1619), the Latin fragment written in his youth:

> Just as the imagination employs figures to conceive of bodies, so the intelligence, to produce spiritual objects, employs certain physical bodies, such as wind and light. From which it follows that,

philosophising in the highest manner, we may lead the spirit via knowledge to the heights ['in sublime'].[41]

What gives this text its particular interest is the fact that immediately after this reference to the *sublimis*, Descartes goes on to comment that the highest truths are to be discovered in the poets, who write under the spell of enthusiasm and imagination:

> It may seem strange that weighty thoughts are to be found rather in the writings of poets than of philosophers. The reason is that poets write under the sway of enthusism and with the force of imagination: there are in us seeds of learning, as there are seeds of fire in a flint, which philosophers extract through reason, and which poets tear out with the imagination, that they may shine more brightly.[42]

This admittedly slim evidence suggests the term, albeit in Latin, was not confined to the field of rhetoric in the narrowest sense, and already in 1619 could refer to the transcending force of the poet's imagination.

We find *le sublime* (and the name of Longinus) similarly linked with the idea of poetic enthusiasm in a French work of the same period, Dom Jean Goulu's *Lettres de Phyllarque à Ariste* (1627-28), which appeared just at the time of the quarrel concerning the 'new' rhetorical style of Balzac's *Lettres*. Some, like Goulu, criticised Balzac for the artificiality of his style; and Goulu quotes Longinus at length in defence of the imitation of great authors as a means to achieve poetic inspiration.

> Car c'est la verité qu'il y en a beaucoup qui puisent l'esprit de ces grans hommes à force de lire & de considerer leurs ouvrages. Et de là comme par un divin enthousiasme sont emportez & ravis à parler plus hautement, & plus sublimement que la condition des hommes ne porte. (II, 244-45)

In this passage (only a part of his quotation from Longinus), Goulu sets against Balzac's studied rhetoric an ideal of eloquence which is at once natural and inspired. Goulu's work provoked in its turn a counter-attack, in which the anonymous author ridiculed his opponent's aspiration to 'l'estage sublime' of naturally-inspired writers who spurn the laborious training and prolonged practice of 'esprits mediocres':

> C'est pour cela qu'il approuve tant [...] la voye par laquelle on parvient à la sublimité de l'éloquence avecque des enthousiasme (sic).[43]

In the course of the quarrel over Balzac's *Lettres*, then, Longinus and *la sublimité* are called to the support of nature, and are deployed against the allegedly artificial rhetoric of Balzac, evidence that already in the 1620s the notion of the *sublime* could be found in a literary context, as well as in discussions of the theory of characters. Later in the century, this same conflict between nature and art, between genius and the rules, will be discussed by Rapin, and he similarly will invoke the authority of Longinus to back the side of nature.[44]

These various occurrences of the term *sublime* in both 'literary' and 'rhetorical' contexts all imply a broadly positive view of the concept. Elsewhere, however, the word is used pejoratively. The *Abrégé de rhétorique*, for example, while avoiding reference to the *stile sublime*, alludes to instances of high-flown language pandering to human pride as 'ces sublimes expressions' (187), opposed here to the naturalness of 'Eloquence Sainte'. This foreshadows Malebranche, who deployed great eloquence in his attack on the immorality of eloquence:

> On pourra reconnaître en quelque façon, que si nous aimons le genre sublime, l'air noble et libre de certains auteurs, c'est que nous avons de la vanité, et que nous aimons la grandeur et l'indépendance; et que ce goût, que nous trouvons dans la délicatesse des discours efféminés, n'a point d'autre source, qu'une secrète inclination pour la mollesse et pour la volupté.[45]

Such pejorative usage of the term, while indirectly acknowledging its 'rhetorical' status, further suggests that *le sublime* was far from having a single or coherent sense. These two pejorative uses of *sublime* both come from texts first published in 1674, the year of Boileau's *Traité du Sublime*. In less serious vein, Molière also records an abusive use of the word. In *Les Précieuses ridicules* (1659), Madelon, having provided her guests with 'les commodités de la conversation', is invited to smell one of their powdered wigs, and exclaims: 'Elle est tout à fait de qualité; le sublime en est touché délicieusement' (I, 279). Somaize's *Dictionnaire des précieuses* translates this for us as 'le cerveau', happily the only known occurrence of the word with this meaning.

It is clearly hazardous to attempt a definition of *le sublime* as employed prior to 1674, especially in the absence of any dictionary,[46] but we should at least avoid the temptation to limit the word to a single or specific meaning. The examples discussed above have demonstrated how *le sublime* could be used to signify different things in different contexts: nowhere is this better seen than in Bary's *Rhetorique françoise* (1653). Bary himself, as we noted, characterises the 'stile sublime' as 'pur, net, [...] orné, bruyant et pompeux'; but in the 'Discours' which prefaces Bary's rhetoric, Le Grand describes Longinus as the rhetorician of the sublime style, 'ce Longinus qui nous a donné des Livres du genre sublime', and he goes on to quote from *Peri hupsous* the *fiat lux* example from Genesis: 'Quelle pompe et quelle grandeur n'apperçoit-on pas dans la pureté de ces mots? que Moïse dit beaucoup, et que Moïse parle peu!' It is true that Bary had specified purity as one of the attributes of the sublime style; but purity, however understood, is not equivalent to brevity, and the example which Le Grand selects from Longinus (and which Boileau was to chose in his 'Préface') presupposes a very different view of the *sublime* from that which Bary gives us. Whether Le Grand and Bary realise it or not, the differences between the definition and the example are irreconcilable. This reaffirms the notion that Boileau, in making his distinction between 'sublime' and 'stile sublime' is not so much redefining the term in a radically new way as attempting to discriminate between the various—and incompatible—uses of the word then current.

We cannot therefore speak of Boileau's originality in the *Traité du sublime* as having been to instigate a shift of the term *sublime* from 'rhetoric' to 'aesthetics'. Firstly, the very words 'rhetoric' and 'aesthetics' may too easily lead us into ambiguity and error when applied to the seventeenth century, unless they are carefully defined. Secondly, *le sublime* was not the only available translation of 'genus grande' in contemporary discussion of the theory of characters, though it was a frequent one. Thirdly, the notion of the high style itself was far from being static, but was gradually evolving in the direction of 'expressive simplicity'. And fourthly, the word *sublime* was current beyond the works of rhetoric, and was used in discussions of literary language where no reference to the theory of characters was implied. Boileau inherits with the word *sublime* an ambivalent, not to say multivalent, term which is in need more of careful clarification than of radical redefinition.[47]

c. THE ROMANTIC SUBLIME

The sublime is now widely discussed by literary critics, and recent interest has focused particularly on the notion of the Romantic sublime.[48] Literary theorists too have devoted considerable attention to the topic, and Neil Hertz's 'A reading of Longinus' (1973), stressing Longinus's concern with the limitations of language, has been especially influential.[49]

This re-evaluation of the rhetoric of the Romantic sublime strongly influenced Louis Marin, whose projected study of the sublime in the seventeenth century was sadly incomplete at his death but who wrote a number of papers connecting the aesthetic of the sublime with Poussin. Marin, like Hertz and de Man, is interested in the sublime as an expression of the ineffable, of something beyond representation: 'Je poserai le sublime comme l'irréprésentable de la représentation'.[50] The storm poses a specifically sublime challenge to the artist, because of the difficulty, impossibility even, of representing it adequately. Interest in the storm as a phenomenon which defies mimesis is at least as old as Pliny, who says in praise of his ideal painter Apelles that 'he even painted things that cannot be represented in pictures—thunder, lightning and thunderbolts'.[51] It is from this perspective that Marin considers two paintings by Poussin, *Grand paysage avec Pyrame et Thisbé* and *L'Orage*. The Romantic sublime may well be a valuable tool for the interpretation of Poussin landscapes, but Marin seems to be claiming more than that in suggesting that the notion of the Romantic sublime was actually current in the seventeenth century, for he quotes Longinus and speaks of Poussin and Félibien as being 'affrontés à la question du sublime et de ses effets pathétiques dans le paysage classique'.[52] There is surely a terminological trap here: when Poussin and Félibien talk about *Pyrame et Thisbé* (the relevant texts are quoted by Marin in full),[53] they on no occasion employ the word *sublime*. This is quite different from describing as 'sublimes' the eighteenth-century *Tempêtes* of Joseph Vernet, where we are merely echoing a term employed by such contemporaries as Diderot.[54]

If we adopt a more historical perspective, it is possible to trace the inspiration of Poussin's *Pyrame et Thisbé* back to the writings of Leonardo da Vinci. Leonardo takes the mimetic theory of art entirely for granted, and is essentially concerned in his fragmentary writings with describing the various techniques by which the painter can produce the most effective representations of nature. He meditates on the subjects which pose the greatest challenge to the painter, such as a battle, night, or a tempest, and in an extraordinary passage in his notebooks, 'How to represent a tempest', he enumerates all the details which would make a picture of a tempest plausible.[55]

Leonardo's notebooks remained unpublished until 1651, when there appeared in Paris a re-arranged selection (including the section on the storm), under the invented title *Trattato della pittura*, and simultaneously by the same publisher a French translation (by Roland Fréart), *Traitté de la peinture*. Appearing as a 'new' work in the middle of the seventeenth century, and concerned as it was with the detailed problems of the imitation of nature, Leonardo's work may well have influenced the early theorists of French classical doctrine (though it is not mentioned by Bray). But while the *Trattato* made Leonardo famous in France as a theorist, he apparently had no discernable influence on seventeenth-century French painters, with the sole but important exception of Poussin, who was well acquainted with Leonardo's writings and evidently influenced by them.[56] The first editions (Italian and French) of the *Trattato* appeared with drawings by Poussin, executed around 1635, which aim to explain certain of Leonardo's ideas, and Fréart's translation contains a flattering dedication to Poussin, *premier peintre du Roi*. The most obvious instance of Leonardo's influence on Poussin is seen in *Pyrame et Thisbé*, where Poussin follows precisely the description of the storm in Leonardo's notebooks.[57]

That Marin should associate this theme with sublimity is entirely understandable. The storm at sea, for example in *Paul et Virginie*, is a characteristic theme of preromanticism;[58] and it has obvious affinities with the views of Edmund Burke, who emphasises both the awe-inspiring powers of nature, and the difficulties of conveying them in art: 'When painters have attempted to give us clear representations of these very fanciful and terrible ideas, they have I think almost always failed.'[59]

It is equally possible, however, to locate the idea of the storm in seventeenth-century painting and writing, where it has a different set of connotations. There is of course a pictorial tradition going back at least to the *Tempesta* of Giorgione (a work known to Leonardo). In his study of Giorgione's *Tempesta*, Edgar Wind produces an iconographical reading of the painting which demonstrates that the storm depicted has emblematic force as a sort of visual pun: in the Italian of the period, *fortuna* could mean both 'fortune' (which ties in thematically with other elements in the picture) and 'storm'—a reading far removed from the Romantic sublime of Burke.[60] For seventeenth-century French writers, on the other hand, the tempest is something of a topos. Dignified by the precedents of the *Odyssey* and the *Æneid*, the subject offers an opportunity for a brilliant *exercice de style*—examples may be found in works as varied as d'Urfé's *L'Astrée*, Camus's *Agathonphile*, Gomberville's *Polexandre*, Madeleine de Scudéry's *Cyrus*, and in Théophile de Viau's ode 'Sur une tempête'.[61]

Finally, it should be remembered that Poussin painted *L'Orage* as one of a pair of paintings, the other being *Un Temps calme*: in this case he seems to be as interested in the juxtaposition of two contrasting themes as he is in the theme of the storm for its own sake. This pair of themes is itself a topos, exploited, for example, by Saint-Amant:

> Que c'est une chose agreable
> D'estre sur le bord de la Mer,
> Quand elle vient à se calmer
> Apres quelque orage effroyable![62]

Precisely the same interest in the contrasting moods of the sea is found in a *devise* by Le Moyne on the subject of eloquence (Fig. 4), and, as we have already seen, at the beginning of Bouhours's *Entretiens* (8).[63]

Is is thus entirely possible to describe Poussin's interest in the theme of the storm within the framework of thought of his own period. Marin, like Monk, reads back onto Boileau a Romantic view of the sublime which is not Boileau's. Any attempt to describe Boileau's aesthetic of *le sublime* should at least start out by trying to locate his aesthetic vocabulary in the context of neoclassical poetics.

III. THE *TRAITÉ DU SUBLIME* AS A TRANSLATION

The most important study of Boileau's concept of the *sublime* is unquestionably Jules Brody's *Boileau and Longinus*. Avoiding entirely the pitfall of superimposing on Boileau the preconceptions of other periods, this study focuses exclusively on the *Art poétique* and the *Traité du sublime*, reading them closely, analysing minutely Boileau's terminology, and comparing the translation at every stage with the Greek original. Brody concludes that for Boileau, as for Longinus, emotion is a basic condition of aesthetic response. *Nature* and *art* are not opposed in Boileau's thought, but subsumed in 'la parfaite habitude du Sublime'; *raison* is not the instrument of logic it is usually taken to be, but a means of insight and a principle of control for the creative writer. Thus *esprit* describes innate potential, but also creative power: it is both an inherited gift and an act of judgement (and it is significant that Boileau uses both *esprit* and *nature* to translate the Greek *phusis*). While it is impossible to do justice to the richness of Brody's study in so brief a summary, the radical originality of this approach is clear; it amounts to a convincing demonstration of the cohesion of Boileau's literary theory and a definitive rejection of the entrenched idea that Boileau's 'preromantic' interest in the sublime is somehow antipathetic to the 'neoclassical' doctrine of his *Art poétique*.

Brody's detailed comparison of the French translation with the Greek original demonstrates how Boileau at times fills out the original, amplifying the meaning in a particular direction—all of which provides us with a fascinating insight into Boileau's understanding of *le sublime*, as we catch him in the act of forging, or at least recreating, a critical term. The passages containing amplifications of especial significance seem to fall into three groups. Firstly, there are those in which Boileau emphasises an allusive, tentative, almost secretive element in the sublime: he speaks of 'une *certaine élévation d'esprit*', or of 'une *certaine* fierté noble', 'ce silence a *je ne sais quoi* de plus grand' (the emphases indicate Boileau's departure from the Greek).[64] Secondly, Boileau points up crucially those passages in the original concerning perfection: 'Le sublime est *en effet* ce qui forme l'excellence et *la souveraine perfection* du discours'; and again 'Comme c'est le devoir de l'art d'empêcher que l'on ne tombe, et *qu'il est bien difficile* qu'une haute élévation *à la longue se soutienne*, et garde *toujours* un ton égal, *il faut* que l'art vienne au secours de la nature: parce qu'en effet, c'est leur *parfaite* alliance qui fait la *souveraine* perfection'.[65] Thirdly, Boileau very frequently underscores descriptions of the emotional impact produced by literature: he stresses the subjective reactions of the reader, he reinforces a comment about the emotive appeal of a particular passage, he gives prominence to the affective aspects of poetical imagery, and he emphasises Demosthenes's ability to engulf his hearer.[66] Very striking in this respect is Boileau's treatment of the passage in which Longinus draws a distinction between persuasion and transport: the argument of the Greek critic survives essentially unaltered, except that Boileau, with numerous amplifications, argues the point more strenuously:

> [Le sublime] ne persuade pas *proprement,* mais il ravit, *il transporte,* et *produit en nous une certaine* admiration, mêlée d'étonnement *et de surprise*, qui est *tout autre chose* que de plaire *seulement*, ou de persuader […]. Il donne au discours *une certaine* vigueur *noble,* une force invincible qui *enlève l'âme* de quiconque nous écoute.[67]

Brody charitably remarks that 'Boileau's licences [are] but a higher form of fidelity',[68] and it is true that in general Boileau merely spotlights certain tendencies already latent in Longinus. Even so, the comparison of the two texts shows vividly how Boileau recreated the sublime for his own purposes, strengthening Longinian assertions concerning the 'sovereign perfection' of sublime speech, and its emotive impact on the reader or listener. Brody sums up thus:

> In Boileau's renderings of Longinus's descriptions of the effects of the Sublime, qualities of intensity, spontaneity, and enthrallment were foremost. The writer's power to cast a spell, create a gripping illusion, was magnified […]. Longinus's Sublime, that inner essence which rivets the attention, was for Boileau 'la souveraine perfection du discours'. His concepts of genre and style, his insistence on naturalness and simplicity, his notion of Tragedy, and his manner of translating the Ancients all were calculated to conserve that perfection and to keep the emotive effects of literature undisturbed, intense, and pure. Every element in Boileau's critical strategy, like his commitment to the Sublime, was born of this impulse.[69]

Brody declares in his conclusion that he has attempted to restore to Boileau the qualities which critics had almost unanimously denied him hitherto, 'originality and unity of thought'.[70]

What Brody's study does not do—and does not claim to do—is to show the cohesion of the concept of *le sublime* (which is not of course the same thing as the cohesion of Boileau's critical system). The great strength of the study is that it concentrates exclusively, as none before had done, on Boileau's critical writings; so exclusively, in fact, that there is not space to look at the contemporary context, so that we lack entirely any foil against which to assess Boileau's critical manœuvres. Brody's study shows the crucial importance of analysing critical terminology with precision, and it helps us to a better understanding of the salient characteristics of Boileau's *sublime* (sovereign perfection, emotive impact, and so forth). It does not, however, pretend to resolve or account for the inconsistencies in Boileau's treatment of the concept, such as the distinction between the sublime and the sublime style, or the question of whether the sublime is a product of thought or of language. Similarly it is hard to speak of the originality of Boileau's critical thought without the context in which to assess it. Brody's synchronic study explains *how* Boileau translated Longinus, but not *why*. In order to address these questions, it is necessary to continue Brody's investigation in a diachronic perspective.

To begin with, we might consider the title that Boileau gives to his translation of Longinus. If Boileau had not elected to translate *hupsos* by *sublime*, the entire eighteenth-century debate on the sublime might not have developed as it did. At a time when Longinus was known principally through Latin translations with such titles as *De grandi sive sublimi, De sublimi genere dicendi* and *De sublimitate,* the French translation of *sublime* might seem inevitable; certainly the manuscript French translation of the 1640s had used *sublimité*. None the less, John Hall had rendered *hupsos* as *the height of eloquence,* and a later English translator as *loftiness,* so that other terms were feasible, at least in English. Perhaps a term such as *haut* or *élevé* would have sounded insufficiently powerful in French, though we noted above Méré's use of *haute éloquence* in a comparable sense. At least one other word was available to Boileau, for he uses it in the sub-title: *Traité du sublime, ou du merveilleux dans le discours.* The very fact that Boileau finds it necessary to add a sub-title at all is perhaps indicative of a certain uneasiness concerning the term *sublime*.

Le merveilleux has first of all the significant advantage of being an established critical term,[71] and it is used principally in this period in discussion of the epic poem. Aristotle had argued that the epic offered greater scope than tragedy for the marvellous (*to thaumaston*, rendered by Le Bossu as *admirable*), on the grounds that its lack of a visual dimension made the marvellous less improbable; Tasso, pursuing this idea further, went on to maintain that the *meraviglioso* was the essential and defining feature of the epic. Such remained the view of all seventeenth-century French critics, whether they were partisans of *le merveilleux chrétien* like Godeau, Le Moyne, Chapelain and Scudéry or whether, like Boileau, they favoured *le merveilleux païen*.[72] Scudéry, for example, considers the *merveilleux* and the *vraisemblable* to be the twin props of the heroic poem, though how precisely each complements the other he does not explain:

> Je suis fortement persuadé que l'histoire Payenne ny l'histoire
> Sainte, ne sont point propres présentement à fournir un Sujet Epique:
> et que la Chrétienne prophane toute seule en nostre temps nous
> peut donner ce merveilleux et ce vraysemblable qui en sont l'âme.[73]

Rapin, too, is at pains to suggest the compatibility of the two terms, though he is not entirely convincing either; at times, indeed, the two terms can appear almost as opposites:

> Le merveilleux est tout ce qui est contre le cours ordinaire de la
> nature. Le vray-semblable est tout ce qui est conforme à l'opinion
> du public.[74]

Thus *le merveilleux* seems to carry with it a suggestion of the improbable, a suggestion which would be altogether inappropriate in the case of the example from Genesis or of Horace's 'Qu'il mourût', since what Boileau wishes to stress with both these examples is not the inherent improbability of either the event or of the remark, but rather the fact that these are both noble conceptions forcefully expressed—so forcefully, in fact, that any improbability goes unremarked.

Furthermore, through its links with the epic poem, *le merveilleux* comes to be associated with the highest of the three characters. Boileau makes it quite clear in the *Art poétique* that the epic poet must use a highly ornamented style, and without such embellishments, the epic will fail:

> C'est-là ce qui surprend, frappe, saisit, attache:
> Sans tous ces ornemens le vers tombe en langueur.[75]

This description of the effect of 'marvellous' devices in the epic poem echoes in part the characterisation of the sublime in the 'Préface', where Boileau writes of 'cet extraordinaire et ce merveilleux qui frape dans le discours, et qui fait qu'un ouvrage enleve, ravit, transporte' (*TS*, 45). The effect described is similar, though perhaps not identical: the epic poem surprises its readers with a fantastic and therefore implausible detail, yet manages to grip them ('saisit, attache') in such a way that they are prepared to suspend disbelief, because they have been drawn into the text to such an extent by sheer force of language. The effect depicted in the 'Préface' applies to all forms of discourse, to unadorned prose narratives as much as to ornate epic poems, and here the concern is shifted decisively towards the affective impact of the language—to the way in which the reader, far from being drawn *into* the text, is impelled to go *beyond* it under the inspiration of fresh emotion ('ravit, transporte').

We may conjecture, therefore, that Boileau preferred to relegate *le merveilleux* to the subtitle of his translation because it was too closely associated both with the genre of the epic and with the corresponding high style of language. The choice of *sublime* as the translation of *hupsos* was not inevitable (although it certainly became so after Boileau); but since *le sublime* was not yet an established critical term in the way that *le merveilleux* was, it offered Boileau greater flexibility of interpretation and allowed him more easily to underscore the affective aspects of language and to suggest that language of strong emotional appeal might as effectively be achieved by simple means as by elaborate rhetoric.

The term *sublime*, though less established than *le merveilleux*, also carries with it its own history. After quoting the passage in which Boileau distinguishes between 'le Sublime' and 'le style sublime', Brody asserts that 'Boileau was the first to use *le sublime* in this specific sense'.[76] This is doubtless what Boileau would have liked his contemporaries to believe, but it is not in fact strictly true. Firstly, as we have already seen, the concept of 'high style' was by then already evolving towards the idea of expressive simplicity, making Boileau's distinction less radical than it might at first seem. Secondly, this selfsame distinction had already been drawn by Tanneguy Le Fèvre in his critical edition of *Peri hupsous* (1663), the first to be published in France. Boileau openly acknowledges his debt to the notes of Le Fèvre's edition,[77] but he passes over in silence the Latin preface, which could be considered to be the most original part of Le Fèvre's work. Le Fèvre's central argument is that the Longinian notion of *hupsos* is entirely distinct from the third of the *genera dicendi* (*hadros*, *megethos*) as described by Hermogenes: 'Nam, quod iam antea dixi, de tertio Genere non agit Longinus'.[78] The Longinian sublime differs from the most elevated of the three styles: firstly, quantitatively, in that it is the highest attainable style, and therefore above *magnitudo*; and secondly, qualitatively, in that whereas grandeur is compared to the body, the sublime is likened to the soul or spirit. In establishing this cartesian dichotomy between sublime style as body, and sublime as spirit, Le Fèvre is apparently arguing that *hupsos* operates on a plane quite independently of the traditional distinctions of rhetorical theory. Elsewhere, however, his terminology can seem confusing, and he continues to link *hupsos* with scenes tending to inspire strong violent emotion, such as violent storms at sea, in the same way that the sublime style of rhetoric had been connected with the strategy of persuasion through emotion. Yet despite the difficulties involved in his argument, Le Fèvre vigorously defends his distinction between sublime and sublime style; in examining possible objections to his position, he denies that Hermogenes had equated the third of the *genera dicendi* with the sublime, and he defends Longinus against the charge that his use of *hupsos* and *megethos* is indiscriminate.

Le Fèvre is entirely aware of the originality of the interpretation that he is proposing: 'Sed, ut ad sententia mea novitatem redeam [...].'[79] He believes that he has rediscovered the true meaning attributed to *hupsos* by Longinus, and that it was Longinus himself who had been the innovator, developing a concept which had been no more than glimpsed confusedly by Caecilius, to whom Longinus is ostensibly replying in his treatise. Le Fèvre concludes by throwing down a challenge to the pre-eminent critic of the day, Jean Chapelain, asking that the latter should give consideration to these arguments. Chapelain, so far as we know, made no reply, and it was to be Boileau, two years after Le Fèvre's death, who was to take up this challenge to discuss the sublime. As we have said, the appearance of Le Fèvre's edition in 1663 may have been a stimulus encouraging Boileau to undertake his translation of Longinus, and the challenge issued in the preface was perhaps a further inducement. It was said that Le Fèvre, the most celebrated Greek teacher of his day, had prized his edition of Longinus above all his other works; he would doubtless have been flattered by Boileau's whole-hearted adoption of his interpretation, even though it goes unacknowledged. The fact of this plagiarism does serve to remind us that Boileau is working within, and reacting against, specific currents of critical thought. A full appreciation of Boileau's *Traité du sublime* and his critical system is only possible when we consider the arguments in the context of contemporary debate.

Maurer is rather harsh on Boileau as a translator, and points to the instances where, for example, metaphors are toned down or attenuated;[80] but this is to ignore the restrictions on poetic language in the classical period, restrictions within which Boileau had to work if he wanted his translation to be taken seriously. His rendering of Sappho into poised alexandrines (*TS*, 68) is a good example of Boileau's ability to tame something just sufficiently to make it palatable to his contemporaries, while still leaving a strong flavour of the original; Racine was to repeat the trick, rewriting the same passage, in *Phèdre*. In fact, Boileau is, as Brody proves, an extremely competent classical scholar, and his translation of Longinus is highly accurate. It is precisely this fact which makes the occasional free renderings in the translation all the more significant, and we should surely give Boileau the benefit of the doubt and assume that he understands the text perfectly, and then ask why he has chosen in a particular instance to highlight a given detail. For all its generally high level of accuracy, there is a sense in which Boileau is knowingly creating the work afresh. He is also crafting a new critical term: he has chosen a word, *sublime*, which is in flux, and which he invents anew—hence the suppression of his crucial debt to Le Fèvre in drawing the distinction between the sublime and the sublime style. It is essential to Boileau's project that the distinction should appear fresh and that his term *sublime* should seem a new one. And so the translation, despite and because of its accuracy and elegance, is much more than a translation. Just as Boileau cribs from Le Fèvre to be able to invent a new critical term, so also he cribs from Longinus to create a new work.

IV. The *Traité du sublime* as neoclassical treatise

Dacier praised Boileau's translation as one of the finest in the French language.[81] But a still greater compliment was paid by Rapin when he spoke of 'la Traduction de Longin, qui est le Chef-d'œuvre de son Auteur, et qui a plus l'air d'original que de traduction'.[82] For a fellow critic to describe the vernacular translation of a classical rhetorician as Boileau's masterpiece is extraordinary, especially given the generally low esteem in which such efforts were generally held. But Rapin explains this paradox by remarking that the *Traité du sublime* is more like an original work than a (mere) translation. Adrien Baillet had exactly the same thought, noting with great acuity that the translation 'est si naturelle, qu'on la prendroit volontiers pour une pièce originale'.[83] This is, we may guess, precisely the effect which Boileau intended:

after all, he did not publish the translation separately (as all the other translations of rhetorical texts had been) but deliberately integrated it into a collection of other 'original' works.

Yet despite the comments of Rapin and Baillet, modern commentators have by and large persisted in regarding the work purely as a translation. The problem derives in part perhaps from a deep-rooted sense of the inferiority of a translation as compared with an original work. But the distinction between an 'original' text and a translation does not stand close scrutiny, and it is quite possible for us to view Boileau's text 'simply' as a work of French classical poetic theory. There are certainly parallel instances in the classical period. La Bruyère, for example, by prefacing his 'original' text with his own translation of Theophrastus in *Les Caractères*, manages to blur the distinction between a translation and an independent creative work.[84] Even the tragedies of Racine which are often so closely based on a classical source—as Racine routinely reminds us in his prefaces—might be considered as very free translations of a classical author. The idea that true freedom, originality, can only be achieved through imitation of the texts of classical antiquity is a Renaissance notion that survives as a vital principle of French classicism. Thus translation may be considered as one significant manifestation of the aesthetic of imitation.

If it is problematic to regard the *Traité du sublime* simply as a translation, then it is surely equally problematic to regard the *Art poétique* as a straightforwardly 'original' work. The accusation that Boileau had plagiarised Horace's *Ars poetica* was made already in Boileau's lifetime—Desmarets remarked that the work should have been called *Traductions de l'Art poétique d'Horace, de Vida et de quelques autres, égayées par quelques satires contres quelques poètes français, tant du siècle passé que du présent*. Boileau responded to his critics in the prefatory 'Au lecteur' of the 1674 octavo and 1675 duodecimo editions of the *Œuvres diverses*:

> Bien loin de leur rendre injures pour injures, ils trouveront bon que je les remercie ici du soin qu'ils prennent de publier, que ma Poëtique est une Traduction de la Poëtique d'Horace. Car puisque dans mon Ouvrage, qui est d'onze cens Vers, il n'y en a pas plus de cinquante ou soixante tout au plus imités d'Horace, ils ne peuvent pas faire un plus bel éloge du reste qu'en le supposant traduit de ce grand Poëte, et je m'estonne après cela qu'ils osent combattre les regles que j'y debite. Pour Vida dont ils m'accusent d'avoir pris aussi quelque chose, mes Amis sçavent bien que je ne l'ay jamais lû.[85]

In fact, Boileau's declaration that he has borrowed 50 or 60 lines from Horace's *Ars poetica* is not strictly true: Boudhors calculates the true figure to be nearer 100 or 110, and in addition there are borrowings from other poems of Horace, so that altogether some 200 lines of the *Art poétique* are indebted to the Roman poet—a considerable number in a poem of only 1100 lines.[86] Given that nearly one fifth of the *Art poétique* is a translation of Horace, and that Longinus was far less well known than

Horace in the classical period, there is a sense in which contemporaries might have looked upon the *Traité du sublime* as the truly original work and seen the *Art poétique* as a mere reworking of Horace.

It is proposed here therefore to read the *Traité du sublime* not as a translation but as a critical treatise of the 1670s, a treatise to which Boileau's contemporaries might have turned for explanation of the current problems of poetic theory. Given the extent to which Boileau willingly and wilfully conflates his own voice with Longinus's, the 'author' of the *Traité du sublime* will be referred to in this section as Boileau-Longinus.

In our study of the background to the literary debate of this period, we have seen how a theory of imaginative literature is vulnerable to attack from two different directions. Firstly, there is the moral objection that poetry, because it imitates reality, is too real, and so obfuscates the proper distinction between truth and falsehood. Secondly, there is the linguistic objection that since language is normally no more than an insipid reflection of the real, it should constantly struggle to achieve a more satisfactory imitation. Imaginative writing is thus caught in a uniquely fragile position, where successful imitation is urged on linguistic grounds, but censured on moral grounds. Linguistic nomenclaturism, pushed to its logical extreme, is necessarily incompatible with a satisfactory account of poetry, for an insistence that words be no more than mere labels for things denies language its aesthetic dimension—and even if language could be savoured for its own sake, such an attitude would encounter the moral objection outlined above. In addition, we have also observed in this period a parallel, if covert, interest in platonist aesthetics.

To what extent, then, is Boileau enabled to address these problems through the *Traité du sublime*? Certainly one element of Boileau's success is that we can forget in reading the *Traité du sublime* that we are reading a translation at all, so skilfully does Boileau assimilate Longinus into the seventeenth century; there is, for example, little of the rebarbative technical vocabulary (*enthymme, syllogisme*) that we find in Cassandre's version of Aristotle's *Rhetoric* and which would have tended inevitably to distance the text from the seventeenth-century reader. In Longinus's attacks on 'enflure' we seem to discern the voice of Boileau condemning the Baroque poets of an earlier generation (*TS*, 52), while the lament that 'on cherche trop la nouveauté dans les pensées qui est la manie sur tout des Ecrivains d'aujourd'hui' (56) seems to fit the seventeenth century as well as it fits the first.[87] Similarly, when Longinus ridicules certain details of the *Odyssey* as 'ces fictions [...] d'assez beaux songes' (67), we could as well be listening to Boileau pronouncing on the contemporary novel. Nor, in all probability, would Boileau have dissociated himself from the exclamation in the last chapter: 'Tant la sterilité maintenant est grande parmi les esprits!' (121). It was one of the aims, perhaps, of the *Traité du sublime* to counter such sterility.[88]

If we now consider the *Traité du sublime* as a critical text of the 1670s rather than as a translation of a first-century Greek treatise, it is not difficult to see how it might serve to counter the moral objection to poetry outlined above. The sublime constitutes a moral value almost by definition (though not entirely so: we have already noted that Malebranche and the author of the *Abrégé de rhétorique* both speak pejoratively of the *genre sublime*), and Boileau-Longinus insists that it is a mark of the sublime that it raises up the soul of the listener, thereby giving it an enhanced view of itself:

> Car tout ce qui est veritablement Sublime, a cela de propre, quand on l'écoute, qu'il élève l'âme, et luy fait concevoir une plus haute opinion d'elle-mesme. (58)

Such might be one source of the sublimity of the *fiat lux* example (64), which so effectively expresses the idea of God's greatness and omnipotence—and what better than a Biblical example to defend imaginative literature against the attacks of those who claimed, like Malebranche, that it was immoral?

Such radical criticism of poetry arose initially, as we have seen, out of a suspicion of the overblown poetic style that allegedly obscured the simple 'unvarnished' truth, and here, too, Boileau-Longinus presents pertinent arguments. Figurative discourse is liable to be 'suspect d'adresse, d'artifice et de tromperie' (84), Boileau-Longinus concedes, but if the figure can be artfully concealed, then the deceit will go undetected. The ideal figure should be felt and not seen:

> Il n'y a point de Figure plus excellente que celle qui est tout-à-fait cachée, et lors qu'on ne reconnoît point que c'est une Figure. Or il n'y a point de secours ni de remede plus merveilleux pour l'empêcher de paroistre, que le Sublime et le Pathetique, parce que l'Art ainsi renfermé au milieu de quelque chose de grand et d'éclatant, a tout ce qui luy manquoit, et n'est plus suspect d'aucune tromperie. (85)

A figure which has been carefully planted will deceive the reader with spurious spontaneity, as Boileau-Longinus remarks with respect to rhetorical questions:

> Par cette Figure l'Auditeur est adroitement trompé, et prend les discours les plus meditez pour des choses dites sur l'heure et dans la chaleur. (87)

The clumsy or inappropriate metaphor is deemed anti-sublime, not because metaphors in themselves should be avoided, but because clumsy metaphors draw attention to themselves (55) and so declare openly their artifice.

Such a justification of figures in their rightful place appears consonant with nomenclaturist language theory. If words are labels for ideas, then grand words should properly be used only to label grand ideas: 'Il faut que les paroles répondent à la majesté des choses dont on traite' (120). Figures similarly mirror the passions, and if the context justifies them, then their use will pass unnoticed. Thus an extravagant hyperbole in Herodotus is defended, 'parce que la chose ne semble pas recherchée pour l'Hyperbole, mais que l'Hyperbole semble naistre du sujet même' (113). 'Enflure'

results, however, when elevated language is employed to reflect an insubstantial sub-
ject, where an apparently solid surface masks a void (52-53), and the 'stile froid' is
caused by indulgence in precious verbal games (55).

There seems, then, to be a plausible argument that by re-establishing a sound
relationship between *res* and *verba*, the excesses of an overblown poetic style might
be excluded, and the pitfalls of an absolute condemnation of figurative discourse
avoided. Nomenclaturism, rigorously applied, seems to lead to a middle position (which
Boileau no doubt found the most congenial, and which Lamy, for example, had an-
ticipated), one which favours the moderate use of figures in appropriate contexts; and
ample support for this view may be found in the *Traité du sublime*.

We have noted how there arose in this period a tension in literary debate be-
tween the moral critique of high-flown ('over-real') language, and the linguistic or
philosophical critique of inadequate or insipid ('under-real') language.
Nomenclaturism, whatever its advantages in an account of figurative discourse, has
an undeniably corrosive effect on any explanation of the aesthetic function of lan-
guage, which is made subservient to preconceived thought, and viewed simply as an
instrument of communication. If language is allowed no autonomy at all, how is the
poet or creative writer ever to achieve fullness of linguistic expression?

If language imitates reality, then the more precise and compelling the imitation
(the closer the link between *res* and *verba*), the more effective will be the language. It
follows therefore that simplicity of style can be seen as more than a logical conse-
quence of this linguistic theory, it can in certain circumstances be seen as a positive
asset. Thus simple words may prove to be more effective in communicating a given
idea than would a more decorative style:

> En effet, un discours tout simple exprimera quelquefois mieux la
> chose que toute la pompe et tout l'ornement [...]. Ajoûtez qu'une
> chose énoncée d'une façon ordinaire, se fait aussi plus aisément
> croire. (100)

The simple style provides not only a more effective use of language, but, as Boileau-
Longinus suggests here, also a more persuasive one.

The role of the 'image' (or tableau) in poetry is, says Boileau-Longinus, to
surprise and to astonish; the role of the image in prose, on the other hand, 'c'est de
bien peindre les choses, et de les faire voir clairement' (77). Notable here is the em-
phasis on the need to show one's subject clearly (thus assuming that language does
not accomplish this effortlessly, of its own accord; language is not transparent) and
also the vocabulary of nomenclaturist theory—the phrase 'peindre les choses', remi-
niscent of Port-Royal theorists, is twice repeated (77, 79). If the picture or image is
successfully achieved, we are uplifted by it, and may perhaps mistake the illusion for
reality, 'il semble que nous voyons les choses dont nous parlons' (76). In this way, it
might be argued, the gap, inevitable in nomenclaturist theory, dividing signifier from
referent is appreciably narrowed, though not bridged. Language, in the nomenclaturist
view, is condemned to the subservient position of being always one step behind real-

ity; but it appears that if language is artfully constructed, the harmful effects of this 'word-lag' can be minimised. Thus by deceiving readers into believing that they are confronted with 'the real thing' and not merely a linguistic artefact, we will come closer to the poetic and philosophical ideal of 'full' expression.

This helps to explain Boileau's somewhat eccentric emphasis on the sublime as 'en effet ce qui forme l'excellence et la souveraine perfection du Discours' (49). The phrase 'la souveraine perfection' is, as Brody points out, grossly inaccurate: the definite article translates an indefinite article in Greek, *tis*; the adjective 'souveraine' is redundant and entirely Boileau's own invention; and 'perfection' translates the two nouns *akrotees* and *exochee*, approximately *distinctiveness* and *excellence*, but not *perfection*.[89] In another passage, Boileau-Longinus describes the qualities achieved by the skilful selection of words: *grandeur, élegance, netteté, poids, force,* and *vigueur* (99). The most interesting word in this list is *netteté*: firstly because it confirms the earlier suggestion that if language is carefully manipulated, it will become, or will appear to become, clear and transparent; and secondly because it is the only word in the list which is mistranslated (Brody does not comment on this detail). The precise sense of the word *eupineia*, here rendered as *netteté*, is the patina on a piece of sculpture or the bloom on a fruit, and is described by Russell as 'in literary criticism [...] [an] attractive [quality] of earlier literature—a sort of archaic charm' (*OTS*, 149), and translated by him as 'old-world charm' (*OS*, 489): *netteté* is obviously an impossible translation. Boileau can be forgiven for having misunderstood this rare Greek term; but the misunderstanding is wholly convenient.

Such signal insistence on 'la souveraine perfection' and 'la netteté', both gross inaccuracies in what is otherwise—especially by the standards of the time—a generally accurate translation, shows how *le sublime* might be seen as achieving for Boileau a fullness of linguistic expression which could overcome the problem of referentiality discussed earlier. The *Traité du sublime* may thus be viewed as an attempt to resolve the various dilemmas confronting poetry in the classical period. On the one hand, it defends poetry against the moral charge that it obscures truth: Boileau-Longinus demonstrates how figurative speech, when used appropriately, need not shock, and suggests moreover that the *sublime* is in itself a guarantor of high moral purpose. On the other hand, the *Traité du sublime* serves to defend poetic language against the charge of inadequacy, showing how clarity, perfection and consequently forceful expression will result from the skilful alignment of *res* and *verba*.

The moral and linguistic problems associated with referentiality are thus reconciled, at least temporarily, in the *Traité du sublime*, and a new theory of poetry is proposed which allies forceful language with truth. Man's highest purpose, suggests Boileau-Longinus in the opening chapter, 'pour nous rendre semblable aux dieux, c'est de faire *plaisir* et de *dire la verité*,'[90] and the purpose of poetry is shown to be not dissimilar. It is above all the alliance between precision (hence forcefulness) and truth which is seen to characterise the *sublime*:

> Dans la Rhetorique le beau des *Images*, c'est de representer la chose comme elle s'est passée, et telle qu'elle est dans la verité. (*TS*, 80)

Such a theory of poetry might be described as an art of the confidence trick. Figurative language is unobjectionable, always providing that it remains out of conscious sight; by confining itself to imitation of 'the movements of nature', it can hope to pass unnoticed. At a higher level, all language, including simple or 'non-figurative' usage, ought ideally to aim to encompass so successfully the object of imitation that the illusion is made real, and the language itself is forgotten. In both cases, the aim is to deceive the reader or listener, to dupe them into believing that language does not exist, and that in fact they are experiencing 'reality' unadulterated. Art is never more perfect than when it is mistaken for Nature; were the artifice evident, Nature would be spoiled:

> Les habiles Ecrivains, pour imiter ces mouvemens de la Nature, se servent des Hyperbates. Et à dire vrai, l'Art n'est jamais dans un plus haut degré de perfection, que lorsqu'il ressemble si fort à la Nature, qu'on le prend pour la Nature même; et au contraire la Nature ne reüssit jamais mieux que quand l'Art est caché. (*TS*, 90)

> Les Figures […] sont les meilleures qui sont entierement cachées. (*TS*, 112)

Nomenclaturism thus entails a paradoxical aesthetic in which the highest aim of the art of language is to foster the illusion that language does not exist.

This is not, however, the entire story as far as the *Traité du sublime* is concerned, for there are also to be found in the work remarks which appear to question some of the basic nomenclaturist assumptions. Boileau-Longinus sometimes describes the sublime as a quality of thought: 'Le Sublime se trouve quelquefois dans une simple pensée' (72); we infer that the words used to reflect a sublime thought will themselves necessarily be sublime. And when Boileau-Longinus speaks of 'farder une pensée' (70), there is again an apparent implication that language and its subject-matter can be separated. But in discussion of the five principal sources of the sublime, this distinction is blurred: *le sublime* is said to derive from '*une certaine Elevation d'esprit, qui nous fait penser heureusement les choses*' (59)—an interesting phrase which emphasises more our response towards the subject than it does the subject itself, but also suggests a quality embracing both the idea and its expression. The second source described ('le *Pathetique*') similarly invokes a quality in the artist, over and above matters of language and content, while the third source ('*les Figures tournées d'une certaine maniere*'), though admitting a difference between 'Figures de Pensée' and 'Figures de Diction', does not acknowledge any precise or hierarchical link between the two (59). Elsewhere, Boileau-Longinus is quite explicit that thought and its expression are mutually dependent upon each other: 'La Pensée et la Phrase s'expliquent ordinairement l'une par l'autre' (99).

This amounts to a denial of the fundamental nomenclaturist assumption that language precedes thought, as well as, by implication, a denial of its corollary in literary theory, the principle of imitation. The consequence is to bring to the fore the materiality of language in a way which had previously seemed unthinkable (and un-justifiable, on theoretical grounds). Thus the fourth source of the sublime is described as '*la noblesse de l'expression*' (59), comprising 'le choix des mots' and 'la diction élégante et figurée'; and the fifth source, embracing all others, is '*la Composition et l'arrangement des paroles dans toute leur magnificence et leur dignité*' (59): in both cases it is the material fact of language which is underlined, though not entirely at the expense of the ideas expressed. In other words, Boileau-Longinus does not appear to be interested merely in the study of *elocutio* in isolation, but rather in the means by which certain forms of expression come themselves to constitute a part of what is being expressed. The focus of attention is thus shifted from decorative to functional rhetoric.[91]

Examples of this in the *Traité du sublime* are abundant. Boileau-Longinus explains, for example, how selection of words serves to do more than merely reflect a preconceived thought and can sometimes help to grip or move the reader, giving the language 'poids' and 'force' as well as elegance and clarity (99). He frequently highlights the musicality of language: he remarks how Plato makes use of a periphrasis in a seemingly simple sentence to create 'une espece de concert et d'harmonie' (98); and again, how Euripides is able to transform an otherwise trivial thought by the way in which he expresses it:

> Cette pensée est fort triviale. Cependant il la rend noble par le moyen de ce tour qui a quelque chose de musical et d'harmonieux. Et certainement, pour peu que vous renversiez l'ordre de sa periode, vous verrez manifestement combien Euripide est plus heureux dans l'arrangement de ses paroles, que dans le sens de ses pensées. (116)

Such a dressing-up of thought is no mere sterile exercise in decorative rhetoric, as the phrase 'en fardant ainsi cette pensée' (70) might imply. In the next example, also from Euripides, Boileau-Longinus describes the functional use of harmonious language, even in expressing a thought which is already elevated: 'Cette pensée est fort noble à la verité; mais il faut avoüer que ce qui luy donne plus de force, c'est cette harmonie qui n'est point precipitée ni emportée (116-17).'

The decisive shift away from the aesthetic of imitation is made manifest in Boileau-Longinus's discussion of music (which, for obvious reasons, had always been more difficult to assimilate into a mimetic explanation of the arts):

> Car bien que [les sons de la Lyre] ne signifient rien d'eux-mesmes, neanmoins par ces changemens de tons qui s'entrechoquent les uns les autres, et par le mélange de leurs accords, souvent, comme nous voyons, ils causent à l'ame un transport et un ravissement admirable. Cependant ce ne sont que des images et de simples imitations de la voix, qui ne disent et ne persuadent rien n'estant, s'il faut parler ainsi, que des sons bâtards, et non point, comme j'ai dit, des effets de la nature de l'homme. (114-15)

Lip-service to the theory of imitation is duly paid with the remark that music imitates the voice; but what is truly significant here is the description of how the specific juxtapositions and combinations of sound—and how could these be said to imitate the human voice?—affect the audience. In this description of the uplifting effects of music, the keynote is not the quality of the imitation so much as the quality of the impact on the listeners.

Boileau-Longinus states unambiguously that the art of language cannot be judged by the criteria of mimesis. A statue may be judged according to how closely it achieves a perfect resemblance, but language cannot be so judged, because it is inherent in man, and therefore a product of nature and not of art—an ingenious defence, which defends the art by pretending it is not an art:

> Dans les ouvrages de l'Art, c'est le travail et l'achevement que l'on considere: au lieu que dans les ouvrages de la Nature, c'est le Sublime et le prodigieux. Or, discourir, c'est une operation naturelle à l'Homme. Ajoûtez que dans une statuë on ne cherche que le rapport et la ressemblance; mais dans le discours on veut, comme j'ai dit, le surnaturel et le divin. (111)

That Boileau fully endorsed this notion of imitation is confirmed by Brossette, who reports Boileau as believing that a certain aesthetic distance is necessary for a work of art to succeed.[92] This rejection of imitation as an aesthetic principle is paralleled by a rejection of referentiality as a linguistic principle: words do not imitate meanings so much as illuminate and even create them: 'Les beaux mots sont, à vrai dire, la lumiere propre et naturelle de nos pensées' (99).

Such a shift away from interest in the quality of imitation inevitably occasions a more closely focused interest in the affective qualities of a work or of a piece of writing. We see this in a very simple way when Boileau-Longinus discusses the sounds of words, and argues that harmonious language is not only persuasive and pleasurable, but also a means of arousing the passions (114). Again, it is claimed that a speech will communicate most effectively when it is able to arouse its audience's emotions: 'Car en réveillant ainsi l'Auditeur par ces apostrophes, vous le rendez plus émû, plus attentif, et plus plein de la chose dont vous parlez' (95). The emphasis is thus shifted away from concern with mimesis, and towards a pragmatic aesthetic which stresses the affective appeal of language. Of course, passion in itself does not constitute the sublime, but it can serve to uplift a speech when employed correctly (and it is striking how much of the vocabulary of this passage—*enthousiasme, fureur noble, feu, vigueur divine*—recalls that of Pléiade poetic theorists):

> J'ose dire qu'il n'y a peut-estre rien qui releve davantage un Discours, qu'un beau mouvement et une Passion poussée à propos. En effet, c'est comme une espece d'enthousiasme et de fureur noble qui anime l'Oraison, et qui luy donne feu et une vigueur toute divine. (60)

Such language does more than merely persuade the audience, it overwhelms them—the terms *dompter* and *soumettre* are especially remarkable:

> [Les Images] animent et échauffent le discours. Si bien qu'estant
> mêlées avec art dans les preuves, elles ne persuadent pas seulement,
> mais elles domtent, pour ainsi dire, elles soûmettent l'auditeur. (80)

This glorification of the power of forceful language brings us back to the problem of the moral ambivalence of rhetoric. Boileau-Longinus seeks to resolve this dilemma by invoking once again the notion of *le sublime*: the sublime uplifts discourse and renders it more persuasive, but in so doing it simultaneously underwrites its moral worth—or, more realistically, it sweeps readers or listeners irresistibly off their feet, so that they become oblivious of the manipulation of rhetoric:

> Le remede le plus naturel contre l'abondance et la hardiesse, soit
> des Metaphores, soit des autres Figures, c'est de ne les employer
> qu'à propos: je veux dire, dans les grandes passions, et dans le
> Sublime. Car comme le Sublime et le Pathetique, par leur violence
> et leur impetuosité, emportent naturellement, et entraînent tout avec
> eux; ils demandent necessairement des expressions fortes, et ne
> laissent pas le temps à l'Auditeur de s'amuser à chicaner le nombre
> des Metaphores, parce qu'en ce moment il est épris d'une commune
> fureur avec celuy qui parle. (101-02)

The moral difficulty posed by rhetoric is effectively avoided here: rather than try to answer the question on these grounds, Boileau-Longinus prefers to shift the focus of the discussion towards language's affective qualities. The description of 'l'excès et la violence de l'amour' (68) in Sappho's poem might well have been deemed immoral by many seventeenth-century critics of poetry; Boileau-Longinus praises the poem, notably for the way in which it achieves its effect on the reader, not through some 'general' imitation of the emotion of love, but through the skilful depiction of certain selected details—again, it is less the quality of the imitation which is in question than the quality of the effect obtained upon the reader.

We noted above the particular insistence in the *Traité du sublime* on the *sublime* as 'la souveraine perfection du Discours'. Boileau-Longinus continues as follows:

> Car il ne persuade pas proprement, mais il ravit, il transporte, et
> produit en nous une certaine admiration mêlée d'étonnement et de
> surprise, qui est toute autre chose que de plaire seulement, ou de
> persuader. Nous pouvons dire à l'égard de la persuasion, que pour
> l'ordinaire elle n'a sur nous qu'autant de puissance que nous
> voulons. Il n'en est pas ainsi du Sublime. Il donne au Discours une
> certaine vigueur noble, une force invincible qui enleve l'ame de
> quiconque nous écoute. (50)

In this passage—'calculated,' remarks Brody, 'to strengthen the assertions of the original'[93] —the sublime may be seen both as a moral force ('une certaine vigueur noble') and as a form of linguistic perfection ('la souveraine perfection'). More than that, however, this discussion of *le sublime* transcends such problems of content and expression, and shifts the arena of aesthetic debate from the mimetic to the pragmatic.

We began by posing the question of why Boileau had undertaken his translation of Longinus, an extraordinary project for an up-and-coming poet and a would-be literary critic in the 1670s. The answer, at one level, is that the *Traité du sublime* provided Boileau with a means of confronting both the double-bind of nomenclaturism, and the twin difficulties concerning the morality of 'over-real' poetry and the efficacy of 'under-real' poetic language. Indeed the *Traité* may be said to go beyond these problems, for it ultimately resolves the difficulties inherent in nomenclaturism by transcending them and proposing a new foundation for an aesthetic theory. With the *Traité du sublime*, Boileau is able to answer critics of the old order and simultaneously to suggest the shape of a new order to take its place.

The new order that Boileau proposes, marking a shift from a mimetic to a pragmatic aesthetic, is one which places much greater stress on the idea of poetic enthusiasm. As we have already seen, there flourished a strong latent current of neoplatonism in seventeenth-century aesthetic theory, but it was a current which classical theorists found hard to express openly—as is demonstrated by their hesitant usage of the term *fureur*. Longinus's treatise, with its discussion of 'cet Enthousiasme, et cette vehemence naturelle qui touche et qui émeut' (59), is clearly amenable to a platonist reading, and, as we noted above, the vocabulary as well as the ideas of Boileau's rendering often recall the platonist poetic theorists of the Renaissance.[94] It is even possible to find in Boileau-Longinus support for the metaphysical ideas underlying the platonist notion of poetic fury:

> [La Nature] a engendré d'abord en nos ames une passion invincible pour tout ce qui nous paroist de plus grand et de plus divin. Aussi voyons-nous que le monde entier ne suffit pas à la vaste étenduë de l'esprit de l'Homme. Nos pensées vont souvent plus loin que les cieux, et penetrent au delà de ces bornes qui environnent et qui terminent toutes choses. (109)

Above all, the *Traité du sublime* neatly side-steps the nexus of problems which had been created by nomenclaturism by emphatically asserting a pragmatic aesthetic, one primarily concerned with the impact of a work of literature on its audience. 'Mais quand le Sublime vient à éclater où il faut,' writes Boileau-Longinus, 'il renverse tout comme un foudre' (50), thus making the prevailing mimetic aesthetic redundant; and as we have already seen, Boileau in his 'Préface' reaffirms the affective qualities of *le sublime*.

We have already noted how Petit makes reference to Longinus in the course of his discussion of poetic fury, and for Petit too the Longinian concept of *hupsos* seems to fit easily alongside the platonist notion of poetic fury. Petit distinguishes poetry borne of art and poetry arising as the fruit of inspiration: 'Prioris character est quicquid in carmine eminet, inflammat, fulgore inusitato legentes rapit' (17), this last phrase recalling Boileau's *sublime*, 'cet extraordinaire et ce merveilleux qui frape dans le discours, et qui fait qu'un ouvrage enleve, ravit, transporte' (*TS*, 45). Nor was Boileau the first (even though he may have thought he was) to have had the idea of drafting Longinus into the service of platonism: he had been anticipated in this strategic manoeuvre by the sixteenth-century Italian philosopher Francesco Patrizi, a renowned anti-aristotelian.[95] There is thus a powerful case for regarding, if not Longinus's treatise, at least Boileau's *Traité du sublime*, as an expression of crypto-platonism.

The role of platonism in classical aesthetics is difficult to quantify, not least because these various currents of thought remain partially submerged, so that their influence is invariably greater than we at first expect. Classical theorists show considerable deviousness in discussing Plato's ideas without appearing to affront rational and aristotelian appearances. Longinus, as we have seen, can be read in a way that brings his thought close to Plato's, so that Boileau's decision to publish a translation of Longinus takes on especial significance. The pretence that the *Traité du sublime* is 'just' a translation provided Boileau with exactly the cover he needed to publish a platonist treatise.

The *Traité du sublime* has the further great advantage from Boileau's standpoint that it provides a new and 'uncontaminated' term, *le sublime*, for the discussion of poetic enthusiasm. Boileau does more in fact than merely appropriate Longinus's treatise: he also invents anew a (crypto-)platonist term, *le sublime*, which is more powerful and more coherent than *le je ne sais quoi*, and less tainted than *la fureur*. It is a measure of Boileau's success that *le sublime* established itself as a critical term so quickly after 1674, and as a term which might be discussed independently of Longinus's treatise.

How does *le sublime* stand in comparison with the term that Bouhours had put forward, *le je ne sais quoi*? For Louis Marin, *le sublime* occupies the same ground as, but is less wide-ranging than, the broader concept of *le je ne sais quoi*: 'le sublime relève du "je ne sais quoi", mais le "je ne sais quoi" ne se réduit pas au sublime'.[96] He focuses on two features of the *sublime* which link it to the *je ne sais quoi*, firstly its indefinability, and secondly its affective impact. The central thrust of his argument is that the *je ne sais quoi* and the *sublime* are both manifestations, during what he calls 'les années charnières 1670',[97] of an attempt to integrate a theory of inspiration into an aesthetic of representation, and he points to the role of enthusiasm and the platonising currents which underlay the reception of Longinus's treatise. Marin describes the *je ne sais quoi* as integrating the notion of inspiration into a mimetic aesthetic theory. But to what extent does the *je ne sais quoi* alone stand for the idea of inspiration? And furthermore, is it sufficient to speak simply of an aesthetic of imitation?

We have noted above:

    i. The overall need to defend the materiality of the sign (against the
    tendency to devalue language altogether at the expense of 'truth');
    and then the mutually inconsistent tensions between
    ii. the need for language to imitate precisely (to achieve fullness of

expression), and

iii. the need for it not to imitate so well as to pose a moral threat (by
confusing fiction with truth).

The *je ne sais quoi* seems well equipped to provide an answer to the second of these
problems (fullness of expression), but not at all able to deal satisfactorily with the
other two (materiality and morality of poetic discourse)—that was why, after all,
Bouhours had found it necessary to introduce into the *Entretiens* the further ideas of
the *devise* and the *bel esprit*. The *sublime* seems to have the distinct advantage of
operating on all three fronts simultaneously. Indeed it does more: Boileau's term both
reconciles the conflicting pressures arising from nomenclaturism, and also transcends
them in the overarching notion of poetic enthusiasm.

The *sublime* and the *je ne sais quoi* are similar, in as much as both are concepts
devised or 'invented' in the 1670s to explain and resolve the same critical dilemma; as
two responses to the same set of problems, it is to be expected that there is a certain
overlap between them. But Marin's claim that the *sublime* is in some sense a 'nar-
rower' version of the *je ne sais quoi* is not convincing—in fact, the reverse is true.
Boileau's concept of *le sublime* embraces the ineffability of Bouhours's *je ne sais
quoi*, and much more besides, most notably a platonist notion of enthusiasm. Bouhours
had needed six juxtaposed dialogues precisely because no single one of his concepts
was fully adequate to the task. The verdict of contemporaries is unambiguous: the *je
ne sais quoi* was soon to vanish from critical debate; the *sublime*, on the other hand,
quickly became and long remained highly contentious. It was clearly the *sublime*
which was found to be the more comprehensive solution to prevailing critical prob-
lems.

The pivotal role of platonist enthusiasm in Boileau's poetic theory is acknowl-
edged by S. Vitanovic, who sums up his view thus:

> Boileau se distingue dans son siècle et s'écarte de la majeure partie
> de ses prédécesseurs et contemporains par le fait même qu'il a
> longuement travaillé et réfléchi le traité *Du Sublime*, ce qui lui a
> permis de se mettre en contact plus étroit avec la tradition
> platonicienne, et des écoles rhétoriques grecques de
> l'enthousiasme.[98]

But Boileau did not need to wait until he had read Longinus to be interested in the
platonist tradition of poetic theory; and he is far from alone among the critics of his
generation in being interested in platonist poetics. The crucial challenge for these
critics, given the hegemony of aristotelian poetics, was to find a critical discourse
which was platonist but not overtly so: discussion of the *énigme* or of the *devise* were
tentative steps in that direction. Boileau's distinctive achievement is to have discov-
ered a strategy for discussing platonism which allows him to challenge the prevailing
tenets of classical poetic theory, while apparently remaining (just) within them. Adopt-
ing the borrowed authority of a seemingly innocuous classical author, he publishes a

treatise on poetic theory with strongly platonist undercurrents, and he adopts a term, *le sublime*, which permits him to discuss openly the notion of poetic fury—and posing all the while as the humble translator.

V. CONCLUSION: THE POETIC THEORY OF THE *ŒUVRES DIVERSES*

Boileau evidently does not envisage the *Traité du sublime* as just one more translation of a classical rhetorician. Rather he has seized on Longinus's treatise, and has exploited the mode of translation, as a means of advocating a poetic theory that is daringly innovative in the context in which it appears. Boileau's great achievement is to produce a 'dynamic translation', one which is almost always highly faithful to Longinus's original but which reads as, and can stand as, an original work. Boileau, in effect, hides behind and speaks through Longinus. This enigmatic style of discourse has obvious advantages for Boileau: notably it allows him to encroach upon the taboo subject of poetic enthusiasm, and without infringing an even greater taboo, the name of Plato. The fact of using a covert form of discourse to describe a platonist aesthetic is obviously highly appropriate. Moreover the appropriation of a classical voice in order to express something which could not be expressed more openly had long been a favoured humanist technique, usually by means of quotation.[99] The practice of excessive quotation came to be much criticised in the second half of the seventeenth century; but Boileau does better than merely quote Longinus: he appropriates his treatise in its entirety.

In the prefatory 'Au lecteur' to the first edition of the *Œuvres diverses*,[100] Boileau states bluntly that the *Art poétique* is indebted for various points to the *Traité du sublime*, and that the two works are intended to be read together:

> J'ay fait originairement cette Traduction pour m'instruire, plûtôst que dans le dessein de la donner au Public. Mais j'ay creu qu'on ne seroit pas fâché de la voir ici à la suite de la Poetique, avec laquelle ce Traité a quelque rapport, et où j'ay mesme inseré plusieurs préceptes qui en sont tirés.[101]

We need to recognise that, notwithstanding the apparently different status of a poem and a translation, the *Art poétique* and *Traité du sublime* function as complementary works.

The two critical works of the *Œuvres diverses*, always published together in Boileau's lifetime, differ inevitably in focus; the *Traité du sublime* is concerned with a general quality of literature, whereas the *Art poétique* is partly concerned with the rules and conventions governing particular genres. But the *Art poétique* is also concerned with the broader question of what constitutes good poetry, and there is some considerable overlap between the two works. At the simplest level we may note that the word *sublime* occurs five times in the *Art poétique*, twice in the first canto, and once in each of the three others. Sometimes the word is employed in a traditional, non-committal way, in the sense of *elevated*, 'un sublime écrivain' (IV, 113), or *serious*, 'un sujet […] sublime' (I, 27), 'un sublime ennuyeux et pesant' (III, 290). More revealing is the remark that Juvenal's works, full of awful truths, 'étincellent pourtant de sublimes beautés' (II, 160): *sublime* here seems to refer specifically to a quality of language, a quality that perhaps transcends the subject-matter. There is finally one use of the *sublime* which appears unambiguously indebted to Longinus, when Boileau apostrophises the would-be poet:

> [...] Soyez simple avec art,
> Sublime sans orgueil, agreable sans fard. (I, 101-02)

The linking of *sublime* with simplicity comes straight from Longinus—'Un discours tout simple exprimera quelquefois mieux la chose que toute la pompe et tout l'ornement' (*TS*, 100)—and is of course an idea to which Boileau had accorded prominence in the 'Préface' to the *Traité du sublime*.

Beyond simple mentions of the term *sublime*, the general thrust of the argument concerning poetry in the *Art poétique* has clear parallels in the *Traité du sublime*. Firstly, the *Art poétique* advocates moderation in the use of figures: rhetorical excess must be avoided (I, 43-44, 63), though figures properly employed may elevate writing (III, 287-90). Connected with this point, secondly, and in line with the injunction to love Reason, 'Aimez donc la Raison' (I, 37), is the emphasis on simplicity; besides the passage quoted above, there are other expressions of this idea in the first canto (e.g. I, 167-70). Thirdly, the poem talks of the need for writing, or at least certain types of writing, to have an emotional impact on the reader, in particular the ode (II, 58ff.) and the epic poem (III, 188). Fourthly, there is some—understandably limited—discussion of the idea of enthusiasm. The poem begins by stressing 'l'influence secrete' of the heavens (I, 3) as a necessary prerequisite for any poet; and later Homer is praised for his 'warmth': 'Une heureuse chaleur anime ses discours' (III, 301). But the role accorded to poetic enthusiasm is severely circumscribed. Boileau warns that inspiration alone is not sufficient, and that it must be founded on a mastery of the art (III, 313-16); and he suggests, for example, that in the case of the ode, 'un beau desordre' is created as a result not of inspiration but of 'l'art' (II, 72).[102] Fifthly, the final canto of the *Art poétique* reaffirms, if it were necessary, the moral function of poetry (IV, 85ff.). Beyond similarities of doctrine in these two texts, it might be argued that they are also stylistically united: Beugnot, for example, has pointed to the omnipresent image of light in Boileau's critical writings—an interesting interpretation, which accords a central position to the *Traité du sublime*, and to the example from Genesis to which Boileau gives so much importance.[103] One might add that this metaphor, 'the light of reason', which is pivotal in Boileau's aesthetic writings, is one with strong resonances in platonist poetic theory.

The similarities between the general strategies of the *Art poétique* and the *Traité du sublime* are obvious: both are concerned to reconcile the seemingly conflicting requirements that poetry should neither over-represent reality, and so be untruthful, nor under-represent reality, and so be unforceful. More revealing, in a sense, are the differences between the two works, or more precisely, the gaps and limitations of the *Art poétique*. Firstly, although Boileau speaks about the emotional impact of the ode and of the epic poem, he is too cautious to extend this idea to humbler or 'lower' genres; thus the idea of forceful and sublime simplicity is evoked but not explored, as it is in the *Traité du sublime*. Secondly, there is no real scope within the framework of the *Art poétique* for Boileau to explore any of the problems generated by nomenclaturism; again, it is left to the *Traité du sublime* to speak about the materiality of poetic discourse and such questions as the sound and harmony of words. Thirdly, and most significantly, the *Art poétique* is excessively cautious in approaching the delicate subject of poetic enthusiasm, notwithstanding the *profession de foi* contained in the first six lines of the poem. Though Boileau gives prominence to the notion at the start, the idea, once launched, is never really followed up—or rather it is only followed up in the *Traité du sublime*. Revealing of Boileau's timidity in the *Art poétique* is his refusal to use the word *fureur* in anything other than a pejorative sense. The term is used just once in an unambiguously positive context, when Boileau speaks of 'l'agreable fureur' (III, 17) of classical tragedy; all other instances of the word are at the least tinged with hostility.[104] The *sublime* provides the perfect cover behind which to continue the debate that Boileau is unable to pursue openly in the *Art poétique*.[105]

In a number of areas, then, the *Traité du sublime* may be seen as consolidating and extending ideas first broached in the (more conventional) *Art poétique*. The major difference which emerges between the *Art poétique* and the *Traité du sublime* is essentially one of emphasis. The *Traité du sublime* is especially appropriate as a vehicle for consolidating the critical thought of the earlier poem, for two distinct reasons: firstly, at the level of content, it allows Boileau to introduce a fresh critical term, *le sublime*, which serves (more successfully than *le je ne sais quoi*) to hold together various otherwise disparate elements, being at once material, moral, and moving; and secondly, at the level of form, the mode of translation allows Boileau to conceal his own voice behind that of Longinus and so to be more outspoken. The *Art poétique* and the *Traité du sublime* together constitute a formidable critical diptych, whose coherence is assured by the pivotal notion of *le sublime*. And of the two works, it is, paradoxically, the *Traité du sublime*, the 'translation', which is the more radical and the more original, and it rightly is given unique prominence on the title-page of the *Œuvres diverses*. Boileau's *Traité du sublime* is the most profoundly innovative text of French classical poetic theory.

NOTES

1. *Essais*, I, 26.
2. *European Literature*, p. 399.
3. See, for example, Scaglione; Moore, 'Boileau and Longinus'; and Litman, who maintains that 'le mot *sublime* [...] introduit des éléments opposés à certains traits fondamentaux de la doctrine classique' (p. 237).
4. Monk, p. 29.
5. See Weinberg, *A History of Literary Criticism in the Italian Renaissance*.
6. See Weinberg, 'Translations and commentaries'.
7. Weinberg, 'Une traduction française'.
8. Fumaroli, *L'Age de l'éloquence*, passim, and 'Rhétorique d'école et rhétorique adulte'.
9. See Fumaroli, 'Le corps éloquent'.

[10.] See Adam, *Histoire*, III, pp. 148-49.

[11.] Balzac, *Œuvres*, II, p. 209; Brody discusses this debt in detail (*Boileau and Longinus*, pp. 15-18).

[12.] This is not mentioned by either Brody or Fumaroli.

[13.] *Boileau and Longinus*, pp. 24-29.

[14.] Quintilian's *Institutio oratoria* in 1663; Aristotle's *Poetics* in 1671; and Cicero's *De oratore* in 1673. Cicero's *Orator* would not appear in French until 1737.

[15.] *Les Vies des poètes grecs*, pp. 7, 23.

[16.] The printed catalogue of the BnF lists 23 editions between 1674 and 1707.

[17.] The first was Batteux's *Les Quatre Poëtiques: d'Aristote, d'Horace, de Vida, de Despréaux* (1771).

[18.] There was one edition with the Greek original, and another with a Greek and an accompanying Latin translation.

[19.] For example Pocock, who devotes three chapters to the *Art poétique*, and scarcely more than three lines to the *Traité du sublime*.

[20.] The same challenge can be levelled at Longinus, who discusses a Greek sentence (from Genesis I, 3, but quoted inaccurately) translated from a Hebrew original (*Peri hupsous*, 9.9). In fact, the original Hebrew makes Longinus's point much more clearly than do either the Greek or French translations. The Hebrew phrase translated as 'Let there be light / there was light' may crudely be transliterated as 'Yeh ohr / vayeh ohr': the single phoneme 'va' (the 'vav conversive') has the function of turning verbs from future to past, and vice versa, producing in this example an extremely neat parallelism. Longinus is thought either to have been a Jew or at least to have been in contact with Jewish culture, so presumably he knew Hebrew, and perhaps had the original in mind when quoting the Greek example. Fleury frequently in his writings describes the beauty of Biblical poetry, and states explicitly that these poems can be appreciated only by those who read them in the original Hebrew (for example, *Opuscules*, II, p. 649).

[21.] 'In discussing the quality of thought and style which marks writing as *hupseelon*, the author breaks free of the rhetorical tradition within which he works, and throws real light on what constitutes literary greatness' (D. A. Russell, in *The Oxford Classical Dictionary* (2nd edition), p. 619). Russell, writing from the viewpoint of the classical scholar, also considers that Boileau was correct to separate *hupsos* from grandiose diction (*OTS*, p. xxxvii).

[22.] See, for example, Genette, 'Figures', *Figures I*; and Todorov, *Théories du symbole*, pp. 65-66.

[23.] Kibédi Varga, *Rhétorique et littérature*, pp. 16-17; and France, *Rhetoric and Truth*, pp. 8-12.

[24.] *Rhétorique et littérature*, p. 12.

[25.] Quoted France, *Rhetoric and Truth*, p. 19.

[26.] This is opposed to, for example, the *mimetic* approach, which stresses principally a work's relationship to the world it supposedly reflects (*Mirror and Lamp*, Chap. 1).

[27.] Brossette, 'Mémoires', pp. 524-25; *TS*, p. 108.

[28.] D. G. Coleman, *The Gallo-Roman Muse*, Chap. 4.

[29.] Du Bellay, *Deffence*, pp. 40, 91; Ronsard, 'Preface sur la Franciade, touchant le poëme heroïque', *Œuvres complètes*, I, pp. 1166, 1172.

[30.] Quoted in Griffiths, *Antoine de Montchrestien*, p. 203, note 2.

[31.] For more detailed discussion of the theory of characters (*charakteeres logou, genera dicendi*), see *OTS*, pp. xxxiv-xxxvii. Barthes uses the phrase 'la roue de Virgile' in discussing this theory ('L'ancienne rhétorique', p. 108), and it has been taken up by more recent critics (France, *Rhetoric and Truth*, p. 10; Charles, *Rhétorique de la lecture*, p. 138). I do not use the phrase here, however, because it is connected with the medieval version of the theory of characters, according to which the three styles are each characterised according to social rank: 'Mais ce qui pour les premiers critiques, était affaire de style est devenu, pour l'école du xⅡe et du xⅢe siècle, affaire de dignité sociale: c'est la qualité des personnes, et non plus celle de l'élocution, qui fournit le principe de la classification' (Faral, *Les Arts poétiques*, p. 88). The same view is expressed by E. de Bruyne (*Etudes d'esthétique médiévale*, II, p. 41). It seems therefore inappropriate to speak of 'Virgil's wheel' in the context of the seventeenth century, when scholars were acquainted with the theory of characters through the texts of classical antiquity.

[32.] See also M. Le Guern, 'La question des styles et des genres dans la rhétorique française de l'âge classique'.

[33.] *Rhetorique françoise*, p. 69.

[34.] *Rhetorique françoise*, p. 265.

[35.] It was first published only in 1938.

[36.] *Rethorique françoise*, p. 250.

[37.] *Rhétorique*, p. 377. Naves is clearly mistaken in suggesting that Lamy is the first French rhetorician to discuss the three characters (*Le Goût de Voltaire*, p. 79).

[38.] *Traité du poëme épique*, 1662, p. 3.

[39.] *Œuvres complètes*, I, pp. 59-60.

[40.] Hepp, 'Esquisse', pp. 369-70.

[41.] Descartes, AT, X, p. 217; my translation. '[…] Unde altis philosophantes mentem cognitione possumus *in sublime* tollere.'

[42.] AT, X, p. 217; my translation.

[43.] *L'Antiphyllarque*, 1630, pp. 28-29.

[44.] *Réflexions*, p. 27.

[45.] *Œuvres*, p. 276 (*Recherche*, II.3.5).

[46.] Nicot's *Thrésor de la langue françoyse* (1606) explains *sublime* by the Latin 'sublimis'.

[47.] The crucial weakness of Monk's approach is that it fails to reckon with the seventeenth-century framework of ideas within which Boileau is thinking. He assumes implicitly that the history of any given idea will describe the inexorable progress of a single, coherent and neatly labelled entity along a predestined path to the present. Wood, writing from the standpoint of a critic of eighteenth-century English literature, similarly attacks Monk's approach as 'seriously biased and narrow' (*The Word 'Sublime'*, p. 7). Wood contends 'that classical oratory is not necessarily devoid of interest in the study of the eighteenth-century sublime', and that 'the sublime of Longinus has several legitimate heirs in the eighteenth century' (pp. 7-8). He concludes: 'Relativity may be the key word in following the long history of the sublime. While Mrs. Langer poses what is probably the central problem for the achievement of the sublime in any age, the artistic unification of form and feeling such as to produce a certain effect, she also allows that this process inevitably results in different forms of the sublime depending on the cultural milieu involved, which fosters its own values and concepts, and symbolizations thereof' (p. 210).

[48.] For example, T. Weiskel's *The Romantic Sublime* (1976). *New Literary History* in 1985, the *Revue d'histoire littéraire de la France* in 1986 and the *Rivista di estetica* in 1987 have all devoted entire numbers to the sublime.

[49.] See Salizzoni, 'Il fondo dell'opera'.

[50.] '*Locus classicus sublimis*', p. 53.

[51.] *Natural History*, XXXV, 96; p. 333.

[52.] '*Locus classicus sublimis*', pp. 57-58.

[53.] *Sublime Poussin*, pp. 73-74.

[54.] In support of his attaching the label 'sublime' to Poussin's storms, Marin quotes Longinus's own definition of the sublime, from near the beginning of the treatise (1.4): 'Mais quand le sublime vient à éclater au bon moment, comme la tempête, il disperse toutes choses'. The translation (Marin's own) is a highly tendentious one: 'tempête' translates *skeeptos*, literally 'thunderbolt' (Liddell and Scott), and not attested at all as meaning 'storm'—Ancient Greek has other words to describe a storm (for example the poetic term *thuella*). On the other hand, *skeeptos* is commonly used metaphorically to speak of an orator's powers; Longinus uses the word again in 12.4, in speaking of Demosthenes's oratory (and of course it is Demosthenes who is depicted, thunderbolt in hand, in the engraving (see frontispiece) which Boileau chose to face the title-page of the *Traité du sublime*). Thus Longinus's reference to a 'thunderbolt' is a well-worn metaphorical usage; his comment is firmly within the domain of rhetoric, and implies no reference to the natural world, as Marin would have us believe.

[55.] *Notebooks*, pp. 186-87.

[56.] See Bialostocki, 'Poussin et le Traité de la peinture'.

[57.] 'Comment il faut representer une tempeste', *Traitté de la peinture*, Chap. 66, p. 17; see Bialostocki, 'Une idée de Léonard'. *L'Orage*, which has come to light since Bialostocki's article, provides further support for his argument; furthermore both pictures are thought to date from 1651, the year of the *Traitté de la peinture*.

[58.] See Van Tieghem, *Le Sentiment de la nature*, pp. 199-211.

[59.] *Enquiry*, p. 63.

[60.] One might add that the theme of the storm seems rather peripheral in Poussin's work overall; his contemporary Gaspard Dughet treated the subject far more frequently (see M.-N. Boisclair), and in general the theme is considerably more common in Dutch art of the seventeenth century than it is in French art.

[61.] Dorival, 'Expression littéraire', p. 45.

[62.] 'La solitude', vv. 141-44; I, p. 44.

[63.] Vernet also painted a pair of thematically contrasted seascapes, *Calm: sunset* and *Storm on the coast*; see Conisbee, *Vernet*, nos 44, 45.

[64.] Brody, pp. 54-55.

[65.] Brody, pp. 99, 104.

[66.] Brody, pp. 95, 110-11, 125, 127.

[67.] Brody, p. 96.

[68.] Brody, p. 97.

[69.] Brody, p. 142.

[70.] Brody, p. 141.

[71.] The term *merveilleux* is inherited from Italian criticism (*mirabile*, *meraviglioso*). Weinberg points to one sixteenth-century critic, Patrizi, who links the term *mirabile* with theory derived from Longinus (*History of Literary Criticism*, p. 785).

[72.] See Sayce, *The Biblical Epic*, pp. 12-17.

[73.] 'Préface', *Alaric*.

[74.] *Réflexions*, p. 39.

[75.] *Art poétique*, p. 101; III, 188-89; see also p. 101; III, 174-75.

[76.] *Boileau and Longinus*, p. 90.

[77.] *TS*, p. 43.

[78.] sig. i–ii v.

[79.] sig. i v.

[80.] See Karl Maurer, 'Boileaus Übersetzung'.

[81.] 'Remarques', *TS*, p. 185.

[82.] *Œuvres*, II, p. 502.

[83.] III, p. 650.

[84.] Perrault, in the *Parallèle* (II, p. 177), does however comment that modern readers have much preferred La Bruyère's original characters to his translations.

[85.] Pléiade, p. 860.

[86.] See Marmier, *Horace*, pp. 99-107.

[87.] On Boileau's reaction to the baroque aesthetic, see Sayce, 'Boileau and the French baroque'; and Wadsworth, 'New views of French classicism'.

[88.] We might, however, speculate on the political implications of the final chapter, in which Longinus argues that a free republic is a necessary prerequisite for a flourishing and sublime literature, and in which he speaks of the limitations of monarchy ('nul Esclave ne pouvoit jamais estre Orateur', p. 121). Earlier in the century Patru and La Mothe Le Vayer had certainly been sensitive to the political repercussions of this final chapter. Surely Boileau cannot have been unaware of the possibility of an unflattering parallel with the contemporary absolutist state? He could easily have omitted this final chapter, which is in the manner of an addendum, without otherwise distorting the arguments of the treatise. Perhaps his scrupulousness as a scholar obliged him to translate the treatise in its entirety.

[89.] See Brody, pp. 98-99.

[90.] *TS*, pp. 49, 163; in response to a criticism of Dacier, Boileau later changed the phrase 'faire plaisir' into the more tenuous *'faire du bien'* (*TS*, p. 163).

[91.] These terms are taken from France, *Racine's Rhetoric.*

[92.] See the conversation between Brossette and Boileau recorded in Brossette's 'Mémoires' (quoted in Chap. 1, note 44). Compare with the discussion above in Chap. 1, and in particular with the lines there quoted from the *Art poétique* (p. 96, III, 1-4).

[93.] *Boileau and Longinus*, p. 96.

[94.] For example, *TS*, p. 60.

[95.] Francesco Patrizi, born at Cherso in 1529, became professor of platonic philosophy at Ferrara, then, from 1592, at Rome; he died in 1597. His major work is his *Nova de universis philosophia* (1591), and from the very beginning his work was based on platonic themes: one of his earliest writings (1553) is concerned with the various kinds of poetic madness. Patrizi was involved in the literary controversies of his time: he gave a lecture on a sonnet of Petrarch, published a pamphlet in favour of Ariosoto, and edited Ruscelli's book on *imprese*; of his *Della poetica*, two sections were published in 1586, and five were left in manuscript (see Kristeller, *Eight Philosophers*, Chap. 7). The *Della poetica* expounds an essentially neoplatonist theory of poetry combined with a strongly anti-aristotelian line on the question of imitation (see Bolzoni). Weinberg sums up the 'Deca ammirabile' as follows: 'All notions of imitation and of verisimilitude have been discredited, and in their place the marvelous has been enthroned as the fundamental characteristic of poetry. It has been related on the one hand to the divine furor, which moves the poet, on the other hand to the effect of admiration, which is felt by the audience. The rules, the chop-logic, the distinctions of the Aristotelians have been rejected, and their place has been taken by a mysticism of poetic wonderment' (*History of Literary Criticism*, II, p. 775). The attack on the mimetic aesthetic is unprecedented in Italian Renaissance theory: 'Even at a time in the sixteenth century when other voices were being raised against Aristotle, none was equal to his in its violence and its passion' (Weinberg, II, p. 769). It is interesting to note how neatly Longinus fits into the overall purpose of Patrizi's thought. 'Patrizi cites Longinus in many contexts, and since he is one of the few sixteenth-century theorists to do so, his collection of "deche" derives a very special tone from this rather unusual influence'; Weinberg notes that the contributions of Longinus to discussions of the *mirabile* harmonise entirely with those of Plato (Weinberg, II, p. 785). Patrizi is quite clearly an individual critic who is in no sense typical of his age. There is no particular evidence of his having influenced French classical theory, though his name was certainly known: Rapin refers to 'Patricius' in the preface to his *Réflexions sur la poétique* (p. 11), though without apparently knowing much about him—he describes him merely as a historian of Aristotle's views. Baillet accords him an article in his *Jugemens des savans* (vol. 4/1, art. 1062), again without apparent first-hand knowledge: he says simply that Patrizi had written in Italian a history of poetry in ten books, and he quotes three views on the work together with Rapin's non-committal description of him as a historian and the views of two earlier Latin authors (both highly favourable). It is unlikely then that Boileau had read Patrizi, who does, however, provide a striking example of a theorist before Boileau who was able to use Longinus as part of his statement of neoplatonism (and anti-aristotelianism): the parallels with Boileau's own critical project are evident.

[96.] Louis Marin, *Sublime Poussin*, Chap. 10, 'Le sublime dans les années 1670: un je-ne-sais-quoi?', p. 210.

[97.] *Sublime Poussin*, pp. 214-15.

[98.] 'La place de la mythologie', p. 27; see also 'Le problème du génie'.

[99.] R. A. Sayce, for example, points to Montaigne's 'use of quotations to slip in subversive thoughts' (*Essays of Montaigne*, p. 37).

[100.] That is, the 1674 quarto and duodecimo editions.

[101.] *Pléiade*, p. 856.

[102.] Rapin tends to the opposite view, favouring *nature* over *art*—and supports it by quoting Longinus! (*Réflexions*, p. 27).

[103.] See Bernard Beugnot, 'Boileau, une esthétique de la lumière'.

[104.] See: II, 74; III, 349; IV, 154; compare use of *furie* (II, 201) and *furieux* (IV, 53).

[105.] Hugh Davidson comes to a different conclusion: 'It seems plain that we must rule out large-scale influence of *On the Sublime* on *L'Art poétique*, influence in the sense that Boileau's manner of treatment, topics, and vocabulary are what they are because of Longinus. Beyond a certain point it is impossible to make Boileau say what Longinus said, or, as an academic exercise, to translate Boileau into Longinus' ('The literary arts of Longinus and Boileau', p. 263). This is perhaps to view Longinus as somehow encapsulating certain truths for all time rather than providing a text which Boileau was conveniently able to commandeer.

5: THE ANCIENTS AND THE SUBLIME

> Que trouvez-vous donc de beau dans l'Antique, interrompit Damon.
> Plusieurs choses, répondit Pamphile; la correction de la forme, la
> pureté et l'élégance des contours, la naïveté et la noblesse des
> expressions, la variété, le beau choix, l'ordre et la négligence des
> ajustemens; mais sur tout une grande simplicité qui retranche tous
> les ornements superflus. (Roger de Piles, 1677)[1]

As a new year's gift for 1675, Mme de Thianges presented the duc du Maine with a
model bearing the title 'La chambre du sublime': it portrays the young prince, sur-
rounded by Mme de Montespan and other members of her coterie at court, under the
protection of three men of letters, Boileau, Racine and La Fontaine, who are gallantly
warding off the unseen hordes of unworthy poets. Significantly, it is Boileau who is
most zealous in defending his aristocratic patrons from the invisible enemy—he is
portrayed wielding a pitchfork. It is tempting to see in this pitchfork, especially given
the title of the allegorical model, a symbol of the *Traité du sublime* published the
previous year. The year 1674 had proved to be a crucial one in Boileau's career, for it
had seen—in addition to the publication of the *Art poétique* and, after a long period of
gestation, the *Traité du sublime*—Boileau's introduction to the king at Court and the
granting of a pension. We know too that Boileau was frequently received at this time
by the group surrounding Mme de Montespan, a group which was subsequently dubbed
la cabale du sublime.[2] The maverick young satirist had suddenly been transformed
into a court poet and critic.

Over the next few decades the *Traité du sublime* generated widespread discus-
sion about the concept and definition of *le sublime*. It is even suggested by Antoine
Adam that the notion is central to the *Querelle des anciens et des modernes*:

> Lorsqu'on ignore les problèmes que se posaient alors les écrivains,
> on peut sourire de cet acharnement à défendre et à illustrer cette
> doctrine du sublime. Mais Boileau savait fort bien qu'il touchait là
> au nœud des controverses contemporaines. Il n'ignorait pas que
> les Modernes ne voyaient dans les enthousiasmes de l'inspiration
> que divagations et délires.[3]

How did this manifest itself? The aim of this and the following chapter is twofold: to
examine the manner in which Boileau's contemporaries and immediate successors
adopted, and often adapted, the idea of *le sublime*; and to investigate more closely the

suggestion that *le sublime* is central to the *Querelle des anciens et des modernes*.

I. BOILEAU AND RACINE

Before moving on to the more general notion of a 'party of the sublime', it is important to consider the especially close relationship which existed between Boileau and Racine, and which must necessarily form the heart of any putative 'sublime party'. France talks of Boileau and Racine as 'the King's poets',[4] and the model of the 'chambre du sublime' provides striking evidence of the fact that contemporaries visualised Boileau and Racine as partners engaged in the same poetic endeavour.

Their alliance seems to have been cemented by opposition, moreover, as Pradon's tedious pamphlets testify. Pradon's *Le Triomphe de Pradon* (1684), included the following year in his *Nouvelles Remarques sur tous les ouvrages du sieur D****, is no more than a facile polemic, but it is interesting as evidence of how Boileau and Racine had come by then—ten years on from the *Œuvres diverses*—to be linked in the public mind, and moreover with the label 'sublime' attached to them. Pradon reports with glee the fact that Dacier had written a criticism of Boileau's translation, and the text is peppered with mocking references to 'Longin' and the 'sublime'. Boileau and Racine he refers to as 'nos sublimes, ou nos Ecrivains du Sublime',[5] and more than once he refers to them as 'les Messieurs du Sublime',[6] on one occasion with a footnote against the phrase, explaining 'On les nommoit ainsi à la Cour'.[7] As late as 1694, Pradon still thinks it worthwhile to bring out the term 'sublime' in an attack on Boileau's Tenth Satire against women: he accuses Boileau himself of lacking 'du sublime' and urges him, with redoubled irony, to imitate the example of Racine, who had achieved le 'solide sublime'.[8] The *Nouvelles Remarques* conclude with an 'Epître à Alcandre', which reiterates the attack on this alliance between dramatist and critic, and reminds us again of their favoured status at Court:

> Si Boileau de Racine embrasse l'interest,
> A défendre Boileau Racine est toûjours pret:
> Ces Rimeurs de concert l'un l'autre se chatoüillent,
> Et de leur fade encens tour à tour se barboüillent.
> Maintenant transplantés du Palais à la Cour,
> Nostre heureux Misanthrope est dans son plus beau jour.
> (114-15)

Raymond Picard describes very well the social and pragmatic nature of this friendship between two men of such contrasting personality. 'Cette solide alliance,' he writes, 'au milieu d'un monde déchiré par les rivalités et les haines, a puissamment servi la carrière des deux hommes'.[9] But does 'le duumvirat de Racine et de Boileau', as Picard dubs it (715), have an aesthetic dimension also?

Racine is obviously concerned with the arousal of emotion, and when in the prefaces to *Iphigénie* and to *Phèdre* he speaks of 'la compassion et la terreur' as 'les véritables effets de la tragédie' (I, 671, 745), the debt to Aristotle is explicit. But of course Racine equally defends simplicity, insisting that this requirement need not exclude passion; the point—which has an obvious parallel in Boileau's theory of the sublime—is argued most clearly in the preface to *Bérénice*:

> Il y avait longtemps que je voulais essayer si je pourrais faire une tragédie avec cette simplicité d'action qui a été si fort du goût des Anciens [...]. Il y en a qui pensent que cette simplicité est une marque de peu d'invention. Ils ne songent pas qu'au contraire toute l'invention consiste à faire quelque chose de rien, et que tout ce grand nombre d'incidents a toujours été le refuge des poètes qui ne sentaient dans leur génie ni assez d'abondance, ni assez de force, pour attacher durant cinq actes leurs spectateurs par une action simple, soutenue de la violence des passions, de la beauté des sentiments et de l'élégance de l'expression. (I, 465-66)

This passage anticipates the central notion of Boileau's 'Préface', as when he writes of 'qu'il mourût' that 'c'est la simplicité mesme de ce mot qui en fait la grandeur' (*TS*, 48). And it is apparent that Racine was acquainted with Longinus's treatise even before the appearance of Boileau's translation: in the first preface to *Britannicus* (1670), Racine paraphrases a remark, not especially concerned with the idea of the sublime, from Longinus (14.2), though without mentioning him by name—the allusion is simply to 'un Ancien' (I, 387). (This is perhaps a further indication of how little known the name of Longinus still was to the wider public in 1670; Aristotle is of course mentioned by name several times in various prefaces).

Boileau's most fulsome public tribute to Racine is the seventh *Epître*, written in 1677. At the very beginning of this poem dedicated to Racine, it is the emotional impact of his writing which Boileau chooses to stress:

> Que tu sais bien, Racine, à l'aide d'un Acteur
> Emouvoir, étonner, ravir un Spectateur! (vv.1-2)

Boileau uses the same word 'ravir' in his 'Préface' to describe the sublime, when he speaks of 'ce merveilleux qui frape dans le discours, et qui fait qu'un ouvrage enleve, ravit, transporte' (*TS*, 45). Racine's ability to achieve the most powerful theatrical and poetic effects with superficially simple language has often been commented upon. R. A. Sayce notably describes 'the use of direct statement to convey deep or violent emotion'; whereas periphrasis is employed mainly to carry narrative and argument, direct statement [...] performs the contrary function of expressing more than itself. It is found at the moments of greatest structural significance or of greatest emotional stress';[10] this notion of simple direct language expressing 'more than itself' could well stand as a definition of Boileau's sublime. As just one example (in addition to those quoted by Sayce), we might take a line spoken by Agrippine to Junie: 'Il suffit. J'ai parlé, tout a changé de face' (*Britannicus*, V, iii). At this point in the final act, Agrippine wrongly believes that she has succeeded in reconciling Néron and Britannicus: the words which she speaks are simple—so simple that they could still pass as colloquial speech; yet the sentiment which they convey, together with the staccato rhythm which brooks no opposition, combine to express powerfully Agrippine's imperious, impatient—and ill-founded—self-confidence (she has already used the phrase 'il suffit' to Britannicus (I, iii). The only seventeenth-century example of *le sublime* in Boileau's 'Préface' is taken from Corneille, of course (perhaps because *Horace* was already an 'established' classic text and therefore less controversial, perhaps on account of the useful moral overtones of 'qu'il mourût'); but Boileau could have found more and better illustrations of the sublime in the works of his immediate contemporary Racine.

Indeed, Racine's poetry may well have influenced Boileau's thinking about the sublime. Certainly there was influence in the other direction. *Phèdre*, the first play to have been written in the wake of the *Traité du sublime*, and exactly contemporary with *Epître VII*, contains one indirect allusion to Longinus which may be seen as a sign of solidarity with Boileau in the emergent debate about the sublime:

> Je le vis, je rougis, je pâlis à sa vue;
> Un trouble s'éleva dans mon âme perdue;
> Mes yeux ne voyaient plus, je ne pouvais parler;
> Je sentis tout mon corps et transir et brûler. (I, 3)

Phèdre's celebrated description of her passion for Hippolyte is an inspired example of creative imitation, for it is calqued on the poem of Sappho cited by Longinus (10.2). These lines of Racine provide an eloquent example of both the theory and practice of the sublime, for they simultaneously allude to Longinus's treatise (the only source of Sappho's poem) and put one of its precepts for the attainment of the sublime into effect. Racine may very well be considered as the ideal exemplum of Boileau's theory of the sublime: it is this shared aesthetic, with Boileau as theorist and Racine as practitioner, which is the foundation of the alliance that lasted until Racine's death.

In his 'Mémoires', Brossette speaks of the friendship between Racine and Boileau, and describes how Boileau persuaded Racine to write differently from Corneille and to use Greek heroes. The story is probably fanciful, but it offers an intriguing image of the critic training the young dramatist in the ways of the sublime:

> M. Racine avoit une facilité prodigieuse à faire des vers, mais c'étoit
> le moyen de n'y jetter pas beaucoup de force [...]. M. Despréaux
> m'a dit qu'il avoit appris à M. Racine à faire des vers difficilement.
> (520)

In his Twelfth *Réflexion critique*, published in 1713, Boileau pays final public tribute to Racine as the sublime author *par excellence*. In this, his final utterance on the subject, Boileau quotes as an example of the sublime four lines spoken by Joad in the opening scene of *Athalie* (vv.61-64): 'En effet, tout ce qui peut y avoir de Sublime paroist rassemblé dans ces quatre Vers: la grandeur de la penseé, la noblesse du sentiment, la magnificence des paroles, et l'harmonie de l'expression' (185).

ii. The reception of the *Traité du sublime*

The anecdotal evidence of the 'chambre du sublime' emphasises the dramatic impact which the *Traité du sublime* had on contemporary critical discussion and on Boileau's standing as a critic, and the work quickly acquired authoritative status. 'Sublimité est un bon mot, que M. Despréaux a rendu meilleur' declares Bouhours, as early as 1675;[11] the classical scholar Dacier judges Boileau's work to be 'une des plus belles traductions que nous ayons en nostre Langue';[12] and when Rapin hails the *Traité du sublime* as 'le Chef-d'œuvre de son Auteur', he does not of course mean Longinus.[13] Nor was this impact shortlived: at the end of the century, Jean Le Clerc— an opponent of Boileau's who had no desire to flatter—writes of 'ce stile merveilleux, dont *Longin* a fait un Traité qui est entre les mains de tout le monde, sur tout depuis qu'il a été traduit en François.'[14]

The repercussions of the *Traité du sublime* are felt in a wide variety of writings, and well beyond the confines of poetic theory. Bernard Lamy, for example, introduces into the third edition of his *Rhétorique* (1688) a discussion of the *fiat lux* example from Genesis:

> Longin, ce célèbre rhéteur, donne cette expression pour exemple
> d'une expression sublime. Or pourquoi est elle belle, si ce n'est
> parce qu'elle donne une haute ideé de la puissance du Créateur; ce
> que Moïse voulait faire: c'était là sa fin.[15]

Such comment does not entirely square with his more old-fashioned usage of the term *sublime* found later in the book, when he speaks of 'le stile sublime' as the highest of the three characters (378), or when he remarks that 'l'obscurité a quelque apparence de grandeur, et [...] les choses sublimes et relevées sont ordinairement obscures et difficiles' (422). In order to make his *Rhétorique* look up-to-date in 1688, Lamy clearly feels it important to include an allusion to Longinus—even if the result is that two different usages of *sublime* have to coexist: 'Il ne faut pas confondre le style sublime et magnifique avec ce qu'on appelle grand ou sublime dans le discours' (386).

In a different field, the art theorist Roger de Piles was a friend of Boileau (and painted his portrait); his discussions of *le sublime* and of *l'enthousiasme* in his writings on art are decisively influenced by the *Traité du sublime*.[16] This summary of de Piles's views, from the section 'De l'entousiasme' of his *Cours de peinture par principes* (1708), shows his debt to Longinus (whom he discusses),[17] and also the extent to which the *Traité du sublime* has helped him evolve a distinctively original theory:

> L'Entousiasme est un transport de l'esprit qui fait penser les choses
> d'une maniere sublime, surprenante, et vrai semblable [...].
> Quoique le Vrai plaise toûjours, parce qu'il est la baze et le
> fondement de toutes les perfections, il ne laisse pas d'être souvent
> insipide quand il est tout seul: mais quand il est joint à
> l'Entousiasme, il transporte l'esprit dans une admiration mêlée
> d'étonnement; il le ravit avec violence sans lui donner le tems de

retourner sur lui-meme. J'ai fait entrer le Sublime dans la définition de l'Entousiasme, parce que le Sublime est un effet et une production de l'Entousiasme. L'Entousiasme contient le Sublime comme le tronc d'un arbre contient ses branches qu'il repand de differens côtez; ou plutôt l'Entousiasme est un soleil dont la chaleur et les influences font naître les hautes pensées, et les conduisent dans un état de maturité que nous appellons Sublime. Mais comme l'Entousiasme et le Sublime tendent tous deux à lever notre esprit, on peut dire qu'ils sont d'une même nature. La difference neanmoins qui me paroît entre l'un et l'autre, c'est que l'Entousiasme est une fureur de Veine qui porte notre ame encore plus haut que le Sublime, dont il est la source, et qui a son principal effet dans la pensée et dans le Tout-ensemble de l'ouvrage; au lieu que le Sublime se fait sentir également dans le général, et dans le détail de toutes les parties. L'Entousiasme a encore cela que l'effet en est plus promt, et que celui du Sublime demande au moins quelques momens de reflexion pour être vû dans toute sa force. L'Entousiasme nous enleve sans que nous le sentions, et nous transporte, pour ainsi dire, comme d'un Pas dans un autre sans nous en apercevoir que par le plaisir qu'il nous cause. Il me paroît, en un mot, que l'Entousiasme nous saisit, et que nous saisissons le Sublime. C'est donc à cette élévation surprenante, mais juste, mais raisonnable que le Peintre doit porter son Ouvrage aussi bien que le Poëte; s'ils veulent arriver l'un et l'autre à cet extraordinaire Vraisemblable qui remuë le cœur et qui fait le plus grand mérite de la Peinture et de la Poësie.[18]

De Piles's use of Boileau-Longinus is considerably more subtle than Lamy's had been, for he has integrated the *Traité du sublime* into his own thought. Once again, the extent of this debt is testimony to the prestige and influence that the *Traité du sublime* had so quickly acquired.

In his *Deffense de la langue françoise pour l'inscription de l'arc de triomphe* (1676), the academician François Charpentier vaunts the merits of the French language, and flatters his readers by suggesting that the qualities of a language reflect those of its speakers (a curious application of mimetic theory!): 'C'est la noblesse des sentimens qui donne [aux Langues] de la Force et de la Sublimité' (sig iii r). This use of the term *sublimité* applied to language, just two years after the appearance of Boileau's translation, can hardly be fortuitous (elsewhere in Charpentier's book Longinus is cited explicitly).[19] But while the remark testifies to the remarkable influence of the *Traité du sublime*, it also suggests that Charpentier either misunderstood, or actively disagreed with, the particular interpretation of Longinus enshrined in Boileau's translation, for the proposition that sublimity is simply the reflection of elevated feeling would make of *le sublime* a moral concept, an approach which in no way accords with Boileau's emphasis on the sublime as a characteristic of literary discourse. Clearly, the *Traité du sublime* was widely known after 1674—but was it widely and uniformly understood?

The impact of the *Traité* on its first readers could not have been as great as it was, if the ground had not already been so thoroughly prepared. Many of the ideas embodied in the thought of Boileau-Longinus had been current in embryonic form for some years, at least among a certain circle of critics. Gabriel Guéret, for example, in his *Entretiens sur l'éloquence de la chaire et du barreau* (1666), speaks of wishing to discover 'quelques secrets de cette eloquence sublime, dont tant de monde est Idolâtre, et que si peu de personnes peuvent aquerir' (2). He contrasts the effeminacy of modern eloquence with the true eloquence of the Scriptures:

> Je sçay bien que la sainteté de l'Evangile n'aime point cette Eloquence coquette qui met tous ses soins à se farder, qui ne se plaist qu'à faire l'agreable, qui est satisfaite pourveu qu'elle ébloüisse les yeux, et dont le dessein le plus ordinaire est de tromper [...]. Elle garde tousjours ce juste temperament qui sans rien perdre de sa force, conserve aux sujets qu'elle traitte un air naturel, et qui sans se rendre suspect d'aucun artifice, sçait bien se servir des grandes figures, et de tous les secrets de l'Art. (10-11)

The rejection of baroque rhetoric and the insistence on the Biblical ideal of expressive simplicity evidently look forward to the *Traité du sublime*. Guéret is prevented from developing a more coherent theory of rhetoric by his uncritical assumption of nomenclaturism: he makes a crude distinction between the eloquence of things and that of words (30), and quotes Plato in defence of the view that rhetoric is dishonest (35). Guéret's work shows none the less how certain of the central tenets of the *Traité du sublime* were already being canvassed in the 1660s; what was lacking was a coherent and persuasive framework in which to give them expression.

The *académie Lamoignon* seems to have played a pivotal role in the early genesis of the translation of Longinus. This group—which had regular Monday meetings at the home of the Premier Président Guillaume de Lamoignon from 1667 onwards—embraced lawyers, theologians and philosophers (prominent among whom was Cordemoy, disciple of Descartes and admirer of Plato, whose views on language have already been considered). The assembly is described by Lalemant in some notes he made on the early meetings of an 'Académie des Belles Lettres', and it included a number of members with literary interests, notably Rapin, Pellisson and Fleury (a friend of Cordemoy), and later Boileau himself, as well as such figures as Menestrier and Bossuet.[20] In 1669 Rapin read a paper comparing Homer and Virgil, soon to be followed by the abbé Fleury on the subject of Plato, and, around 1670, Bossuet on the subject of Biblical poetry. In these various discussions, writes E. T. Dubois, 'the sublime was discussed as a category of rhetoric, and what is more important, it was gradually set apart as an independent aesthetic emotion and expression'.[21]

The correspondence of Bussy-Rabutin and Rapin further illustrates the extent to which these ideas were 'in the air' in the early 1670s. When Rapin wishes to praise Bussy's style, he praises its 'antique' simplicity:

> J'ai assez de connoissance de l'Antiquité pour voir, Monsieur, que
> vôtre maniere d'écrire est la vraie, et que vous êtes le seul qui aiez
> trouvé l'art d'écrire simplement sans paroître bas, et d'être naturel
> sans être plat.[22]

Though he does not use the word *sublime*, Rapin's notion of good style is close to the sublime of Boileau's 'Préface'. The following year, Rapin asks Bussy how he understands the 'genre sublime':

> Quelle ideé vous avez du genre sublime, et de cet air de majesté
> qui est essentiel à la belle poesie, où les petits genies ne peuvent
> atteindre que par de vains efforts qui vont dans le galimatias? Car
> tous nos poetes tombent dans ce defaut, pour être destituez de cette
> noblese d'expression qui est necessaire à la poesie.[23]

Bussy's response emphasises the need for powerful poetic discourse; and though he, like Rapin, speaks of a 'genre sublime', he is really concerned with a quality of poetic discourse rather than the definition of the highest of the three characters:

> Je croy comme vous, M. R. P., qu'il n'y a point de poetes françois
> qui ayent ce grand air de majesté dans leurs vers, qui fait le genre
> sublime de la poesie, et vous remarqués fort bien qu'il consiste
> dans la noblesse de l'expression, et moy j'ajoute dans la justesse. Il
> est vray qu'on ne voit point de belle ode françoise; ceux qui en ont
> fait n'avoient pas assés de feu; ils auroient été plus propres a
> l'eglogue.[24]

This exchange between Bussy and Rapin anticipates many of the views of Boileau-Longinus; the very word *sublime* had become currrent in critical discussions while Boileau was working on the *Traité du sublime*.

Rapin's *Réflexions sur la poétique* appeared in the same year as the *Traité du sublime*, so although not influenced by it directly, they are the product of the same intellectual milieu. In his *Du Grand ou du sublime dans les mœurs* (1686), Rapin was later to develop the notion of the sublime as a moral concept, and so in a direction deliberately contrary to the example of Boileau's literary term: 'Rien n'est plus nouveau que le dessein de cet Ouvrage,' he writes in the 'Avertissement' to this work. 'On n'en a peut-être jamais traité de pareil; car l'idée, qu'on se forme du Sublime est tellement attachée au discours, qu'on a de la peine à le mettre ailleurs'.[25] Even so, it may be some tribute to Boileau's influence that Rapin cannot refrain altogether in the *Réflexions* from mention of the sublime, a topic which, as we have seen, had already been broached in his correspondence with Bussy-Rabutin. The term *sublime* is used in his *Défense des fables*, in which Rapin defends the right of the Christian poet to use 'la fable païenne', declaring that poetry must be 'sublime and élevé'.[26] Longinus is mentioned and cited in the *Réflexions* on a number of occasions,[27] and there are several occurrences of the word *sublime*. Homer is described as having 'l'esprit [...] le plus sublime' (16), Virgil as attaining '[le] caractère le plus sublime du vers héroïque' (29). Speaking more of style, Rapin writes that 'l'ode demande du sublime dans les grands sujets' (131). Such uses of the term are conventional enough, but elsewhere in the *Réflexions*, Rapin comes closer to the conception of Boileau:

> Les poètes grecs sont remplis de ces grandes pensées: c'est aussi par la grandeur de leurs sentimens, qu'ils se sont particulièrement signalez dans leurs ouvrages. Démétrius et Longin les proposent sans cesse pour modèles à ceux qui s'étudient au genre sublime. (45)

And again:

> [Homère] est le seul qui ait trouvé le secret de joindre à la pureté du style toute l'élévation et toute la grandeur dont la poésie héroïque peut estre capable. C'est aussi pour cela que Longin le propose toujours comme la règle du genre sublime. (49)

The spirit of both these statements is in line with Boileau's conception of the *sublime* (elevated discourse without the need for elevated language), yet Rapin on both occasions uses the phrase 'genre sublime'. It recurs once more, in a context which makes it absolutely clear that Rapin is not referring to the 'sublime style' of rhetoric, when he states that Du Bartas and Ronsard 'ne furent pas assez habiles pour mettre le genre sublime du vers héroïque dans les choses, plutost que dans les paroles' (96). This use of *genre sublime* could clearly lead to confusion—hence the need for Boileau's distinction in the 'Préface' between *sublime* and *style sublime*.

Adam describes the literary ideals of this group as being characterised by a concern with expressive simplicity and the ideal truth, and a dislike of the contemporary concern with purity and good taste.[28] 'Contre cette poésie raisonnable, pure et exacte, ils rappellent la nécessité de la grandeur et de la force,' he writes. 'Un mot résume cette exigence: le sublime' (III, 136). Participants in the meetings of the *académie Lamoignon* were clearly liable to be receptive to the ideas of Boileau-Longinus, a point that Adam makes very forcibly:

> Le *Traité du sublime* répondait aussi de façon directe aux préoccupations de l'académie de Lamoignon, il développait des thèses que Claude Fleury et Rapin venaient de reprendre [...]. Lorsqu'on a compris quel était le sens véritable de la controverse entre les partisans de l'Antiquité et le parti des Modernes, on se rend compte à quel point le traité de Longin offrait un intérêt d'actualité.[29]

Boileau's translation thus (re-)launched a concept which continued to be debated, directly or indirectly, by many prominent literary figures of the period, among them Rapin, Bouhours, Fleury, La Bruyère and Bossuet. Boileau's translation attracted scholarly interest in its own right: in due course Dacier's 'Remarques' were appended to the *Traité du sublime* (1683), and later Boileau's replies to them (1685). Most of these critics may readily be labelled as 'Anciens'; this lends at least a superficial unity to the disparate discussions concerning the sublime, and we are led to wonder to what extent there emerges from these debates a coherent theory of the sublime, and whether perhaps the 'party of the sublime' might not be coterminous with the 'party of the Ancients'. In order to consider these questions, the remainder of this chapter will examine the different directions in which, in the wake of the publication of the *Traité du sublime*, writers sought to extend or re-orient Boileau's idea of *le sublime* as a concept of poetic discourse.

III. *LE SUBLIME* AS LITERARY CONCEPT AFTER 1674

A. THE BIBLICAL SUBLIME

Bossuet remained always closely identified with the cause of Boileau and Racine, and this despite the fact that his theological beliefs caused him to distrust literature (he was after all the author of *Maximes* against the theatre). He had known Boileau since the period of the *académie Lamoignon*, and was Racine's spokesman in the affair following La Bruyère's *discours de réception*. Fontenelle, in his *Eloge de Malézieu*, emphasises Bossuet's prominence within this grouping:

> La Cour rassembloit alors un assez grand nombre de gens illustres par l'esprit: MM. Racine, Despréaux, de la Bruyère, de Malézieu, de Court; M. de Meaux étoit à leur tête. Ils formoient une espèce de Société particulière, d'autant plus unie qu'elle étoit plus séparée de celle des Illustres de Paris, qui ne prétendoient pas devoir reconnoître un Tribunal supérieur, ni se soumettre à des jugements, quoique revêtus de ce nom si imposant de jugements de Cour. Du moins avoient-ils une autorité souveraine à Versailles, et Paris même ne se croyoit pas toujours assez fort pour en appeler.[30]

Bossuet's paper for the *académie Lamoignon* on the subject of biblical poetry had expressed the essence of his thinking about eloquence: disdain for rhetorical ornament, and conviction that Christian truth is best expressed simply.[31] Bossuet's aesthetic doctrines are perhaps best gleaned from his sermons, in several of which he discusses openly the function of pulpit rhetoric, as here:

> Au reste, n'attendez pas de moi tous ces ornements de la rhétorique mondaine; mais priez seulement cet Esprit qui souffle où il veut, qu'il daigne répandre sur mes lèvres ces deux beaux ornements de l'éloquence chrétienne, la simplicité et la vérité, et qu'il étende par sa grâce le peu que j'ai à vous dire.[32]

Strongly opposed to the view that pleasure is the sole aim of rhetoric, Bossuet is fierce in his defence of simplicity:

> Si notre simplicité déplaît aux superbes, qu'ils sachent que nous craignons de leur plaire, que Jésus-Christ dédaigne leur faste insolent, et qu'il ne veut être connu que des humbles. Abaissons-nous donc à ces humbles; faisons-leur des prédications dont la bassesse tienne quelque chose de l'humiliation de la croix, et qui soient dignes de ce Dieu qui ne veut vaincre que par la faiblesse.[33]

Simplicity is not merely the most truthful form of expression, it is also the most powerful: 'Une seule parole de l'Evangile a plus de pouvoir sur nos âmes que toute la véhémence et toutes les inventions de l'éloquence profane.'[34] This last remark comes from a sermon of 1652; Boileau's theory of *le sublime*, elaborated some twenty years later, is scarcely more than a secularisation of this same notion of eloquence.

Bossuet's 'Sur le style, et la lecture des Pères de l'Eglise pour former un orateur', written around 1670, is derivative and of little interest. There is however one later work in which Bossuet speaks in a more individual voice: the extended preface 'Dissertatio de Psalmis' to his *Liber Psalmorum* (1691), the second chapter of which is entitled 'De grandiloquentia et suavitate Psalmorum' (xl-lv). *Grandiloquentia*, says Bossuet, arises from two things, firstly from subject matter, 'rerum sublimitas', and secondly from the proper choice of words—the deepest thoughts are often expressed with the greatest simplicity (xli). He talks of concision as a source of powerful language, and admires discourse which is so vivid that we seem to see not the image ('imago') but the thing itself ('res ipsa'). The words *sublimis* and *sublimitas* occur on several occasions, and always in Boileau's sense of the *sublime*, as in this example from Psalm 148: '*Ipse dixit, et facta sunt: ipse mandavit, et creata sunt*; prorsus ex dignitate atque ex sublimitate Mosis' (xliv). That Longinus should have found the *sublime* exemplified in Holy Scripture is obviously essential to Bossuet's theory of eloquence. One of Bossuet's sermons begins with the following prayer:

> O Dieu, donnez-moi des paroles, non de celles qui flattent les oreilles et qui font louer les discours, mais de celles qui pénètrent les cœurs et qui captivent tout entendement sous l'autorité de votre Evangile.[35]

The abbé Claude Fleury, who had early been an important figure in the *académie Lamoignon*, remains one of the more neglected authors of French classicism, although (or perhaps because) his writings are voluminous. His literary principles were first expounded in the *Dialogues sur l'éloquence judiciaire*, written in 1664; later works include *Discours sur l'Ecriture sainte*, *Discours sur la prédication*, and *Discours sur la poésie des Hébreux*. Fleury does not discuss the *sublime* specifically; even the term occurs only rarely in his writings (and then not always in Boileau's sense). But the premisses of his literary judgements are profoundly similar to those which inform

Boileau's theory of the sublime—both, after all, derive from the same intellectual milieu.

Fleury regards modern poetry as for the most part frivolous, and he upholds the Bible as the supreme example of eloquence: 'Rien n'est si éloigné du galimatias pompeux des modernes. Nous donnons en grands mots de petites choses, et ils disoient les choses les plus grandes en termes familiers'.[36] The first requirement for great poetry is that the subject matter should be significant, for no amount of verbal felicity can disguise an insubstantial subject.

> Il faut donc ou condamner tout-à-fait la Poésie, ce que ne feront
> pas aisément les personnes savantes et équitables: ou lui donner
> des sujets digne d'elle, et la réconcilier avec la véritable Philosophie,
> c'est-à-dire avec la bonne morale et la solide piété. (II, 659)

The Bible is often most forceful when it is most simple, he contends; and he analyses the way in which Abraham's sacrifice is narrated, with direct speech for God's commands to Abraham, to reveal the technique by which this effect is achieved: 'Mais faisant parler l'un à l'autre, on s'imagine voir la chose, et l'esprit a le loisir de se reposer et de considérer l'obéissance d'Abraham' (II, 638). As is evident from this example, Fleury is not interested in anodyne simplicity, but rather in how words can be made to work, and he discusses also the use of metaphor in the Scriptures. He writes interestingly about the difference between prose and poetry, and is passionate in the defence of poetry. Plato's name occurs in the course of the discussion of poetry, and Fleury is at pains to point out that Plato did not condemn all poetry (II, 660). He also talks in some detail about the untranslatability of great poetry, which, through no necessary fault of the translator, loses its beauty in another language—an awareness absent from Boileau's 'Préface' (II, 657).

It is abundantly clear from these few examples that Fleury is highly sensitive to the materiality of poetic language; he is interested in poetic discourse as a form of expression in which subject matter and style have fused and become inseparable. In a variant on the 'Enfin Malherbe vint' commonplace,[37] Fleury singles out not the 'purity' of Malherbe's verse, but rather its sound:

> Malherbe est le premier de nos Poëtes, qui a fait des vers agréables
> et doux, parce qu'il est le premier qui a observé l'harmonie des
> paroles, c'est-à-dire, ce qui les fait sonner le mieux à nos oreilles,
> et la cadence des vers. Au lieu que du Bartas a fait des vers dont le
> sens est très-beau et le son très-choquant.[38]

Fleury's writings about poetry are thus fully consonant with Boileau's view of *le sublime* (though they did not have as great an influence, being for the most part published posthumously). The *Discours sur la poésie des Hébreux*, after describing the characteristics of poetic diction, uses the term *sublime*—perhaps a nod in Boileau's direction:

> Les pensées qui sont revêtues de cette élocution et de ces figures, ne sont pas seulement véritables, solides et utiles, comme on n'en peut douter, sachant que le Saint-Esprit les a inspirées; mais encore très-souvent belles, brillantes, sublimes, délicates.[39]

Fénelon's aesthetic ideas have been studied in depth by A. Pizzorusso and although, like Fleury, he provides no extended discussion of *le sublime* as such in his works, the premisses and assumptions of his poetic theory are clearly in close sympathy with those of Boileau-Longinus. Fénelon's 'Discours à l'Académie' delivered upon his election to that body in 1693 is an eloquent statement of his literary aesthetic:

> Depuis que des hommes savants et judicieux ont remonté aux véritables règles, on n'abuse plus, comme on le faisait autrefois, de l'esprit de la parole; on a pris un genre d'écrire plus simple, plus naturel, plus court, plus nerveux, plus précis. On ne s'attache plus aux paroles que pour exprimer toute la force des pensées [...]. L'esprit même se cache, parce que toute la perfection de l'art consiste à imiter si naïvement la simple nature, qu'on la prenne pour elle [...]. On a senti même en nos jours que le style fleuri, quelque doux et quelque agréable qu'il soit, ne peut jamais s'élever au-dessus du genre médiocre, et que le vrai genre sublime, dédaignant tous les ornements empruntés, ne se trouve que dans le simple.[40]

This description of 'le vrai genre sublime' as an ideal of poetic discourse combining forcefulness with simplicity would clearly have found favour with his fellow Academician Boileau. Fénelon reiterates his views in the *Lettre à l'Académie* (1714, published 1716):

> Pour le genre sublime et véhément [saint Augustin] ne veut point qu'il soit fleuri [...]. J'avoue que le genre fleuri a ses grâces; mais elles sont déplacées dans les discours où il ne s'agit point d'un jeu d'esprit plein de délicatesse et où les grandes passions doivent parler. Le genre fleuri n'atteint jamais au sublime [...]. Je veux un sublime si familier, si doux et si simple que chacun soit d'abord tenté de croire qu'il l'auroit trouvé sans peine, quoique peu d'hommes soient capables de le trouver.[41]

Fénelon is perhaps the author most strongly identified with the poetic theory of Boileau-Longinus, so the overt praise of the *Traité du sublime* in his *Dialogues sur l'éloquence* (c.1679, published 1718) comes as no surprise: 'Je ne crains pas de dire que [le *Traité du sublime*] surpasse à mon gré la *Rhétorique* d'Aristote' (*Œuvres*, I, 9). The influence of the *Traité du sublime* makes itself felt throughout the *Dialogues*, as Fénelon uses the 'Ancient' idea of powerful simplicity as a model for understanding the rhetoric of the Scriptures: 'Pour sentir [l'éloquence de l'Ecriture], rien n'est plus utile que d'avoir le goût de la simplicité antique' (I, 66).

The interest of theologians in what we may term the biblical sublime is not confined exclusively to the Ancients. The prominent Jansenist Louis Isaac Le Maître de Sacy devoted many years of his life to the Port-Royal translation of the Bible, and as part of this project he published in 1682 *La Genèse traduite en françois*. One section of the preface is entitled 'Simplicité sublime de l'Ecriture' and begins thus: 'On ne s'arrestera pas ici à representer ce qu'il y a de grand dans le stile de cette histoire, qui estant meslé avec une simplicité divine, porte par tout un caractere de verité' (sig. o vi r); Sacy then goes on to name Longinus and to paraphrase the long passage from the seventh chapter of Boileau's *Traité du sublime* (acknowledged in a marginal reference) which cites and discusses the *fiat lux* example:

> Cet Auteur Grec remarque dans ces paroles quelque chose de grand
> et de merveilleux. Surquoy celuy qui l'a traduit depuis peu en nostre
> langue fait cette sage reflexion:«On n'appelle point proprement
> sublime dans un discours ce qui n'a rien d'extraordinaire ny de
> surprenant [...].» (sig. o vi v)

Such an extended quotation from the *Traité du sublime* in the preface to a translation of the Scriptures (Sacy's preface moves on immediately from Boileau-Longinus to St Augustine) suggests that Boileau's poetic aesthetic had also found favour with the Jansenists.

It is not the explicit concern of any of the writers considered here to develop Boileau's theory of the sublime; it is sufficient to note that they perpetuate in their writings views that Boileau clearly shared. It is however significant to note that Boileau's staunchest support comes from those Ancients most eminent as theologians. Boileau's *sublime* may not be a moral term as such, but it is a literary term with definite moral underpinning. In a curious but genuine compliment, Fénelon wrote to Bossuet: 'Vous êtes plein de fentes par où le sublime échappe de tous côtés.'[42]

Adam's original insight into the connection between the Ancients and the cause of the *sublime* has been widely accepted; Litman, for example, has chapters on La Bruyère, Rapin and Fénelon (curiously, he omits Bossuet and Fleury) which show clearly the link between the Ancients and the *sublime*. Much more interesting, in a sense, are the cases of those Ancients who opposed Boileau's view of the sublime—a crucial facet of the debate which Adam and Litman ignore entirely.

B. SCHOLARLY OPPOSITION TO THE *TRAITÉ DU SUBLIME*

It is plainly not the case that the Ancients who wrote on *le sublime* were united in agreement with Boileau. Dacier's scholarly 'Remarques' on (i.e. criticisms of) the translation of Longinus are not overtly hostile—it is in some sense a tribute to Boileau that such a prominent classical scholar should have deemed the *Traité du sublime* worthy of such close scrutiny—but they provided welcome ammunition to the likes of Pradon. Boileau sought to save face by publishing the 'Remarques', together with his rejoinders in due course, alongside his translation. Dacier's 'Remarques' were clearly an embarrassment to Boileau, even though irrelevant as regards his main critical purpose, and Pradon suggests, maliciously perhaps, that Boileau intervened with Dacier to ask him to mitigate the tone of his comments.[43]

More openly hostile was the attack of Pierre Daniel Huet in his *Demonstratio evangelica* (1679), in which he denied the sublimity of expression (though not of subject matter) in the *fiat lux* passage of Genesis. Boileau inserted a predictable response into the 'Préface' to the *Traité du sublime* in the 1683 edition of his *Œuvres*, and probably thought the matter resolved. Huet, however, wrote a response to his response in the form of a letter which came eventually to be published by Le Clerc in the *Bibliothèque choisie* of 1706, and this led to the tenth *Réflexion critique* (written 1710, published posthumously 1713), aimed at both Le Clerc and Huet.[44] The exchange did not produce arguments of great significance, but it certainly demonstrates Boileau's stubbornness in debate: Huet was a celebrated scholar who had begun the preparation of the classical editions *ad usum Delphini*, and Boileau was evidently stung by his criticism.

C. BOUHOURS'S DELICATE RESPONSE

Dacier and Huet each, in their different ways, made scholarly criticisms of details in the *Traité du sublime*. However much they may have irritated or even embarrassed Boileau, they were clearly not questioning his entire project in translating Longinus, and Boileau eagerly rebutted the criticisms in both cases. A more oblique and delicate form of attack came from Bouhours in *La Manière de bien penser dans les ouvrages d'esprit* (1687). We have already considered Bouhours's only partly successful attempt to resolve contemporary critical problems in the *Entretiens*. The term which he launched in that work, the *je ne sais quoi*, had had nothing like the success or the impact which the *sublime* had enjoyed in the wake of the *Œuvres diverses*, and *La Manière de bien penser* marks Bouhours's attempt to rebut the *Traité du sublime* and to regain the critical initiative.

Though an Ancient, and though introduced to the Lamoignon circle by his fellow Jesuit Rapin, Bouhours was never a central figure of the *académie*, and was certainly never identified with the *cabale du sublime*. Unlike Rapin, he remained perhaps closer to the stylistic ideals of a previous generation and of his master Le Moyne, upholding the rhetorical tradition of Counter-Reformation Jesuit polemic which favoured a slightly more orotund, less austere poetic style. Bouhours sensibly realises that he cannot ignore the *Traité du sublime* after such success, and *La Manière de bien penser* contains many allusions to Boileau's work.

Longinus's treatise is quoted at regular intervals, mostly in innocuous contexts,[45] and on one occasion Bouhours even throws a bouquet in Boileau's direction: 'Voicy un endroit que le Traducteur de Longin a rendu admirablement [...]' (371). But a slightly different note is struck as the conversation turns to the legitimacy of an elevated style: when Eudoxe quotes Longinus to support a complete condemnation of inflated style, Philanthe counters with the example of Martial—and Martial gets the last word (343-44). Just as Boileau had earlier spoken through the voice of Longinus, so Bouhours now apparently conceals himself behind the figure of Martial. (Nor is this the only occasion on which an example from Longinus is contradicted: compare 107-08.)

Use of the term *sublime* is again a tacit acknowledgement of Boileau's presence—though not necessarily a flattering one. E. T. Dubois notes that Bouhours 'refers explicitly to Boileau's translation of Longinus and adds literary examples of his own to those offered by Boileau';[46] but on closer inspection these supplementary examples turn out to be somewhat insidious. Eudoxe's praise of the style of the Scriptures ('sa simplicité a tant de sublime', 59-60) is entirely in accordance with Boileau's notion of the sublime (though neither Boileau not Longinus is mentioned at this point). Later Eudoxe returns to the idea: 'L'Ecriture Sainte est un fonds de pensées nobles, grandes et sublimes' (167). On this occasion, he quotes the *fiat lux* example and Longinus's analysis of it—but there is still no mention of Boileau: Longinus's treatise is quoted in the margin, in Latin (168), as though oblivious of the fact that it was the *Traité du sublime* which had given this example its contemporary prominence. Eudoxe goes on moreover to argue that in certain circumstances forceful expression can contribute to 'la hauteur de la pensée' (*hauteur* is of course the most literal rendering of *hupsos*), and he quotes in support of his contention various examples from the Scriptures. Longinus's Genesis example, though quoted, is thus relativised, and with the additional biblical examples Bouhours distances himself from Boileau's theory of the sublime.

Bouhours returns to his oblique attack only a few pages later, when Philanthe cites the elder Horace's 'Qu'il mourût' as a notable instance of a powerful *pensée*: 'Ce qu'il mourust exprime la générosité Romaine d'une manière vive et touchante, qui frappe l'esprit, et émeut le cœur en mesme temps' (174). This is a good instance of Bouhours's technique of strategic silence. The example comes of course straight from Boileau's 'Préface' (where it is Boileau's sole original example of the *sublime*), so it might seem curious that there is no mention of Boileau, nor even a marginal reference to the *Traité du sublime* (marginal references are used very widely throughout the book). More curious still is the fact that Philanthe's/Bouhours's analysis of the example studiously avoids the word *sublime*: is Bouhours suggesting that the impact of *qu'il mourût* can be explained without the need of recourse to the theory of the sublime? Our suspicions only increase when a page or so later we do find the expressions 'la sublimité' and, twice, 'les pensées sublimes' (176-77) used to describe this category of example: Bouhours acknowledges the term, yet refuses to apply it to Boileau's celebrated example.

Elsewhere too we find 'la sublimité', 'des pensées sublimes' (107), used to refer to grandeur of thought, and while this is certainly one source of the Longinian sublime (and Bouhours here gives a marginal reference to Longinus, 107), it is hardly the central characteristic of Boileau's conception of the *sublime*. Under *sublime* in the 'Table des matières' we find a cross-reference to *penseés nobles*—and to a discussion (111-13) in which the word *sublime* does not occur once.

On other occasions 'le sublime' is used to refer (critically) to the hyperbolic style of Gracián (327) or to the conceited Italian verse of Bernini ('le sublime vicieux', 364), thus according the *sublime* a sense entirely opposed to the one which Boileau had intended. To disprove the sublimity of Gracián, Bouhours ironically quotes Longinus—in the Latin version (328).

This implied critique of the *sublime* becomes overt in the conclusion of Eudoxe's explanation of *la délicatesse*: 'D'où l'on peut conclure que la délicatesse ajoûte je ne sçay quoi au sublime et à l'agréable' (216). Later Eudoxe dwells on the charms of la naïveté, again at the expense of the *sublime*:

> Le grand, le sublime n'est point naïf, et ne le peut estre: car le naïf emporte de soy-mesme je ne sçay quoi de petit, ou de moins élevé. Ne m'avez-vous pas dit, interrompit Philanthe, que la simplicité et la grandeur n'estoient pas incompatibles? Oüi, reprit Eudoxe, et je vous le dis encore; mais il y a de la différence entre une certaine simplicité noble et la naïveté toute pure: l'une n'exclut que le faste, l'autre exclut mesme la grandeur. (297)

Thus Bouhours outlines a critical concept (*la délicatesse* or *la naïveté*) which embraces *le sublime* but includes much else besides. Boileau's two examples of *le sublime* in the 'Préface' (*fiat lux* and *qu'il mourût*) are both woven into Bouhours's discussion, but in a manner which divorces them from Boileau's conception of the *sublime*. Bouhours's stylistic ideal, infused with such values as *le joli*, is ultimately irreconcilable with the more austere notion of the biblical *sublime* that had grown up in the *académie Lamoignon*. And on this point there is complete unanimity between the two interlocutors of the dialogue:

> Comme la noblesse des pensées, poursuivit Eudoxe, vient, selon Hermogene, de la majesté des choses dont elles sont les images, ainsi que nous avons veû: leur agrément peut venir, selon Démétrius, de la nature des objets qui plaisent d'eux mesmes, tels que sont les fleurs, la lumiére, les beaux jours, et toutes les choses qui flattent les sens.
>
> C'est sans doute pour cela, repartit Philanthe, que Voiture a des pensées si jolies: car personne n'a mieux mis en œuvre ce que la nature a de plus délicieux et de plus riant. Vous avez deviné justement ce que je pensois, repartit Eudoxe. (178-79)

Demetrius is set against Longinus (Roman against Greek), *la délicatesse* and *la naïveté* set against *le sublime* (feminine nouns against a masculine one): the aesthetic of *le sublime*, while not actually denied, is at the very least relativised. To praise so extravagantly the poetry of Voiture is to devalue the significance of those neoplatonist notions of *fureur* and *enthousiasme* which are at the core of Boileau's aesthetic.

D. LA BRUYÈRE AND THE BIBLICAL SUBLIME

The first edition of *Les Caractères* (1688) contains no specific mention of *le sublime*, though the general character of many fragments in 'Des ouvrages de l'esprit' is clearly in keeping with Boileau's poetic theory: 'Combien de siècles se sont écoulés avant que les hommes, dans les sciences et dans les arts, aient pu revenir au goût des anciens et reprendre enfin le simple et le naturel!' (70; cf. 72). But in the fourth edition of the following year (1689), La Bruyère tackles the subject of *le sublime* head-on:

> Qu'est ce que le sublime? Il ne paraît pas qu'on l'ait défini. Est-ce une figure? Naît-il des figures, ou du moins de quelques figures? Tout genre d'écrire reçoit-il le sublime, ou s'il n'y a que les grands sujets qui en soient capables? Peut-il briller autre chose dans l'églogue qu'un beau naturel, et dans les lettres familières commes dans les conversations qu'une grande délicatesse? ou plutôt le naïf et le délicat ne sont-ils pas le sublime des ouvrages dont ils font la perfection? Qu'est-ce que le sublime? Où entre le sublime? (90)

The fragment is a curious one, not least for the way in which it is cast entirely in the interrogative form. Eight questions in all—but are they rhetorical questions? Garapon interprets the fragment as meaning simply that *le sublime* is by definition undefinable (90, n. 1), recalling those (equally unsuccessful) seventeenth-century attempts to grapple with *le je ne sais quoi*. Litman, on the other hand, reads the fragment as a résumé of the ideas of Boileau, Bouhours and Rapin, so sees it as a wholly unoriginal restatement of the 'Ancient' view of *le sublime* (though he nuances this later by noting La Bruyère's emphasis in other fragments on strong emotions and on the link between these and Christian eloquence) (131-40). Thus neither Garapon nor Litman find anything of significance in La Bruyère's contribution.

La Bruyère's questions are surely ingenuous: his readers would have known that Boileau had at least attempted a definition of *le sublime* in his 'Préface', just as they would have known that 'les Figures tournes d'une certaine maniere' (*TS*, 59) were described by Boileau-Longinus as one of five sources of sublimity. La Bruyère's true target becomes evident when he turns to the minor genres, and asks whether the eclogue or the letter are capable of attaining *le sublime*, or only *le naïf* and *le délicat*. It can hardly be coincidental that La Bruyère chooses the same two terms which Bouhours had advanced in *La Manière de bien penser*; but whereas Eudoxe had rather patronisingly suggested that 'la délicatesse ajoûte je ne sçay quoi au sublime' (216), La Bruyère here reverses the proposition by suggesting with a leading question ('plutôt') that 'le naïf et le délicat' constitute merely a paler version of *le sublime* fit only for the lesser genres.

Boileau's distinction in the 'Préface' between *le sublime* and *le style sublime*— 'le Sublime *se peut* trouver dans une seule pensée, dans une seule figure, dans un seul tour de paroles' (my emphasis, 45)—leaves ambiguous the question of whether *le sublime* is appropriate to all genres, and it is this weakness which Bouhours had been able to exploit. Behind the feigned innocence of his questions, La Bruyère is obviously responding in the fourth edition of 1689 to Bouhours's work of 1687. (Litman's suggestion that La Bruyère is summing up the views of Bouhours is misguided.) Where Bouhours had tried to establish *le naïf* and *le délicat* as an alternative aesthetic to *le sublime* (thereby enfeebling the concept), La Bruyère insists on the supremacy of *le sublime* (again, in a fragment added in 1689):

> Le sublime ne peint que la vérité, mais en un sujet noble; il la peint tout entière, dans sa cause et dans son effet; il est l'expression ou l'image la plus digne de cette vérité. (90)

As the final clause of this sentence makes clear, *le sublime* is concerned with ultimate truth; *le naïf*, it is implied, cannot aspire to these heights. This concern with 'l'expression la plus digne de la vérité' has also a neoplatonist resonance, and other additions to the 1689 edition reinforce this identification with Boileau's theory of *le sublime*. This is most notable in a fragment in 'De la chaire' underlining the need for *enthousiasme* in pulpit rhetoric:

> Un prédicateur devrait [...] se livrer [...] à son génie et au mouvement qu'un grand sujet peut inspirer [...]; jeter [...] par un bel enthousiasme, la persuasion dans les esprits et l'alarme dans le cœur, et toucher ses auditeurs d'une toute autre crainte que celle de le voir demeurer court. (457)

The word *sublime* may not appear here, but the description recalls Boileau-Longinus none the less. From the first, *Les Caractères* presented a view of poetic language typical of the Ancients, but the fourth edition of *Les Caractères* marks a decisive contribution to the debate about *le sublime*, rebutting Bouhours's notion of *la délicatesse* and reaffirming the idea of the biblical sublime as envisaged by Boileau, Bossuet, Fleury and Fénelon.

IV. CONCLUSION

No attempt has been made here to provide an exhaustive description of the discussions concerning the sublime prompted by the *Traité du sublime*, but enough has been said to form some general conclusions about the pattern of that debate. It is evident first of all that the *Traité du sublime* had an enormous impact on contemporary opinion. Brossette acknowledges the repercussions the work had had in a letter to Boileau in 1708:

> Votre traduction mérite de grands éloges, non-seulement par elle-même, mais parce qu'elle a donné lieu à quantité d'excellens Ouvrages que plusieurs savans ont fait depuis ce temps, sur Longin; et je ne craindrai point d'en dire trop en assurant que Longin est plus connu dans le monde par votre Traduction, qu'il ne l'étoit auparavant par lui-même.[47]

Certain of the central ideas of the *Traité du sublime* were earlier current in writers (notably Fleury) associated with the *académie Lamoignon*. The great success of the *Traité du sublime* seems to have been to crystallise those ideas in one all-embracing term: *le sublime*. The speed with which the term gained common acceptance suggests that it corresponded very precisely to a perceived contemporary need. Other critical terms which were tried out by Bouhours, *le je ne sais quoi* (pre-1674), and *la délicatesse* (post-1674), failed to make a comparable impact, partly because they were less inclusive, partly because they lacked the inestimable advantage (in the eyes of the Ancients anyway) of being legitimised by an author of antiquity.

Paradoxically, however, the very success of the *Traité du sublime* in promoting discussion of *le sublime* worked also to confuse or adulterate the definition of the concept: the profusion of critics who took up the term produced a profusion of definitions and alleged clarifications. Among the many minor authors who discuss *le sublime*, we may take as an example the abbé Morvan de Bellegarde (1648-1734), a prolific author whose writings include works on the Bible (for example, *Réflexions sur la Genèse*, 1699) and many translations of Christian writers. He was a disciple of Bouhours, and although he left the Jesuits after seventeen years as a member of the Society—apparently because of his attachment to cartesianism—he sides clearly with the Ancients; in his *Lettres curieuses de littérature et de morale* (1702), for instance, he defends Homer by criticising those who apply modern notions of *vraisemblance* and the *bienséances* to earlier periods.

The earlier *Réflexions sur l'élégance et la politesse du stile* (1695) contain a section 'Du stile sublime' (375-85). He quotes at length the passage from Boileau's 'belle preface' on the distinction between the sublime and the sublime style, including the *fiat lux* example, but he does not seem to have understood Boileau's argument, and in the examples which he goes on to give (drawn mainly from Racine, Tallemant des Réaux and Fléchier) he appears to equate the *sublime* essentially with nobility of expression; he even finds an instance of the sublime in Fontenelle's *discours de réception*. When in 1705 Bellegarde published an anthology of *pensées choisies* arranged alphabetically by subject (including an entry 'Sublime'), he entitled it *Le Sublime des auteurs*. We can only guess what Boileau's response might have been to this ultimate trivialisation of the critical term he had shaped. Nowhere in his voluminous writings does Bellegarde ever express an original thought on the subject of *le sublime*, and therein lies the interest of his contribution. It is a mark of the success of Boileau's *Traité du sublime* that by the end of the century *le sublime* had become established in the literary critical canon of the Ancients. Bellegarde had nothing new to say about *le sublime*, but evidently felt duty-bound to discuss the term—a back-handed compliment to Boileau, since Bellegarde so manifestly misunderstood the central thrust of the *Traité du sublime*.

Bellegarde may not have grasped the theory underlying *le sublime*, but he was anxious to display the credentials appropriate to an Ancient, and it is clear that those who participated in the debate about *le sublime* were Ancients rather than Moderns. This generalisation needs to be hedged in three ways, however.

Firstly, the discussion concerning the *sublime* is not a concerted debate about Boileau's critical thought. Some authors (such as La Bruyère) seem to misunderstand

Boileau, some (Bossuet) seize on particular aspects of his thought, some (Rapin) develop the idea of the *sublime* in entirely new directions. Perhaps not surprisingly, the single most radical component of Boileau's critical thought—his commitment to a neoplatonist theory of poetic fury—remained undiscussed: either it had been mis-understood, or it was doubted, or simply it was still thought too contentious. The debate about the sublime grew haphazardly away from Boileau's original ideas.

Secondly, debate about the sublime was not confined to the ranks of the An-cients but affected rhetorical and artistic theory more widely: both Bernard Lamy and Roger de Piles adopted and absorbed certain of Boileau's ideas, as did (in a quite different domain) Le Maître de Sacy.

Thirdly, there are opponents of the *sublime*, or at least of Boileau's conception of it, even within the ranks of the Ancients (Dacier, Huet, Bouhours).

Are there perhaps other approaches to these debates which would show more clearly the cohesion and allegiances of the various parties? It seems difficult to iden-tify with any precision a religious dimension to discussion of the sublime: a number of the participants in the *académie Lamoignon* appear to have had Jansenist leanings, but of course not all—the Jesuit Rapin is an obvious counter-example. The Jesuit–Jansenist controversy is more evident in the writings of Bouhours than of Boileau. None the less, the aesthetic of the sublime as exemplified by the Jansenist Le Maître de Sacy might be seen as a continuation in a different form of the Calvinist aesthetic of simplicity.[48]

Another line of approach might be to look for some political or social dimen-sion to the discussion of *le sublime*. The alliance between Boileau and Racine was grounded, at least in contemporary public perception, in their attachment to the Court: this seems to fit with A. Niderst's view of the *Querelle* as a struggle between a Versailles or Court party (the Ancients), and a Paris party (the Moderns), a view he supports with a remark from Fontenelle's *Eloge de Malézieu* quoted above. The extensive comments, recently discovered, of Boileau and Racine on Perrault's *Epître au Roi* clearly reaffirm—if it were necessary—the political rivalry which existed between the two factions.[49] It is not at all evident, however, that the political differences be-tween Versailles and Paris help to illuminate the literary debate. This impression is confirmed by a more recent study of Niderst's which attempts to refine this political opposition, in which he surprisingly ranks Fleury with the Moderns, on account of his political allegiance to Colbert.[50]

There are also perhaps certain institutional divisions between the two parties. While the Moderns seem to have scored a number of successes in the various struggles to elect their supporters to the Académie française, the more 'scholarly' Académie des Inscriptions et des Belles-Lettres was apparently more favourable to *le sublime*. Nor, finally, can we ignore the purely personal tensions latent in the *Querelle*. The full extent of these private antagonisms is imperfectly understood but, for example, Soriano has shown ('Les contes gais') how Boileau and Perrault exchange scarcely-veiled insults concerning the former's impotence and the latter's homosexuality, and all in the course of dutiful discussion of *le sublime*.

Such antagonisms emphasise the divide between the two sides in the *Querelle*; they do not however illuminate the notion of *le sublime*, which is best understood as the crucial episode in a debate about the nature of poetic discourse. The passage from the *Eloge de Malézieu* quoted above is interesting for the way in which it shows how a Modern, Fontenelle, groups together so insistently the names of Racine, Boileau, La Bruyère and Bossuet, the old *cabale du sublime*. It confirms at least the notion of a correlation between the Ancients and those critics and authors interested in the *sublime* (though the linking of their names predates the *Traité du sublime*, since it goes back to the *académie Lamoignon*).

Adam is therefore surely correct in proposing a link between the Ancients and the *sublime*, but the proposal is misleading unless heavily qualified. When Litman, following Adam, writes that 'le sublime devint donc une question centrale de la querelle des Anciens et des Modernes' (240), he implies a simple equation between adherents of the sublime and supporters of the Ancients which underestimates the true complexity of the situation. It is certainly true that most writers on the sublime are to some degree associated with the Ancients, but the Ancients, as we have seen, are not united and are not uniformly partisans of the sublime—being an Ancient is a necessary condition for being interested in *le sublime*, but not a sufficient one. This alone is not enough to support the idea that *le sublime* is at the heart of the *Querelle*. To argue that, it is necessary also to demonstrate that the Moderns set out deliberately to oppose the poetic theory of the Ancients.

NOTES

[1.] *Conversations sur la connoissance de la peinture*, pp. 42-43.

[2.] See Adam, *Histoire*, III, pp. 152-53; and Picard, *Carrière de Jean Racine*, pp. 262-65.

[3.] Adam, *Histoire*, V, p. 76. This claim is echoed, but not explained further, by Theodore Litman: 'Sans nul doute, le sublime est à la base de la célèbre querelle' (*Le Sublime*, p. 161).

[4.] France, *Rhetoric and Truth*, Chap. 5.

[5.] *Nouvelles Remarques*, p. 98.

[6.] For example, *Nouvelles Remarques*, p. 25.

[7.] *Le Triomphe*, p. 22.

[8.] *Réponse à la Satire X*, pp. 3, 14.

[9.] *La Carrière de Jean Racine*, p. 264.

[10.] 'Racine's style', pp. 75-76.

[11.] *Remarques nouvelles*, p. 80.

[12.] 'Remarques', *TS*, p. 185.

[13.] *Œuvres*, II, p. 502.

[14.] *Parrhasiana*, p. 115.

[15.] *Rhétorique*, pp. 42-43; text of 1688 edition; this passage, and the whole chapter in which it occurs, are absent from the 1675 and 1676 editions.

[16.] See T. Puttfarken, *Roger de Piles' Theory of Art*, 'Enthusiasm, the Sublime, and the influence of Boileau', pp. 115-24.

[17.] *Cours de peinture par principes*, p. 120.

[18.] *Cours de peinture par principes*, pp. 114-17.

[19.] For example, pp. 280-81, 294-95.

[20.] See J. Le Brun, 'Le Père Pierre Lalemant et les débuts de l'Académie Lamoignon'. The 'Préface' to the 1683 edition of Boileau's *Œuvres diverses* contains a fulsome eulogy of Guillaume de Lamoignon, who had died in 1677; this 'Préface' reappeared in the editions of 1685 and 1694, then in 1701 in the 'Avis au Lecteur' preceding *Le Lutrin* (Boileau, Pléiade, pp. 189-90, 857). On Boileau's relations with the Premier Président, see Pléiade, p. 1007. Bussy-Rabutin and Rapin frequently discuss Guillaume de Lamoignon in their correspondence, always in the most flattering terms.

21. 'Some definitions', p. 77.

22. 24 juillet 1671; Bussy-Rabutin, *Correspondance*, 43-44.

23. 22 septembre 1672; *Correspondance*, 74.

24. 11 octobre 1672; *Correspondance*, 76.

25. *Œuvres*, II, p. 499.

26. Quoted in E. T. Dubois, 'Some definitions', p. 81.

27. See pp. 27, 42, 45, 49, 129.

28. *Histoire*, III, pp. 134-38.

29. III, p. 149.

30. Quoted in Niderst, *Fontenelle*, p. 365.

31. See O. Grosheintz, *L'Esthétique oratoire de Bossuet*; and J. Truchet, *La Prédication de Bossuet*, Chap. 3, 'Bossuet théoricien de l'éloquence sacrée'.

32. Quoted in Grosheintz, p. 21.

33. Quoted in Grosheintz, p. 41.

34. Quoted in Grosheintz, p. 23.

35. Quoted in Grosheintz, p. 39.

36. *Opuscules*, II, p. 640; Dubos was later to express a similar idea.

37. See Chap. 1, note 19.

38. II, p. 670.

39. *Opuscules*, II, pp. 647-48.

40. I, p. 535.

41. *Lettre*, pp. 42, 50, 75.

42. Quoted in Adam, *Histoire*, V, p. 93.

43. Pradon, *Nouvelles remarques*, pp. 9-10.

44. See Boileau, Pléiade, pp. 1105-06.

45. See pp. 107-08, 158-59, 168, 328, 371-72, 380.

46. 'Some definitions', p. 78.

47. *Correspondance entre Boileau et Brossette*, p. 275.

48. In the sixteenth century, simplicity of poetic style is generally regarded as a characteristic of Protestant writing (see M. Raymond, *L'Influence de Ronsard*, I, pp. 339-50). Calvin, in his advocacy of simple attic prose, forms part of the sixteenth-century anti-ciceronian movement; he supports this position with an essentially religious argument, that God's truth is embedded in the natural order of God's language: 'La langue est créée de Dieu pour exprimer la cogitation à ce que nous puissions communiquer ensemble. Pourtant, c'est pervertir l'ordre de Dieu de circuire par ambages à l'entour du pot pour faire rêver les auditeurs et les laisser dans un tel état' (quoted by L. Wencelius, *L'Esthétique de Calvin*, p. 345). For Calvin, the message of the Scriptures possesses a beauty and a power which has no need of the adornment of human rhetoric; the truth is self-evident: 'L'Escriture a de quoy se faire cognoistre, voire d'un sentiment aussi notoire et infaillible comme ont les choses blanches et noires de monstrer leur couleur, et les choses douces et amères de monstrer leur saveur' (*Institutes*, 1560; quoted by F. M. Higman, *Style of John Calvin*, p. 161). Wencelius concludes his study of Calvin's views on style with the suggestion that 'il y a quelque chose de calvinien dans l'idéal des Lettres du siècle de Louis XIV' (*L'Esthétique de Calvin*, p. 419), a view which has been often echoed. Clearly there are similarities between Calvin's aesthetic and Boileau's; but there are also fundamental differences. Calvin has an entirely utilitarian and didactic view of literature, and he sees the sole role of language as being to convey the truth as straightforwardly as possible—unlike Ronsard, he believes implicitly in nomenclaturism. This is precisely the view upheld by the Moderns, the view vehemently opposed by Boileau (see P. Burke, 'Two faces of Calvinism'). Calvin is not interested, as Boileau is, in the aesthetic dimension of simple poetic discourse; in the context of Protestant propaganda, simple everyday language is a means by which Calvin hopes to convey his message more effectively and more widely.

49. See Soriano, *La Brosse à reluire*.

50. 'Les Gens de Paris et les Gens de Versailles', pp. 164-65.

6: THE MODERNS AND THE COUNTER-SUBLIME

Les concerts de l'Opera ne sont que quelque apparence de son
dans la gorge de quelques femmes. (François Lamy)[1]

I. THE QUERELLE AND RECENT CRITICAL DEBATE

After many years during which the subject had been scarcely discussed, the
Querelle des anciens et des modernes began to attract renewed critical interest in the
last quarter of the twentieth century. In his *Crise de la littérature française sous Louis
XIV* (1976), Bernard Magné undertook a wide-ranging survey of French literature
from the 1660s to the end of Louis XIV's reign, including a detailed study and reinter-
pretation of the *Querelle*—perhaps the most significant treatment of this subject since
the (now outdated) works of Rigault and Gillot. Magné criticised these latter works
(694-95) for presenting the *Querelle* incoherently as a sequence of discontinuous
battles over disparate issues (inscriptions, *le merveilleux*, Homer); and he is equally
critical of the general notion that the *Querelle* is no more than the French facet of the
more widespread *crise de la conscience européenne* described by Paul Hazard.

Magné prefers to view the *Querelle* not as an appendage to the *grand siècle* but
as an ideological conflict having its roots in the 1660s, and so covering almost the
entire personal reign of Louis XIV (895-96). The triumph of French culture in this
period engenders an inevitable rivalry with the still-considerable prestige of the cul-
ture of the ancient world, and while the Ancients defend the values of humanism, it is
left to the Moderns to extol the virtues of nationalism in the cause of what Magné
terms 'cette idéologie royale-nationale' (893). From this ideology, literature cannot
be exempt:

> La solution humaniste n'est plus adaptée aux réalités
> contemporaines, car elle est devenue incompatible avec l'idéologie
> dominante. La suprématie absolue du monarque et de la nation ne
> tolère aucun domaine réservé. Elle exige que dans la poétique aussi
> ait lieu une révision des valeurs. (898)

Magné is insistent that those who would see in the *Querelle* the reflection of some
wider philosophical opposition are simply the dupes of this royal ideology. The *Querelle*
is about literature, he says, not about philosophy:

Osons exiger le retour aux textes, à tous les textes, du moins à tous les textes repérables, qui nous rappellent d'emblée une évidence: la discussion n'est pas philosophique, elle est littéraire. Elle porte sur la langue, sur les diverses formes du discours littéraire ou, comme on disait alors, sur l'éloquence et sur la poésie, sur les œuvres écrites et à écrire. Tout le reste, c'est-à-dire les autres disciplines artistiques, et surtout les sciences et les techniques, ne vaut que comme preuve ou exemple. La question *de fond* peut schématiquement s'énoncer ainsi: étant donné qu'il existe dans les ouvrages de l'esprit un point de perfection, quand et par qui a-t-il été atteint? La réponse des humanistes du siècle précédent reste encore valable pour les Anciens et l'abbé du *Parallèle* la résume parfaitement: 'Les vrais amateurs des anciens assurent qu'ils ont atteint la dernière perfection' (I, 12). Au contraire, les Modernes placent cette dernière perfection sous le règne de Louis XIV. (897-98)

To deny flatly, as Magné does, the view that the Moderns are 'des opposants discrets au régime' is to contradict an interpretation of long standing. Alain Niderst, however, has recently reasserted the traditional view that the Moderns were in opposition to the King, and pointing to the political and social divisions dividing the two camps, he argues that the *Querelle* was founded on rivalry between *la Cour* and *la Ville*. The partisans of the sublime, the Ancients, were known in a contemporary phrase as the 'gens de Versailles', yet Magné suggests they are in opposition to the Versailles ideology; Perrault, on the other hand, supposedly a supporter of the new ideological régime, could not have appeared at Versailles: 'Les Perrault, exilés de Versailles depuis 1680, et les adversaires de la politique actuelle du roi, avaient des motifs de s'unir contre les thuriféraires du Pouvoir'.[2] Niderst has since refined his thesis with a suggestion that in the years 1678-1686 the Ancients (including Bossuet and Mme de Maintenon) were part of a clan supporting the minister Louvois, while the Moderns may be identified with the clan which supported his rival Colbert.[3]

The connection between the party of the Ancients and the Court was in fact to become closer: the 'Messieurs du sublime', Boileau and Racine, were appointed *historiographes du roi* by the King in 1677. The task of recording for posterity the history of his reign was one to which the King naturally attached great importance; there was considerable jostling for the post, and much resentment directed against the two bourgeois on whom the choice eventually fell.[4] They themselves do not appear to have felt any contradiction between their admiration of the literature of antiquity and their glorification, through literature, of the contemporary royal régime; Magné makes no mention of the fact that Louis chose two of the most prominent Ancients to glorify his reign. The ideological divide which Magné claims to exist between Ancients and Moderns is perhaps too simply drawn to be totally plausible.

On the question of *le sublime* Magné maintains that Litman's thesis is 'incomplète et inexacte' (766) because it accords too much importance to what he sees as a single thread in a much wider debate:

> Ainsi, pour Th. Litman, la Querelle, loin de refléter une interrogation générale sur le rôle de la littérature ancienne dans la culture moderne, n'apparaît plus que comme un cas particulier du débat sur le sublime, qui devient la notion à partir de quoi tout s'ordonne. Ce renversement de perspective, outre qu'il n'explique en rien l'existence de la Querelle sous le règne personnel de Louis XIV, conduit à surestimer l'importance du sublime, en tant qu'il exprime les valeurs, ou certaines valeurs, défendues par les Anciens, et, inversement, à sous-estimer la force du courant moderniste. Voir dans toute cette période une montée, et même un triomphe du sublime, quelque peu contrarié par les attaques rationalistes des Perrault, Fontenelle et autres La Motte, c'est donner une image renversée du réel [...].
>
> Ce n'est qu'en étudiant sa fonction au sein de la crise de l'humanisme qu'on peut retrouver les significations du sublime, qui apparaît alors, pour l'essentiel, comme une tentative pour réhabiliter une littérature gréco-latine violemment contestée par les Modernes au nom d'une vérité intellectuelle et morale dont le xvıı^e siècle est le dernier dépositaire. (766-67)

Magné's argument has been quoted at length, since this chapter will endeavour to defend a different interpretation, one which attributes a much greater importance to the role of *le sublime* in the *Querelle*. In order to make out a convincing case for a *Querelle du sublime*, it is necessary firstly to show exactly (as Litman does not) how the Moderns attempted to refute Boileau's theory of *le sublime*.

Secondly, in order to make sense of this attack, this chapter will seek to locate these discussions in a broader context of debate about the nature of literary language. Magné's interpretation, situating the *Querelle* in a wide-ranging opposition between humanism and nationalism, is strikingly inconsistent in one respect. He insists that the *Querelle* is in essence literary, and castigates critics for overlooking this fact and for viewing it in grand philosophical terms; yet when he comes to consider *le sublime* he makes no real mention of the concept as a theory of literary language, and instead proposes to view it 'au sein de la crise de l'humanisme'—precisely the kind of explanation by broad generalisation that he warns against elsewhere.

II. FONTENELLE

We tend not to think of Fontenelle primarily as a poetic theorist: his longevity and his eighteenth-century fame as Secretary of the Académie des Sciences obscure his seventeenth-century career as a man of letters. Niderst, however, draws attention to the importance and complexity of this early phase of Fontenelle's literary career. A poet before he was a philosopher, he collaborated with Thomas Corneille in two opera librettos, and wrote two plays, a comedy and a tragedy. The list of his works dealing with, or at least touching upon the subject of poetry, is extensive: *Description de l'empire de la poésie, Sur la poésie en général, Réflexions sur la poétique, Discours sur la nature de l'églogue, De l'origine des fables*, and *Digression sur les Anciens et les Modernes.*

It comes as a surprise to discover how little *le sublime* is discussed in this large corpus of works; despite the acclaim which had greeted Boileau's *Traité du sublime*, the work is scarcely mentioned by Fontenelle. There are, in the writings listed above, a total of only four occurrences of the word *sublime*; each use of the term is casual and pejorative in intent. In his *Description* (published in the *Mercure galant*, 1678), a rather laboured allegorical description of the poetical terrain, Fontenelle speaks of 'des montagnes de la rêverie. Ces montagnes ont quelques pointes si élevées, qu'elles donnent presque dans les nues. On les appelle les *pointes des penseés sublimes*' (III, 32). In the *Eglogue*, Fontenelle is critical of Ronsard for choosing the eclogue as a form by which to praise princes 'dans tout le sublime dont on est capable' (III, 62), meaning, in context, an exaggerated and overblown style. Arguing in *Poésie* that, to use fabulous images correctly, the poet must innovate, Fontenelle exclaims: 'Notre sublime consistera-t-il toujours à rentrer dans les idées des plus anciens Grecs encore sauvages' (III, 41); and a few pages later, 'Combien de choses sublimes [la poésie] n'a-t-elle pas dites sur le souverain Etre, le plus inaccessible de tous aux efforts de l'esprit humain' (III, 46)—for once, the use of *sublime* is not obviously pejorative, but the term is employed here to describe subject-matter rather than poetic style, and in the context of a discussion of poetry as 'la difficulté vaincue'.

In none of the examples cited does Fontenelle refer to Boileau's *sublime*. In *Poésie*, he uses the term loosely to refer to elevated writing, while in the earlier examples, referring to overblown diction, and to sublimity of thought (as opposed to sublimity of style), the term *sublime* is used precisely as it had always been used prior to Boileau. Such a conspicuous avoidance of Boileau's re-definition of the term is surprising, and suspicious.

On one occasion only does Fontenelle openly discuss *le sublime*, in the 'Préface' to the *Histoire des oracles* (1686), when he is speaking of his own style:

> Les matières que j'avais en main m'ont invité à une manière d'écrire
> fort éloignée du sublime. Il me semble qu'il ne faudrait donner
> dans le sublime qu'à son corps défendant; il est si peu naturel. (II,
> 90)

The discussion is brief enough, but the implicit dismissal of Boileau's theory of *le sublime* is evident: to speak of the *sublime* as 'peu naturel' is to ignore the whole thrust of the *Traité du sublime* and its emphasis on the idea of forceful simplicity.

Even so, one single sentence of near-explicit criticism in the whole corpus of Fontenelle's writings on poetic theory hardly constitutes an all-out attack on Boileau's theory of the sublime. Much more remarkable is the fact that on the frequent occasions when he discusses the power of elevated language, Fontenelle skirts around *le sublime* and avoids using the word. In the *Description*, for example, Fontenelle speaks slightingly of 'la haute poésie':

> La haute poésie est habitée par des gens graves, mélancoliques,
> renfrognés, et qui parlent un langage qui est, à l'égard des autres
> provinces de la poésie, ce qu'est le bas-breton pour le reste de la
> France. Tous les arbres de la haute poésie portent leurs têtes jusques
> dans les nues. (III, 31)

'La haute poésie' is manifestly 'la poésie sublime' by another name ('high' being the literal translation of the Greek *hupsos*); the avoidance of the word *sublime* is all the more extraordinary when we recall that the *Description* appeared just four years after the *Traité du sublime*. These elevated poets are mocked for being serious and difficult to understand, and high-flown metaphor is made the defining characteristic of the high style; in both these respects, Fontenelle's high style is of course at odds with the sublime style, clear and simple, advocated by Boileau. Fontenelle can hardly be unaware of this. The passage can only be read as a (not very) veiled attack on Boileau, an attack all the more devastating because its object remains unnamed throughout.

Certainly it is in this sense that Alain Niderst reads the above passage, on the basis of 'internal' evidence.[5] The reading is only confirmed by the presence elsewhere in Fontenelle's writings of this same technique of strategic omission. One example occurs at the beginning of the *Réflexions sur la poétique*, where the idea that there exists 'un certain art de plaire qui est au-dessus de tout' is treated with scorn:

> Mais qu'est-ce que cet art de plaire? Il ne se définit point: on l'attrape
> par hasard; on n'est pas sûr de le rencontrer deux fois; enfin, c'est
> une espèce de magie tout-à-fait inconnue. (III, 1)

This view is of course in contrast with the claims of Boileau-Longinus that '[le Sublime] produit en nous une certaine admiration mêlée d'étonnement et de surprise, qui est toute autre chose que de plaire seulement' (50). The attack on Boileau is two-pronged: Fontenelle first mischievously equates any aesthetic seeking to transcend the rules with 'un art de plaire'; and having distorted Boileau's *sublime*, he then proceeds to ridicule it.

The same rhetorical sleight of hand is evident in *De l'origine des fables*, when Fontenelle describes how the first men, out of ignorance, saw miracles everywhere:

> A mesure que l'on est plus ignorant, et que l'on a moins
> d'expérience, on voit plus de prodiges. Les premiers hommes en
> virent donc beaucoup [...]. Quand nous racontons quelque chose
> de surprenant, notre imagination s'échauffe sur son objet, et se
> porte d'elle-même à l'agrandir et à y ajouter ce qui y manquerait
> pour le rendre tout-à-fait merveilleux, comme si elle avait regret
> de laisser une belle chose imparfaite. De plus on est flatté des
> sentimens de surprise et d'admiration que l'on cause à ses auditeurs;
> et on est bien aise de les augmenter encore, parce qu'il semble
> qu'il en revient je ne sais quoi à notre vanité. (II, 388-89)

We are reminded here irresistibly of Boileau's definition of *le sublime*: 'Il faut donc entendre par Sublime dans Longin, l'Extraordinaire, le Surprenant, et comme je l'ai traduit, le Merveilleux dans le discours' (46). Fontenelle has taken over the terms 'surprenant' (also 'surprise') and 'merveilleux', but attributing to them a sense entirely opposed to that intended by Boileau; there is, of course, no mention of *le sublime*.

III. PERRAULT

Fontenelles's technique of indirect attack is anticipated in Charles Perrault's first significant piece on poetic theory, *Le Génie: Epistre à M. de Fontenelle* (1686). The poem employs numerous phrases which at first sight appear consonant with the idea of *le sublime* ('ce beau feu', 'cette divine flamme', 'une sainte fureur', 172-73), but which on closer inspection turn out to be critical commonplaces describing a more 'rational' literary aesthetic. The word *sublime* occurs once only, near the beginning of the poem ('les figures sublimes', 172), and in an unmistakably pejorative context—a clear snub to the *Traité du sublime*.[6]

If Fontenelle's *Description* is the first attack by a Modern on the *Traité du sublime*, the major polemical work of the Moderns is still Perrault's *Parallèle des anciens et des modernes* (1688-97), and so we turn naturally to this manifesto if we are trying to measure the prominence of *le sublime* in the *Querelle*. Cast as a dialogue between the Chevalier, the Abbé (both Moderns) and the Président (an Ancient), the second part (1690) of this four-part work deals entirely with the subject of eloquence, while the third (1692) is devoted exclusively to poetry, including a stinging attack on Homer.

Litman asserts with confidence that the conception of the sublime plays an important role in Perrault's thought (161); the Ancients sought to make the sublime invulnerable, he claims, by placing it 'beyond the rules', and the Moderns needed therefore to expose the hollowness of this pretension by establishing a rule-based poetics: 'Pour Perrault,' writes Litman, 'le sublime représente surtout une menace redoutable pour sa théorie du progrès dans l'art de la poésie' (169). Litman cites a number of passages from the *Parallèle* in support of this claim. The Abbé, for example, denies that inspiration is essential to the epic poem: 'Car il ne faut pas s'imaginer que le talent de faire d'excellens vers, ny mesme l'enthousiasme dont on veut que soient saisis ceux qui les font, ayent seuls fait donner un nom si honorable à ce genre de Poésie' (III, 94). Later, the Chevalier is critical of odes which, in the 'ancient manner', eschew regularity and finish with a different subject from the one with which they had started: 'Il y a long-temps que je suis choqué de cette maniere antique, quoy qu'on dise qu'il y a de l'enthousiasme, et une espece de transport divin à en user ainsi' (III, 179).

Litman's interpretation of these and similar passages is open to challenge on two fronts. Firstly, the opposition between rules and inspiration, that is, between art and nature, is hardly an original one, and goes back to the Renaissance and to classical antiquity. This distinction alone can hardly explain the keenness of the debate between Perrault and Boileau. Secondly, Litman fails to comment on the fact that in only one of the passages which he quotes as attacks on the sublime is the word *sublime* actually used. Elsewhere, as in the passages quoted above, we find such terms as *enthousiasme* or *transport divin*; it is highly tendentious to assume as Litman does—and as Perrault would have wanted him to do—that these are synonymous with *sublime*.

Perrault's general opposition to the notion of poetic enthusiasm is evident, but it is necessary to consider the precise ways in which the term *sublime* is used in the *Parallèle*. The first occurrence is in a discussion of the rhetoric of Demosthenes, when the interlocutors discuss the opening lines of the *Fourth Philippic*, not perhaps an especially noteworthy choice.[7] The Président, as spokesman of the Ancients, predictably emphasises the power of simplicity in the passage: 'Admirons la simplicité majestueuse qui regne dans les ouvrages de Demosthene, preferable mille fois à toute l'abondance et à tous les ornemens de ceux qui l'ont suivy' (II, 173).[8] The Abbé retorts that there are two kinds of simplicity, a type which results from poverty of invention as well as the forceful kind described by the Président, and that 'la simplicité de Demosthene que nous venons de voir n'est point majestueuse' (II, 173). Furthermore, the Abbé argues, even if this simplicity had been successfully achieved, it would still not have been appropriate in the circumstances of the present speech, which requires something more grandiloquent.

> Quand on voudra examiner de près ce que nous avons leu de Demosthene, on trouvera que la mauvaise mediocrité y a plus de part que la bonne, mais quand elle seroit toute excellente et de la bonne espece, je dis qu'il falloit autre chose que de la simplicité dans un discours aussi celebre, qui se prononçoit devant le peuple d'Athenes, et où il s'agissoit de la plus importante de ses affaires. Il falloit là du *sublime* et de l'heroique, où pouvoit-il plus à propos deployer les grandes voiles de l'Eloquence, et employer ses plus nobles figures et ses plus beaux ornemens. La grande Eloquence a toûjours esté comparée ou à un grand Fleuve ou à un Torrent, et jamais à un petit Ruisseau qui n'humecte qu'à peine son lit et ses rivages. (my emphasis; II, 180-81)

The arguments of the Abbé, that there are good and bad forms of simple expression, and that sometimes even successful simplicity is inappropriate, are implicitly hostile to Boileau's theory of the sublime, according to which the greatest expressivity may be achieved through simplicity. In effect, this is the view that the Président begins to put rather tentatively before being overwhelmed by the Abbé's response; but he is not permitted to use the word *sublime*. Indeed, when the term does occur, it is in the mouth of the Abbé, a Modern, and he uses the word to refer to inflated diction, almost as a synonym for *enflure*—that is, in a sense entirely opposed to that of Boileau-Longinus. Perrault is scoring a debating point at Boileau's expense, and he does this not only by offering a theory of poetic language which is clearly at variance with Boileau's own, but also by wilfully affecting to ignore Boileau's redefinition of the term *sublime*, and continuing to employ the word in its traditional sense.

The second occurrence of the word *sublime* is again in the mouth of a Modern. After discussing passages from Demosthenes and Cicero, the Abbé proposes that they consider an example drawn from a contemporary orator, and he quotes a long passage from Le Maître. 'Voilà qui me plaist,' exclaims the Chevalier, 'voilà qui me remplit l'esprit agreablement, et voilà comme je veux que l'on parle, cela est abondant sans estre diffus, sublime sans estre obscur et vigoureux sans estre emporté' (II, 245). Where Boileau had advocated a style of poetic language which would bowl over the astonished reader with its emotional force, what the Chevalier here seems to be espousing is something altogether more modest, a style which is pleasing, clear and moderate; again, the term *sublime* is used to refer to an aesthetic which is emphatically not Boileau's. Thus in the whole of the third dialogue, which is devoted exclusively to eloquence, the spokesman of the Ancients never once pronounces the word *sublime*. Indeed, the term is only used twice, once by each of the Moderns, and on both occasions it quite unambiguously signifies a poetic aesthetic opposed to Boileau's theory of the sublime.

References to the sublime are scarcely more abundant in the following (fourth) dialogue, devoted to poetry. The term first appears, not unexpectedly, in a long discussion of Homer. After detailing the Greek poet's various transgressions, the Abbé consents—in deference to the views of the Président—to consider what are thought to be among Homer's finest lines, and they agree to examine those passages selected for praise by Longinus. 'Je ne puis pas refuser cette proposition;' says the Président, 'Longin est un trop grand personnage, pour ne pas approuver son choix' (III, 117). The gullible Président has of course been lured into a trap: almost all of Longinus's quotations of Homer occur in Chapter 7, 'De la Sublimité dans les pensées', which examines thoughts extraordinarily conceived and expressed—only one facet of the Longinian sublime, and certainly not a prime characteristic of Boileau's *sublime* either. To compound the distortion, the Abbé then selects only two of the ten or so Homeric passages discussed in the treatise, and on the basis of this highly selective sample, he argues that both passages contain absurdly exaggerated images. The first describes the goddess Discord as having her head in heaven and her feet on earth, the second compares the leap of the gods' horses to the distance a man can see looking out from the coast. 'Voilà une chose bien mal-aisée,' says the Chevalier self-contentedly, 'que de faire des exagerations de la nature de celles que Longin donne pour des modeles du sublime' (III, 119).

The word *sublime* occurs three times in these discussions (III, 117, 119, 121), always with reference to the two Homeric images which are comprehensively criticised, and it inevitably takes on a pejorative colouring. The Président, were he more than a token Ancient, might have pointed out to his two interlocutors that the two examples selected are untypical of those found elsewhere in Longinus, and highly misleading with regard to Boileau's discussions of *le sublime*. He might further have pointed out that, though the name of Boileau is never uttered, the quotation of the two examples from Homer is taken word for word from Boileau's translation of Longinus.[9] In the event, it is left to Boileau himself to indicate to Perrault this unacknowledged quotation in the fourth *Réflexion critique.*

The only two other occurrences of the word *sublime* are when discussion turns to lyric poetry and so to Pindar. The Abbé opens the attack:

> Il faut croire qu'il est bien sublime, puisque personne n'y peut atteindre, soit pour l'imiter, comme dit Horace, soit pour l'entendre, comme dit Jean Benoist l'un de ses plus excellens Interpretes, qui assure qu'avant luy les plus savans hommes n'y ont presque rien compris; et qui a fait voir par ses interpretations forcées, qu'il n'y entend rien non plus que les autres. (III, 160-61)

To which the Président replies, rather feebly:

> Vous voyez cependant la reputation que Pindare s'est acquise jusques dans les derniers temps, où pindariser signifie, dire les choses d'une maniere noble et sublime. (III, 161)

The Abbé's use of *sublime*, equating it with incomprehensibility, is obviously ironic and inaccurate. More damaging to Boileau's cause is the inadequacy of the so-called Ancient's reply: the Président falls back limply on tradition, using the term *sublime* in an undefined way which fails to distinguish his sense from the deliberately fraudulent non-sense of the Abbé.

Litman is clearly correct in identifying Perrault as an opponent of the aesthetic of *le sublime*, but he never explains how this opposition is articulated. In most of the examples that he cites as hostile to the sublime, the word *sublime* does not even occur: the absence of any sustained treatment of *le sublime* is precisely one of the most surprising features of the *Parallèle*. In a work which devotes six hundred pages to matters of poetry and eloquence, and was published only some fifteen years after the *Traité du sublime* which had provoked such widespread debate, we would naturally expect the sublime to figure largely in the discussion, if only to be refuted. There is, instead, a conspiracy of silence. Even the word *sublime* occurs on only seven occasions in the entire book, and only once in the mouth of the 'Ancient'; and when the term is used, it is in a sense different from Boileau's, referring pejoratively to Homer or mocking the linguistic density of Pindar.

This does not mean that the *Traité du sublime* is ignored. The example of Pindar had also been discussed by Longinus, in Chapter 29 (indeed, it was Boileau who first identified the verse quoted as being from Pindar), while the examples from Homer are, as we have seen, quoted verbatim from Boileau's translation. These oblique references to the *Traité du sublime* occur always at those moments when the term *sublime* is being deliberately misused, so as to constitute an indirect attack on Boileau. More powerful still is the invisible attack elsewhere in the *Parallèle*, where Perrault contrives to talk of poetry and eloquence at great length without ever using the word *sublime*. Given the extent of contemporary debate, this silence can only be seen as a deliberate strategy.

Fontenelle and Perrault thus emerge as the two principal contemporary antagonists of Boileau's theory of *le sublime*. They share not only a common cause but also a common strategy. Both authors affect to disregard the *sublime* in their writings, and make only passing, and usually pejorative, reference to the concept. This critique of the sublime is a powerful one. To have attacked the *Traité du sublime* head-on would have embroiled Fontenelle and Perrault in discussion of a classical author who manifestly had great merits as a critic. By instead discussing poetry and eloquence over many pages without ever having recourse to the word *sublime*, Fontenelle and Perrault aim to demonstrate that the term is redundant, a decorative but dispensable frill deployed by the Ancients to add mystique to their creed. It is obviously more damaging to Boileau's cause, and more effective as propaganda, to show *le sublime* to be an irrelevance than to try to argue that the concept is ill-conceived or ill-defined. Both Fontenelle and Perrault opt to counter Boileau's theory of the sublime with a strategic silence.

IV. BOILEAU'S REPLY: *RÉFLEXIONS CRITIQUES I-IX*

Boileau's *Œuvres diverses* were frequently republished, and in 1694, twenty years after the first edition, they were reprinted in a two-volume edition greatly enlarged by the addition of new works: the *Satire X*, the *Ode sur la prise de Namur*, eight epigrams, and a series of nine *Réflexions critiques sur Longin*. The full title of the *Réflexions* makes clear that they are a response to Perrault: *Réflexions critiques sur quelques passages du rhéteur Longin où, par occasion, on répond à quelques objections de Monsieur P*** contre Homère et contre Pindare*. Critics have paid little attention to this work, generally dismissing it as an ephemeral piece of polemic: 'A proprement parler,' says Rigault, 'les *Réflexions sur Longin* sont un répertoire des bévues de Perrault. Boileau n'y aborde aucune question, n'y soutient aucune doctrine' (250).

At first approach, this work appears to be a sustained attack on Perrault and in no sense a reflection upon Longinus. Each *réflexion* begins with a sentence taken from Boileau's own translation of Longinus, but in every case the particular passage selected is intrinsically unimportant, even trivial, and serves only as a pretext to launch an aggressive discussion. Antipathy between Boileau and Perrault stretched back over a number of years;[10] Boileau was clearly smarting at Perrault's remarks in the *Parallèle*, and he devotes much energy in the *Réflexions* to the scoring of return points. He chides Perrault for not taking the advice of his friends before publishing the *Parallèle* (55-56); in response to Perrault, he defends—sometimes in excessive detail—particular criticisms he had levelled against Scudéry or Saint-Amant (59-60, 85); he even attacks Charles Perrault's brother, Claude. Above all, Boileau repeatedly and mercilessly exposes Perrault's ignorance of Greek and his imperfect grasp of Latin by analysing carefully certain of the passages from ancient authors which are scrutinised in the *Parallèle*. 'Ainsi voilà plus de vingt bévûes que Monsieur P. a faites sur le seul passage d'Elien,' (66) exclaims Boileau at one point, and he begins the 'Conclusion': 'Voilà un leger échantillon du nombre infini de fautes, que Monsieur P. a commises en voulant attaquer les défauts des Anciens' (110). Throughout the *Réflexions* he refers to Perrault as 'le Censeur', he ridicules him for his lack of scholarship, and, in self-defence as much as attack, he uses a quotation from Régnier to suggest that a true pedant is someone who criticises authors he cannot properly understand.

The scholarly scrap is of strictly limited interest, but an important question remains: in what sense are these *Réflexions sur Longin*? The title of the work leads us to expect some consideration of *le sublime*, especially since the work, in the 1694 edition, was placed immediately after the *Traité du sublime*. But there is no discussion of *le sublime* as such; and even the word *sublime* only occurs on a couple of occasions: Boileau speaks in passing of 'sublimes figures' (101) in Pindar, and of 'les endroits les plus sublimes' (105) in referring to elevated subject matter, but that is all. When, elsewhere, he speaks of Quinault, Boileau prefers to use a different word altogether: 'Ces vers n'estoient pas d'une grande force ni d'une grande élévation' (67). Is Rigault right then to see this work as nothing more than a polemical pamphlet?

Closer examination suggests that there are traces of earlier debates that transcend the purely polemical. To begin with, there is the curious fact that the *Réflexions* are not really about Longinus and apparently make no mention of the *sublime*. We have already seen how Perrault in the *Parallèle* had used an indirect means of attacking *le sublime*, and it seems that Boileau answers irony of form with irony of form, matching Perrault's elliptical attack with an equally elliptical response. Boileau is clearly sensitive to Perrault's devious use of the dialogue form, for he comments on it explicitly in the *Réflexions* (86-87); so we are warned to expect an equally devious response. The title *Réflexions sur Longin* is deliberately ironic.

The substance of the attack on Perrault and the *Parallèle* is contained in Boileau's discussions of Homer (*Réflexions III, IV, V, IX*) and of Pindar (*Réflexion VIII*). Perrault had of course cited many other classical writers (including Plato, Demosthenes, Cicero, Horace, Terence and Virgil) in the course of the *Parallèle*, but Boileau limits his remarks to just two authors; moreover he draws attention to this fact in the 'Conclusion': 'Je n'ay mis icy que [les fautes] qui regardent Homere et Pindare' (110). It was precisely in discussing these two authors, and only these two, that Perrault had had occasion to use—or more accurately, to misuse—the term *sublime*. These passages had presented an implied attack on Boileau's theory of the sublime, and what Boileau does here is to systematically examine and expose Perrault's scholarship while discussing precisely the same passages. Thus Boileau demonstrates that the attack on the sublime is both ill-conceived and inaccurate; but he does this without once using the word *sublime*, and his defence of sublimity is as elliptical as Perrault's attack had been.

The *Réflexions sur Longin* turn out to be about the sublime after all, for Boileau is not merely attacking Perrault, but also defending himself against criticism of *le sublime*. In piecing together the fragmentary remarks of different sections, it can be seen that the first nine *Réflexions* mark a modest development in Boileau's concept of *le sublime* in their consistent concern with the nature of literary language. Boileau at one moment interrupts an attack on Perrault to describe the historical origins of the asiatic style (88-89). On another occasion, when he is arguing that the only sure guarantee of literary worth is the approbation of posterity, he remarks that if Ronsard is no longer admired, this is not because taste or the language have changed, but rather because of some inherent defect in Ronsard's own language:

> [La chûte de ces Auteurs] n'est venuë, que de ce qu'ils n'avoient point atrappé dans ces Langues le point de solidité et de perfection, qui est necessaire pour faire durer, et pour faire à jamais priser des ouvrages. (93)

This of course begs the question of what precisely is the 'point de solidité'. Boileau taunts Perrault that if he cannot 'feel' the beauties of Homer or Plato, his taste is at odds with the consensus of twenty centuries, and he might as well renounce his literary career: 'Il faut trouver moyen de voir [le merveilleux], ou renoncer aux belles lettres ausquelles vous devez croire que vous n'avez ni goust ni génie, puisque vous ne sentez point ce qu'ont senti tous les hommes' (95). This use of *sentir* would not withstand close scrutiny, and Boileau wisely avoids the argument elsewhere in the *Réflexions*.

The most common attack used against Perrault is to question his competence: his opponent should not presume to judge the style of Greek authors whom he cannot read in the original. Boileau scores a nice point when he notes that a passage of Longinus on Homer to which Perrault had taken particular objection turns out not to be by Longinus at all, but an interpolation of the translator: '[Mr P.] n'a jamais leu Longin, selon toutes les apparences, que dans ma traduction' (76). Time and again he ridicules Perrault for mistakes arising from his lack of Greek and his inadequate Latin:

> Quand je dis cela neanmoins, je suppose que vous sachiez la langue de ces Auteurs; Car si vous ne la sçavez point, et si vous ne vous l'estes point familiarisée, je ne vous blâmerai pas de n'en point voir lez beautez: je vous blâmerai seulement d'en parler. Et c'est en quoi on ne sauroit trop condammer Monsieur P. qui ne sçachant point la langue d'Homere, vient hardiment lui faire son procez sur les bassesses de ses Traducteurs, et dire au Genre humain qui a admiré les ouvrages de ce grand Poète durant tant de siecles, Vous avez admiré des sottises. (95)[11]

Boileau insists that the beauty—*le sublime*—of any literary work can only be appreciated in the original language. The quality of a passage resides not just in the ideas expressed but also in the particular words chosen to express them; style and content are indistinguishable. This notion underlies all Boileau's comments on the failings of Perrault's criticism; and by stressing in this way the purely linguistic component of *le sublime*, Boileau refines the theory which he had expounded twenty years earlier in the *Traité du sublime*.

V. THE TRIUMPH OF NOMENCLATURISM

That Boileau felt it necessary to fight on in defence of *le sublime* is not surprising. The deadening influence which nomenclaturism exercised over poetic theory, and which the *Traité du sublime* was attempting to combat, became if anything more oppressive around the turn of the century, as the double bind by which poetic discourse could be censured for imitating both too well *and* too poorly became increasingly apparent.

On the one hand, Malebranche's *De la recherche de la vérité*, published in the same year as the *Traité du sublime*, includes an attack on the rhetorical exploitation of imagination and the passions in such writers as Montaigne; the treatise as a whole presents a not unsophisticated view of eloquence (Malebranche was influenced by Augustine as well as by Descartes), but its ideas were soon simplified and systematised, notably by the Benedictine François Lamy.[12] Earlier cartesian mistrust of rhetoric was thus revived, and in the late 1690s the debate was rekindled (with Gibert as the principal antagonist of François Lamy), and for over a decade all the old arguments about the ambivalent morality of rhetoric were freshly rehearsed.[13] On the other hand, the publication of Locke's *Essay concerning Human Understanding* (1690, French trans. 1700), with its third Book devoted entirely to a discussion 'Of Words', could be read as reaffirming earlier cartesian concerns about the 'efficacy' of language.

In the course of the eighteenth century, the tide began to turn against nomenclaturism, as philosophers—starting with Locke himself—became increasingly doubtful about the notion that things or ideas could be found to correspond to all words, and as they began to explore more exactly the form and structure of language.[14] In the meantime, however, the first two decades of the eighteenth century may be said to mark the high-water point of nomenclaturism in France. The pre-eminence of nomenclaturist thinking about language had precisely the consequence which Boileau, who died in 1711, had feared and foreseen ('J'ai souvent ouï dire à M. Despréaux que la philosophie de Descartes avait coupé la gorge à la poésie'): namely, a *mise en cause* of the value and utility of poetry.[15]

The consequences of nomenclaturism for rhetorical and poetic theory can best be gauged in the writings of the abbé de Saint-Pierre and the abbé de Pons. In 1703 Boileau was reportedly much concerned to learn from his friend the abbé Renaudot that the abbé de Saint-Pierre was planning to write a *Traité du sublime*.[16] Saint-Pierre (1658-1743), only later to become celebrated as a utopian thinker and reformer, had been a member of the Académie française since 1695, and was known to be Modern in his sympathies; any *Traité du sublime* from this close friend of Fontenelle was certain to be critical of Boileau. In the event the work was never published, perhaps never completed, and no trace of it appears to remain among his manuscripts.[17] It is not difficult to guess the broad line of approach that Saint-Pierre would have adopted, however. An unpublished maxim (written 1687-92) gives an early clue to his thinking about rhetoric:

> La véritable éloquence est celle du bon sens simple et naturel: celle
> qui a besoin de figures et d'ornements n'est fondée que sur ce que
> la plupart des hommes ont des lumières fort courtes et font
> qu'entrevoir les choses.[18]

His 'Observations sur la beauté des ouvrages d'esprit', published in the *Mercure de France* in 1726, start from a resolutely Modern position to elaborate a rationalist, even utilitarian, view of rhetoric. Horace's dictum is deftly twisted against classicism when Saint-Pierre insists that the beauty of a work is achieved through a combination of 'le plus agréable' and 'le plus utile'.[19] The most useful is that which is the most morally improving; thus *Phèdre* is criticised because Racine renders pitiful a protagonist whom we ought to find odious (319). The most agreeable idea or sensation is one which is novel:

> La beauté dans l'expression demande une ressemblance exacte entre
> une belle pensée, entre un beau sentiment, et l'expression de cette
> pensée et de ce sentiment. Il y faut de la brièveté, mais il faut surtout
> que la pensée soit belle, et par conséquent nouvelle et importante
> [...]. La partie essentielle du beau, c'est la nouveauté. (322-23)

Saint-Pierre's emphasis on the importance of novelty (which may well have influenced Houdar de La Motte)[20] means that he cannot believe in the absolute nature of aesthetic judgements. What was new in a previous age cannot be new in the present one, and even what strikes a young man as new—and therefore beautiful—will not necessarily affect him in the same way when he is older and more experienced: 'C'est une supposition fausse que de supposer qu'il y a des ouvrages d'une beauté absolue, indépendante, éternelle' (326).

Despite certain incidental points of contact—the moral function of rhetoric, the importance of 'la justesse' in both thought and expression—Boileau's theory of poetic discourse is quite different from Saint-Pierre's. Boileau believes that Longinus, among others, has established an absolute and enduring standard of beauty; and the theory of *le sublime* presupposes a much more sophisticated understanding of literary language than the utilitarian nomenclaturism of Saint-Pierre.

Saint-Pierre's aesthetic indeed leaves no room for *le sublime*. It is entirely likely that his 'Observations' are the work to which Renaudot was referring when he spoke of a putative *traité du sublime*: it would be a typical strategy of the Moderns to have attacked Boileau's concept of *le sublime* by conspicuous avoidance of the term at every turn.

If Saint-Pierre attacks Boileau obliquely, the abbé Jean-François de Pons (1683-1732) chooses outright confrontation. He shows his Modernist colours in his 'Dissertation sur les langues en général, et sur la langue françoise en particulier', published in *Le Nouveau Mercure* in 1717, in which he uncompromisingly asserts the impossibility of understanding dead languages (33-47). In the following year, 1718, he published in the same journal his 'Réflexions sur l'éloquence', a work which marks the absolute supremacy of nomenclaturism.

The *Logique* of Arnauld and Nicole had presented a far from simple picture of the relationship between words and ideas:

> La pureté du langage, le nombre des figures, sont tout au plus dans l'éloquence ce que le coloris est dans la peinture, c'est-à-dire, que ce n'en est que la partie la plus basse et la plus materielle: mais la principale consiste à concevoir fortement les choses, et à les exprimer en sorte qu'on en porte dans l'esprit des auditeurs une image vive et lumineuse, qui ne présente pas seulement ces choses toutes nues, mais aussi les mouvements avec lesquels on les conçoit. (276)

This notion of the vivid depiction of a strongly felt idea is crucial because it acknowledges the fact that words cannot simply mirror thoughts or things; by softening the absolute rigours of nomenclaturism, Arnauld and Nicole avoid a totally reductive explanation of language. Bossuet's explanation of rhetoric is predictably subtle:

> Trois choses contribuent ordinairement à rendre un orateur agréable et efficace: la personne de celui qui parle, la beauté des choses qu'il traite, la manière ingénieuse dont il les explique; et la raison en est évidente. Car l'estime de l'orateur prépare une attention favorable, les belles choses nourrissent l'esprit, et l'adresse de les expliquer d'une manière qui plaise les fait doucement entrer dans le cœur.[21]

This account of 'la manière ingénieuse' by which thought finds expression in language goes far beyond nomenclaturism—as we would expect from a supporter of Boileau's *sublime*. However even works more sympathetic to the Moderns, such as Bernard Lamy's *Rhétorique* and Malebranche's *De la recherche de la vérité*, reiterate the concerns of Arnauld and Nicole concerning the role of 'les mouvements' in shaping our conception of ideas: 'Il est certain que nous parlons selon que nous sommes touchés,' writes Bernard Lamy. 'Les mouvements de l'âme ont leurs caractères dans les paroles, comme sur le visage'.[22]

When Perrault comes to consider the definition of eloquence in the *Parallèle*, he has l'Abbé quote the various views of Cicero, only to ridicule them (II, 41-42)—significantly, there is no mention of Demosthenes, with whom Cicero is unfavourably compared by Longinus. Through the voice of the Abbé, Perrault instead proposes his own definition of eloquence, 'l'Art de bien parler selon la nature du sujet que l'on traite, et selon les lieux, les temps et les personnes' (II, 43). In stressing the communicative function of language, Perrault moves closer to a more narrowly nomenclaturist account, perhaps because he wishes to realign the definition of rhetoric and to make of it an art which can help popularise the whole system of new scientific thinking.[23]

Whatever Perrault's motives, he points the way for the abbé de Pons, whose definition of eloquence is untroubled by nuance: 'L'Eloquence est l'Art de bien penser et de bien exprimer ses pensées' (7). Pons adopts the Port-Royal notion of words as signs established 'pour le commerce mutuel des pensées' (8), and pursues it rigorously to its logical end:

> Il n'y a aucun rapport Phisique, entre les pensées de nôtre esprit & les figures, ou caractéres variés qui en sont les signes: Un mot n'est pas plus beau par lui-même, qu'un autre mot: Une expression n'est, ni plus noble, ni plus brillante qu'aucune autre; mais, comme nos pensées ont par elles-mêmes des dénominations distinctes: Que les unes sont belles, vrayes, nobles, lumineuses; les autres, communes, fausses, ignobles, confuses; nous déférons stupidement aux signes les honneurs dûs aux choses signifiées.
>
> On croit avoir bien loüé nos bons Ecrivains, lorsqu'on a dit de l'un, qu'il écrit noblement, qu'il est fécond en expressions hautes et sublimes; de l'autre, qu'il écrit élégamment, qu'il est riche en expressions fines, galantes et délicates: On propose ces Auteurs pour modeles; voilà, dit-on, comme il faut écrire?
>
> J'aimerois autant, qu'on loüa le célébre Lully, d'avoir élégamment notté ses Operas. (8-9)

If words are merely the signs of thoughts or ideas, they cannot be intrinsically beautiful; when we speak of beauty of style, says Pons, we are confusing the idea or thing being evoked with the sign itself—and it is hardly by chance that 'expressions sublimes' are singled out for ridicule, especially as he repeats his attack in this term:

> Il n'y a aucun rapport entre les mots des Langues, et les pensées dont ces mots sont les signes. Le mot, *Dieu*, institué chez nous pour la plus haute des idées, auroit pû être le signe de l'idée la plus abjecte: Telle autre expression, qui est le signe d'un sentiment sublime, auroit pû être fixée à un sentiment vulgaire. Je fais hommage de mon respect et de mon admiration à l'idée grande, au sentiment sublime; mais, je ne confonds pas dans mon hommage, les vains simulacres, les signes arbitraires qui me les présentent; il y auroit à cela, si j'ose le dire, une espèce d'Idolâtrie.
>
> Longin (Chap. 25. Traduction de Despreaux), dans son Traité du Sublime, conseille l'usage des *beaux mots; parce qu'ils sont la lumière propre et naturelle de nos pensées. Il faut néanmoins*, continuë-t-il, *prendre garde à ne pas exprimer une idée basse, en termes grands et magnifiques, si ce n'est dans la Poësie*.
>
> Que nous dites-vous, Monsieur le Rheteur? Vous distinguez dans les Langues, des expressions belles et des expressions laides; mais, à quelle marque reconnoissez-vous les

> unes et les autres? Les beaux mots sont, à vôtre avis, la lumiere
> propre et naturelle des pensées; c'est-à-dire, que les pensées ne
> sont point lumineuses par elles-mêmes, et qu'elles empruntent tout
> leur éclat des signes qui les représentent? Vous deffendez à l'Orateur,
> d'exprimer des choses basses en termes magnifiques, tandis que
> vous le permettez au Poëte? (11-12)

The linguistic theories of Pons proclaim a kind of *degré zéro de la rhétorique*, the notion that language is necessarily 'transparent'. The rise of this view, which Boileau had foreseen, inevitably spelt the demise of his aesthetic of *le sublime*. Pons takes the words of Boileau-Longinus and turns them inside out: 'Les mots ne sont point la lumière propre et naturelle de nos pensées, ils n'en sont que les signes arbitraires' (12).

Nomenclaturism, which took wing in the wake of the *Grammaire générale et raisonnée*, reaches its logical (if absurd) climax in the writings of the abbé de Pons. His attack on Boileau-Longinus is patently absurd, yet—within his own terms of reference—entirely consistent. Boileau's cautious attempt to reassert a platonist strand in thinking about poetry is inconceivable within the narrowly rational confines mapped out by the Moderns. Platonism would eventually re-emerge near the end of the century as an important element in poetic thinking, but only after many decades during which philosophers, grammarians and poets had worked to discredit nomenclaturism.

VI. *RÉFLEXIONS CRITIQUES X-XII*

In so far as the *Querelle* is essentially a debate about the nature of literary language, the concept of *le sublime* may be said to be at its heart: in this sense it is legitimate to describe the *Querelle des anciens et des modernes* as a *Querelle du sublime*. Boileau evidently identified closely and possessively with the concept of *le sublime*, which continued to preoccupy him until his death. In the last year of his life he wrote three further *Réflexions critiques* (X-XII), different in tone and style from the previous nine, and published posthumously in 1713.

The tenth *Réflexion* is the least interesting of the three, being given over to a long and rather tedious attack on Le Clerc and Huet who, many years earlier, had questioned the presence of *le sublime* in the much-quoted sentence from Genesis.[24] Boileau, in response, condescendingly reiterates the distinction between *le sublime* and *le style sublime*, but without adding significantly to what he had written previously in the 'Préface'.

The eleventh *Réflexion critique* does, however, break new ground. The most significant recent attack on *le sublime*, apart from the unpublished work of the abbé de Saint-Pierre, had come from a younger ally of Perrault and Fontenelle, Houdar de La Motte. In his 'Discours sur la Poësie en général, et sur l'Ode en particulier' (1707), La Motte attacks Boileau, though without naming him: 'Mais je ne sçais si la nature du Sublime est encore bien éclaircie. Il me semble que jusqu'à présent on en a plutôt donné des exemples que des définitions' (34-35). He goes on to quote what had by now become the canonical example of *le sublime*, 'Dieu dit que la lumière se fasse', only to conclude that this is sublime because of the truth which it encapsulates: an interpretation diametrically opposed to Boileau's. On this occasion, however, Boileau decides to counter-attack indirectly, and he makes no comment on this section of the 'Discours'. Instead, he picks up La Motte's criticism of a line from the *récit de Théramène*, and defends Racine from the criticism that his use of metaphor had been excessive and inappropriate.[25] Boileau insists as ever on the affective impact of literary language: 'Lors qu'un endroit d'un Discours frappe tout le monde, il ne faut chercher des raisons, ou plutost de vaines subtilitez, pour s'empescher d'en estre frappé' (183).

The twelfth and final *Réflexion* is very short. Realising the need for a more forthright explanation of *le sublime* in the face of so many attacks, Boileau attempts a more watertight definition than the one he had given in his 'Préface' thirty-six years earlier:

> Le Sublime est une certaine force de discours, propre à eslever et à ravir l'Ame, et qui provient ou de la grandeur de la pensée et de la noblesse du sentiment, ou de la magnificence des paroles, ou du tour harmonieux, vif et animé de l'expression; c'est-à-dire d'une de ces choses regardées separément, ou ce qui fait le parfait Sublime, de ces trois choses jointes ensemble. (184)

Boileau provides one final example, and quotes four lines from *Athalie*; this alone, he says, suffices to prove Racine's superiority over Corneille. Eleven years after his death, Racine is still Boileau's closest ally in the *cabale du sublime*.

In his 'Discours sur la Poësie', La Motte is categorical about the subservience of poetic enthusiasm to reason:

> Enthousiasme tant qu'on voudra, il faut qu'il soit toujours guidé par la raison, et que le Poëte le plus échauffé se rappelle souvent à soi, pour juger sainement de ce que son imagination lui offre. (28-29)

The prevailing climate of rationalism made it increasingly hard for Boileau to defend the concept of *le sublime*; a figure such as Pierre Bayle who stands apart from the *Querelle* typically has no time for poetry, which he regards as a frivolous occupation.[26] The essence of what Boileau had fought for is perhaps best summed up in the eleventh *Réflexion critique*: 'La Poésie porte son excuse avec soy' (180). It was not an argument likely to cut much ice with the likes of La Motte or the abbé de Pons.

The final three *Réflexions critiques* provide striking testimony to the fact that *le sublime* remained at the forefront of Boileau's critical preoccupations right to the end of his life. Thirty-six years had elapsed since the publication of the *Traité du sublime*, and still Boileau worked to fend off attackers of *le sublime* and to refine his earlier thoughts in the 'Préface'; in these late critical works, there is never allusion to the arguments of the *Art poétique*. In his own mind, and in the minds of his contemporaries, Boileau was intimately identified with *le sublime*.

If the extent of Boileau's identification with *le sublime* is striking, so too is the speed with which the concept of *le sublime* went into decline after 1711. Discussion of *le sublime* naturally outlived Boileau, but already within a decade of his death we find the term being used in ways quite different from that in which he had employed it in the *Traité du sublime*. The abbé Du Bos, for instance, in the *Réflexions critiques sur la poésie et sur la peinture* (1719), talks of *le sublime* in connection with the phrase *qu'il mourût*, but then develops the notion in an altogether original direction, speaking of 'un sublime de rapport', and citing in support Molière's *Misanthrope* (I, 84-88). In the same year Marivaux published an article in the *Mercure*, 'Sur la pensée sublime', in which he too discusses *qu'il mourût*, and again he elaborates the idea of the *sublime* in an entirely individual way.[27] Neither author appears to be wishing to attack Boileau or what we may term the Classical Sublime; by 1719 the term seems merely to have broken away from the sense which Boileau-Longinus had given it. When, in 1722, the abbé Desfontaines writes that 'la clarté est souvent l'écueil du sublime',[28] thus establishing *le sublime* and *la clarté* as opposites, he looks forward to what we may call the Romantic Sublime which was to enter the mainstream of French thought only in the last third of the eighteenth century, heralded by Burke's *Enquiry*: 'In reality a great clearness helps but little towards affecting the passions, as it is in some sort an enemy to all enthusiasms whatsoever' (60).

VII. CONCLUSION: IMAGES OF THE SUBLIME

The greatest stumbling-block for French classical critics in their attempt to shape a coherent theory of eloquence is, as we have seen, their mimetic model of language, their view that words function as pictures of reality. It seems apposite therefore to conclude by considering the literal image of the Classical Sublime, as part of the seventeenth-century iconographical tradition of eloquence.

In the early 1680s, Charles Perrault commissioned a series of eleven paintings from the most prominent painters then working in the capital, to create a *Cabinet des Muses* for his Paris home. In fact, Perrault left his house in 1685, when it was cleared to make way for the Place des Victoires, so the commissioned pictures may never even have been hung as intended. Perrault was not, however, deterred from publishing a precise description of the project: *Le Cabinet des beaux-arts* (1690) contains engravings of the eleven paintings, together with extensive explanations of each—the iconographical importance of the project was evidently at least as important to Perrault as its actual realisation.

The one painting of the eleven to have survived is *L'Eloquence*, by René-Antoine Houasse (Fig. 6), and engraved (rather poorly) for *Le Cabinet des beaux-arts* by Jean Bonnart (Fig. 7). The subject of eloquence has a well-established iconographical tradition. The Dijon painter Philippe Quantin, for example, painted *La Muse Polymnie* (before 1628) for a *Chambre des Muses* in a château near Saulieu in Burgundy; the muse, whose name is inscribed on a column, is described as dressed in white, and wearing a diadem of pearls in her hair; the right hand is held aloft, the left clasps a closed book on which is written 'Suadere'; on the ground, books and a recumbent column.[29] Ripa's influence here is paramount: the description of 'Polinnia' in the *Iconologia* (347-48; Fig. 8) includes mention of the white dress (purity and sincerity), the pearls worn around the head (gifts and virtues), the raised right hand (the appeal of eloquence), and the left hand holding a book inscribed with the word 'Suadere' (persuasion as rhetoric's ultimate goal).

Not all painters follow Ripa quite so slavishly as Quantin, but it is clear that the *Iconologia* provided the essential inspiration for paintings on this subject, even before the translation of the *Iconologia* into French (first part 1636-37, both parts 1644). The *Polymnie* of Le Sueur and Pierre Patel (Fig. 9), painted for the hôtel Lambert in the early 1650s, depicts the muse holding a triangle, but this work is unusual, indeed unprecedented, precisely because it owes nothing to Ripa.[30] The *Allégorie de la rhétorique* by Le Sueur's contemporary, La Hyre (c. 1650; Fig. 10), draws on Ripa unashamedly. The pearls worn around the head and the white dress are attributes of Ripa's Polyhymnia, as is the motto 'Ornatus persuasio', which appears to be a variant of 'Suadere'; certain other details, however, such as the garland worn around the head (eloquence), and the sceptre with two winged serpents (wisdom), the open raised right hand, and the open book (necessity of study) held in the other derive from Ripa's several descriptions of 'Eloquenza';[31] he equally rejects other attributes, such as the thunderbolt which figures so prominently in de Bie's engraving of 'Eloquence' in Baudoin's Ripa (Fig. 11). Thus La Hyre follows Ripa, but selectively and creatively, combining chosen features from the various sections devoted to Polyhymnia and Eloquence.

Michel Dorigny's *Polymnie, muse de l'Eloquence* (Fig. 12), dating from around 1650 (and formerly attributed to Simon Vouet), again uses attributes from Ripa (white dress, pearls, raised index finger of right hand, book inscribed 'Suadere'), but adapts the *Iconologia* in a more startling fashion than do either of Vouet's other two disciples Le Sueur and La Hyre.[32] The volume inscribed 'Suadere' is not held by the muse but by a putto, while a second putto acts as Eloquence's secretary, symbolizing the connection of the written with the spoken word; at the muse's feet lies a tame lion, symbol of strength and sweetness combined; and, perhaps the most interesting innovation of all, in the background on the left a Roman emperor harangues his troops, his right arm outstretched, his left hand holding a laurel wreath. In an original imitation of Ripa, the Muse's raised right-hand index finger (from Ripa's 'Polinnia') is combined with the emperor's open raised left hand (from Ripa's 'Eloquenza'). To complement the statuesque female figure of eloquence, Dorigny has introduced a male figure symbolizing the power of eloquence in action: thus the theory and practice of eloquence are shown in complementary juxtaposition.

This figure of the orator in action anticipates the engraving (by Paillet and Vallet) which Boileau chose to serve as the frontispiece to the *Traité du sublime*.[33] It is clear, if we are to believe Brossette's report of the matter,[34] that Boileau's choice of frontispiece was careful and deliberate. He intended it, so Brossette tells us, to represent Demosthenes—'un Orateur véritablement né au Sublime' (*TS*, 108), and Longinus's pre-eminent example of an orator whose words are overwhelmingly powerful (and, perhaps not coincidentally, the orator roundly attacked by Perrault in the

Figure 6. René-Antoine Houasse, *L'Eloquence*, c.1681-83
(Brest, Musée des Beaux-Arts).

L'ELOQUENCE.

Figure 7. J. Bonnart, engraving, of R.-A. Houasse, *L'Eloquence*.

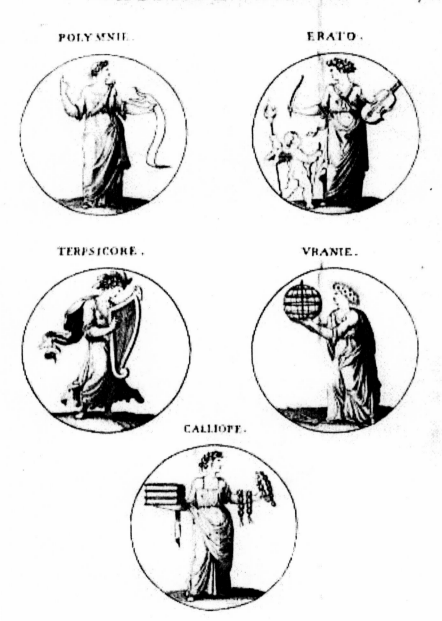

Figure 8. Jacques de Bie, 'Polymnie', engraving, from Ripa, trans.
Baudoin, *Iconologie* (Paris, 1644).

Figure 9. Le Sueur and Pierre Patel, *Polymnie*, c.1650-52 (Paris, Louvre).

163

Figure 10. La Hyre, *Allégorie de la rhétorique*, c.1650 (private collection).

ELOQVENCE. XLIX.

En'eſt pas ſans raiſon, que pour exprimer ſes diuers
effects, on la peint armée d'vn Morion, enuironné
d'vne Couronne d'or, d'vn Corcelet, & d'vne Eſpée,
qu'elle porte à ſon coſté; Outre que de l'vn de ſes bras, qu'elle

H ij

Figure 11. Jacques de Bie, 'Eloquence', engraving, from Ripa, trans. Baudoin,
Iconologie (Paris, 1644).

Figure 12. Michel Dorigny, *Polymnie, muse de l'Eloquence,*
c.1650 (Paris, Louvre).

Parallèle).[35] In the engraving, as in Dorigny's picture, the orator is placed left, raised up, and facing right; the raised index finger of the left hand also echoes Dorigny, and suggests a debt to Ripa (albeit with the wrong hand!). But where Dorigny's orator is a secondary and poorly lit figure, in Paillet's image the muse has been eliminated and it is the orator who becomes the focus of attention. In two important respects, this image is quite unlike any of the earlier representations of eloquence. Firstly, Paillet depicts the audience in some detail so as to emphasise the impact of the orator's eloquence; and in contrast to the calmness of the Muses, the audience here is shown in a state of emotional frenzy. Secondly, the orator wields in his right hand a thunderbolt, a powerful (and masculine) symbol of the force of rhetoric.

The thunderbolt is in part a reference to Demosthenes, whose forceful eloquence is discussed on several occasions in the *Traité du sublime*, twice with reference to 'le foudre' (Chapters 10 and 28). The powerful concision of Demosthenes is contrasted with the more prolix Cicero:

> On peut comparer ce premier [Demosthene], à cause de la violence, de la rapidité, de la force et de la vehemence avec laquelle il ravage, pour ainsi dire, et emporte tout, à une tempeste et à un foudre. (*TS*, 72-73)

A later passage on Demosthenes speaks of 'cette force et cette vehemence', 'ses tonnerres', 'ses éclairs', and concludes:

> Et certainement il est plus aisé d'envisager fixement, et les yeux ouverts, les foudres qui tombent du Ciel, que de n'estre point émû des violentes passions qui regnent en foule dans ses Ouvrages. (*TS*, 108)

The thunderbolt as symbol of powerful oratory is not of course confined to either Longinus or Demosthenes, and the metaphor was a commonplace of Greek and Roman criticism, as Boileau obviously knew.[36] Equally important, the symbol was familiar to authors of Renaissance emblematic handbooks, such as Ripa and Valeriano. In his description of 'Eloquenza', Ripa writes graphically of the overwhelming power of 'il folgore', the attribute given prominence in the engraving made for Baudoin's edition of 1644 (Fig. 11).[37] Ripa also refers to Valeriano's *Hieroglyphica*, the vast anthology of ancient systems of symbols which was still being republished in France, in both Latin and French, in the early decades of the seventeenth century.[38] Valeriano describes a range of meanings associated with the thunderbolt: strength, power, fame, speed, clemency, and, of course, the force of eloquence.[39] The image of thunder was associated with ancient orators like Pericles, says Valeriano, because of the way in which they moved their audience, and because of the power and authority of their words; this image unquestionably has its source in the Scriptures, he claims, citing several examples of thunder used as an image of the persuasive Heaven-sent voice. Thunder as a symbol of forceful or even religious eloquence had thus been a commonplace of Renaissance emblematists, but, as we saw, it appears to have been systematically avoided by the seventeenth-century painters of eloquence who otherwise depended on Ripa.

The image of *le foudre* is pivotal to the picture of poetic discourse which Boileau wishes to paint; it occurs indeed in the opening chapter of the *Traité du sublime*: 'Quand le Sublime vient à éclater où il faut, il renverse tout comme un foudre' (*TS*, 50). The presence of the symbol in the frontispiece to the *Traité du sublime* is more than merely illustrative: given the striking absence of the image from earlier depictions of eloquence, it is a daring innovation.

Charles Perrault commissioned his own image of eloquence as part of his *Cabinet des Muses* less than a decade after the appearance of the *Traité du sublime*, and the published engraving of the picture was published with Perrault's own detailed explanation in *Le Cabinet des beaux-arts* (11-14). The Muse at the centre of the canvas recalls in some respects the Muses of the earlier part of the century: she holds a caduceus in her left hand, like La Hyre's Muse, and, like Dorigny's Muse, she is waited on by attentive cherubs. The purple dress, the golden crown, the raised index finger of the left hand, the open book, all are attributes familiar from Ripa, and place the picture squarely in the tradition of depictions of eloquence.

In other respects however Houasse's image breaks very definitely with that tradition. The books presented as icons of eloquence bear the names of their authors, all of them seventeenth-century and French: Balzac, Le Maître, Ogier and Pascal (Perrault explains that he has deliberately avoided naming living authors (14)). Most extraordinary of all is the setting of the picture. Allegorical pictures had traditionally been set in some unspecified scene of classical antiquity, thus reminding viewers of the unsurpassed authority of the classical authors; the picture of La Hyre shows a temple and a pyramid in the background, that of Dorigny some (rather chipped) classical columns and, again, a temple. Houasse also shows (undamaged) columns, but these are neoclassical rather than classical, and they are propping up the Louvre, which has now taken the place of the temple. The identity of the location is confirmed by the scene (background, left) showing Louis XIV presiding at a meeting of the Académie française (of which body Charles Perrault had been secretary since 1671). 'C'est là que l'Eloquence épanche avec profusion ses plus riches tresors,' simpers Perrault, 'pour répondre en quelque sorte a la majesté du Prince qui l'écoute, et a la dignité du Corps qu'elle fait parler' (12). The impact of the picture is thus unashamedly Modern. The Ancient symbolism enshrined in Ripa's iconology is used, paradoxically, to proclaim the superiority of the Moderns, the literalism of the portrait of the Académie undermining the symbolic potential of the Muse and turning her into a harmless and powerless anachronism.[40]

One other detail of Houasse's picture requires comment. In the background on the right, a group of some six boys are apparently learning the practice of eloquence. It is a curious, almost deliberately obscure detail of the picture: the figures are so much shorter than those on the left that they must be assumed to be children, and they are dressed in a way (barefoot, apparently wearing togas) which hardly seems French, and so jars with the French setting. Perrault in his commentary is not at all helpful:

'On void d'autres Genies dans l'éloignement qui s'exercent a haranguer et ce chemin est peut estre le plus seur et le plus court pour se rendre habile' (12). In some ways this detail recalls Dorigny's picture with its half-hidden image of the emperor haranguing his troops—except that in Dorigny's image the eloquence is for real, and not the mere amusement of children. Perhaps this detail might be seen as an iconographical refutation of the frontispiece to the *Traité du sublime*: the orator who is the central and dynamic figure of Paillet's image becomes in Houasse's picture a juvenile and entirely incidental figure.

Whether or not Perrault intended his image to be an explicit riposte to Boileau, it is abundantly clear that it represents a view of eloquence antithetical to that of the Classical Sublime. Paillet's image, commissioned by Boileau, and Houasse's image, commissioned by Perrault, represent the opposing views of sublime and counter-sublime which stake out the divide between Ancient and Modern in the *Querelle*. In Houasse's picture, while children play at eloquence, the academicians soberly and rationally debate the subject with their sovereign. The watchword of Perrault's literary aesthetic is *la raison*. 'L'air seul de son visage,' he writes of the Muse, 'imprime du respect par tout ou la raison à quelque autorité' (11). And to accompany Bonnart's engraving after Houasse in *Le Cabinet des beaux-arts*, Perrault penned the following verses:

> En vain la puissance des Armes,
> Avec le force de mes charmes,
> Ose entrer en comparaison.
> Tout cède au pouvoir de bien dire,
> Et s'exerce un supreme empire,
> Par tout ou regne la Raison. (11)

History, at least in the short term, was on the side of Perrault. Paillet's picture does not appear to have been reproduced except in subsequent editions of Boileau's works; Houasse's picture, on the other hand, was engraved more than once, and an engraving (by P. Klopper) of the central part of the picture was adopted as the frontispiece of the third edition of Bernard Lamy's *Rhétorique* (1688)—the very edition, ironically enough, which first shows the influence, albeit garbled, of the *Traité du sublime*. Perrault's chosen image of eloquence thus represents more than just an alternative to the Classical Sublime: it marks the failure of a quasi-platonist aesthetic such as the Classical Sublime to make its mark in a climate of increasingly assertive poetic rationalism.

NOTES

[1.] François Lamy, *De la connoissance de soi-mesme* (1697), p. 7.
[2.] Niderst, *Fontenelle*, p. 365.
[3.] See Niderst, 'Les Gens de Paris et les Gens de Versailles'.
[4.] See Picard, *La Carrière de Jean Racine*, pp. 313-25.
[5.] *Fontenelle*, pp. 87-89.

[6.] See also below, note 36.

[7.] Longinus frequently refers to Demosthenes, and he quotes at length from *On the Crown* (*TS*, Chap. 14) and from the *First Philippic* (*TS*, Chap. 16), but he does not single out the *Fourth Philippic* for particular comment.

[8.] In the *Oxford Classical Dictionary* (2nd edition), G. L. Cawkwell writes of Demosthenes: 'In many instances he produces a great effect by the use of a few ordinary words. In his most solemn moments his style is at its plainest and his language most moderate. A master of metaphor, he uses it sparingly, and hardly at all in his most impressive passages' (p. 332). As a brief definition of the *sublime*, Boileau could hardly have done better.

[9.] Compare *Parallèle*, III, p. 118, with *TS*, p. 62.

[10.] See Hans Kortum.

[11.] Compare pp. 71, 92, 98, 99, etc.

[12.] See Carr, 'Rhetorical theories of Malebranche' and 'François Lamy'.

[13.] See Tocanne, *L'Idée de nature en France*, pp. 436-46.

[14.] 'We begin from the position commonly accepted in the seventeenth century, the position of Locke, Wilkins, and the linguists of the Royal Society, that words are signs for ideas (or things). The first and most obvious line of dissent began with Locke himself who admitted that there are certain classes of words which for one reason or another do *not* name ideas. As time went on more and more classes were added to the list of exceptions until by the end of the eighteenth century the principle that words stand for ideas no longer seemed a profitable starting point for the theory of language' (S. K. Land, *From Signs to Propositions*, pp. 184-85).

[15.] See Mercier, 'La querelle de la poésie', and Menant, *La Chute d'Icare*.

[16.] The abbé Eusèbe Renaudot writes to the comte d'Ayen (6 July 1703): 'M. des Préaux est dans une petite inquiétude sur ce que je lui ay apris qu'il avoit un concurrent, qui alloit sur ses vieux jours l'anéantir par un traité du sublime qui couroit déjà les ruelles, et l'auteur est l'abbé de Saint-Pierre. Il est vray dans le fond qu'il a travaillé sur cela, et le poète, comme vous savez, croid tout fort aisément, mais non pas qu'on puisse l'égaler; en quoy il ne se trompe pas, sur plusieurs sujets, mais surtout à l'égard de celui-là' (L. G. Pélissier, 'Les Correspondants du duc de Noailles', p. 642). See also Boileau, Pléiade, pp. 675, 1147.

[17.] There is no mention of a *Traité du sublime* in any of the three large collections of the abbé de Saint-Pierre's manuscripts, in the Bibliothèque publique, Neuchâtel; the Bibliothèque municipale, Rouen; and the Archives nationales, Paris. It is possible, though unlikely, that it survives elsewhere.

[18.] M. L. Perkins, 'Unpublished maxims', p. 500.

[19.] 'Observations sur l'éloquence', pp. 320-21. References are to the manuscript version of the 1726 text, edited by L. Kerslake, which Saint-Pierre re-entitled 'Observations sur l'éloquence'.

[20.] Compare: 'Je crois que le Sublime n'est autre chose que le vrai & le nouveau réünis dans une grande idée, exprimés avec élégance & précision [...]. Tout le monde convient aujourd'hui que sans le vrai, il ne peut y avoir de solide beauté, ni par conséquent de Sublime [...]. La nouveauté n'est pas moins nécessaire au Sublime; car il est de son essence de faire une impression vive sur les esprits, & de les frapper d'admiration. Le moyen sans nouveauté de produire ces grands effets?' (Houdar de La Motte, 'Discours sur la poësie et sur l'ode', pp. 35-36).

[21.] Quoted in Grosheintz, p. 23.

[22.] *Rhétorique*, p. 157; see also Malebranche, I, pp. 250-51.

[23.] See H. M. Davidson, 'Fontenelle, Perrault'.

[24.] Voltaire would later take the part of Huet and Le Clerc, in his article "Genèse" in the *Dictionnaire philosophique* (*Œuvres complètes* (Oxford), Vol. 36, pp. 147-49).

[25.] This criticism of the *récit de Théramène* was later (but only after Boileau's death) voiced by Fénelon (*Lettre à l'Académie*, p. 93).

[26.] See H. E. Smith, pp. 22-27.

[27.] *Journaux*, pp. 56-72.

[28.] Quoted in Marivaux, *Journaux*, p. 50.

29. Described by Quarré, p. 11.

30. Rosenberg Henderson, p. 568.

31. *Iconologia*, pp. 126-29.

32. See also M. Fumaroli's description of this picture (facing the frontispiece of the paperback edition of *L'Age de l'éloquence*).

33. See frontispiece; the engraving was made after a drawing by Antoine Paillet (Paris 1626-1701), a painter of portraits and of historical scenes, among which the conquests of Louis XIV. The image was engraved by Guillaume Vallet (Paris 1632-1704), who specialized in engraving religious and historical subjects. Boileau chose in Paillet and Vallet two prominent artists of the time: both were *académiciens* (1659 and 1664 respectively), Paillet was also *Peintre ordinaire du roi*; both exhibited in the Salon of 1673, so just prior to the publication of this engraving: perhaps the drawing and/or engraving were exhibited in the Salon?

34. 'Mémoires', pp. 524-25.

35. *Parallèle*, II, pp. 39, 158-76, 180-84. There is of course no title or explanation accompanying the engraving, but is seems that Paillet, a recognised portrait-painter, followed Boileau's instructions to depict Demosthenes: the orator's profile bears a similarity, for example, to an antique bust of Demosthenes drawn by Rubens and published in 1638 as one of a set of eight engraved portraits of classical figures.

36. Pericles was always said to have 'thundered and lightened', and the notion of *fulmen eloquentiae* is found in both Cicero and Quintilian (see *OTS*, pp. xxxix and n. 1, 62, 111). Even Charles Perrault in *Le Génie* speaks of 'la foudre' in connection with Pericles and Demosthenes (p. 173); however, in discussing 'la foudre et les éclairs' with no allusion to the concept of *le sublime*, Perrault deliberately undermines one of the central pillars of the *Traité du sublime*.

37. '[Il] folgore della sublime, che hà forza d'atterrire, et di spaventare ciascuno [...]. Per lo fulmine si mostra, come narra Pierio Valeriano nel lib. 43 che non con minore forza l'eloquenza d'un huomo facondo, et sapiente, batte à terra la pertinacia fabricata, et fondata dall'ignoranza nelle menti de gli stolidi prosuntuosi, che il fulmine percuote, et abbatte le torri, che s'inalzano sopra gl'alti edifitii' (Ripa, *Iconologia*, p. 127).

38. There are editions of the *Hieroglyphica* published in Lyon in 1602, 1610 and 1626; and of a French translation, Lyon, 1615. The first French translation had been published in Lyon, 1576.

39. *Commentaires hieroglyphiques*, II, pp. 280-86.

40. Perrault may have had particular reason in the early 1680s for wishing to lavish praise upon the King: Racine and Boileau were becoming increasingly hostile, and the growing power of Louvois and the death of his protector Colbert (1683) led to the end of his career at Court and the removal of his government stipend; henceforth Perrault was to devote much more of his time to writing.

CONCLUSION: TOWARDS THE ROMANTIC SUBLIME

Ils abordèrent la question du sublime. Certains objets, sont d'eux-mêmes sublimes, le fracas d'un torrent, des ténèbres profondes, un arbre battu par la tempête. Un caractère est beau quand il triomphe, et sublime quand il lutte. 'Je comprends' dit Bouvard 'le Beau est le Beau, et le Sublime le très Beau.' Comment les distinguer? (*Bouvard et Pécuchet*, Chap. 5)

In 1733 there was published in Verona a handsome small folio edition of *Peri hupsous*, presenting in parallel columns on opposite pages the Greek text alongside translations in Latin (by John Hudson), Italian (by Anton Francesco Gori) and French (by Boileau):[1] for the eighteenth century, Longinus clearly enjoyed the status of a 'classic'—as too did Boileau's translation. But as Longinus became more prominent in the pantheon, so the term *sublime* became more widely used, and more varied in its applications.

'Il y a le sublime qui commence': thus Montesquieu on seeing the Masaccio frescoes in the Brancacci chapel of Santa Maria della Carmine in Florence (II, 1356). His use of the term *sublime* in the late 1720s to describe this example of early Renaissance art, celebrated for its use of perspective and chiaroscuro to achieve strikingly realistic portrayals of psychologically plausible human figures, is manifestly indebted to Boileau's aesthetic of *le sublime*. But only forty years later, Diderot is employing the same term in the *Salon de 1767* to describe the very different aesthetic of Joseph Vernet.[2] For Diderot, Vernet's stormy seascapes epitomise the sublime of Edmund Burke's *A Philosophical Enquiry into the Origin of our Ideas of the Sublime and Beautiful* (1757), recently translated into French (1765).[3] Diderot's use of the term *sublime* has virtually no point of contact with Montesquieu's use of the word forty years earlier; the divide between Masaccio's simple but powerful realism and Vernet's emotional pre-Romanticism marks a divide between what we may term the Classical Sublime and the Romantic Sublime.

Discussion of *le sublime* certainly flourished in the intervening years, and the reactions to Boileau's *Traité du sublime* became increasingly eclectic.[4] Silvain's *Traité du sublime* (1732) provoked a flurry of works in the 1730s by the abbé Prévost, le Père Castel and Rémond de Saint-Mard. Charles-Hugues Lefèvre de Saint-Marc's five-volume edition of the complete works of Boileau (1747) gave particular prominence to the *sublime* by including in the critical apparatus extensive extracts from earlier writings on the *Traité du sublime*; and this edition was the principal source of

172

Jaucourt's workman-like article 'Sublime' in the *Encyclopédie* (Vol. XV, 1765), which appeared in the same year as the French translation of Burke's *Enquiry*. Diderot's *Salon de 1767*, written under the influence of Burke, may be said to mark the first French appearance of the Romantic Sublime, and so a decisive break with the earlier aesthetic and poetic preoccupations of classicism. The Classical Sublime continued to shape critical discussion, as for example in Marmontel's article 'Sublime' written for the *Supplément à l'Encyclopédie* (Vol. IV, 1777), but outside the ideological context within which it had been conceived, the concept had been emptied of its energy.

This is well illustrated in the critical writings of Voltaire. Steeped in the literary culture of the seventeenth century, Voltaire naturally associates Racine with the *sublime*: 'Je regarde Racine comme le meilleur de nos poëtes tragiques, sans contredit, comme celui [...] qui seul a été véritablement sublime sans aucune enflure.'[5] His remarks on a passage in Corneille's *Nicomède* reveal however the extent to which his use of the term *sublime* has become banal:

> Ce morceau sublime, jeté dans une comédie, fait voir combien le reste est petit [...]. Ce vrai sublime fait sentir combien l'ampoulé doit déplaire aux esprits bien faits. Il n'y a pas un mot dans ces quatre vers qui ne soit simple et noble [...]. Il fallait que toute la pièce fût sur ce ton héroïque. Je ne veux pas dire que tout doive tendre au sublime, car alors il n'y en aurait point; mais tout doit être noble.[6]

Despite Voltaire's emotional attachment to the literature and literary values of *le siècle de Louis XIV*, his absolute rejection of poetic enthusiasm—which he equates with fanaticism—make him totally uncomprehending of the latent neoplatonism with which Boileau had invested the term; writing in 1771, Voltaire remains untouched by the influence of Burke:

> La chose la plus rare est de joindre la raison avec l'enthousiasme [...]. L'enthousiasme raisonnable est le partage des grands poëtes. Cet enthousiasme raisonnable est la perfection de leur art: c'est ce qui fit croire autrefois qu'ils étaient inspirés des dieux, et c'est ce qu'on n'a jamais dit des autres artistes.[7]

To say that the Classical Sublime and the Romantic Sublime were two discrete concepts might seem obvious, were it not for the fact that recent scholarly interest in the Romantic (also Gothic) Sublime as a concept attempting to represent the unrepresentable and to break beyond the confines of rational discourse has revived (albeit differently) earlier attempts to read a Romantic aesthetic back onto classicism. The two concepts, though both grounded in a notion of inspiration, are however fundamentally distinct. At the level of genre, the Classical Sublime is exclusively a (French) literary concept, whereas the Romantic Sublime is a (European) aesthetic concept which is as much concerned with painting as with poetry. The Classical Sublime relishes an ideal of clarity, whereas the Romantic Sublime finds pleasure in terror and obscurity, as here, in Diderot's *Salon de 1767*:

> Tout ce qui étonne l'âme, tout ce qui imprime un sentiment de terreur conduit au sublime [...]. L'obscurité ajoute à la terreur [...]. La clarté est bonne pour convaincre, elle ne vaut rien pour émouvoir. La clarté, de quelque manière qu'on l'entende, nuit à l'enthousiasme.[8]

In strictly linguistic terms, Classical poetic discourse is concerned with the nature of the linguistic sign, the perfect mapping of *signifiant* onto referent; Romantic poetic discourse, on the other hand, arises from what is not or cannot be expressed, from the gap between *signifié* and referent. Thus the Classical interest in the *je ne sais quoi* and the Romantic concern with the ineffable are, from a linguistic standpoint, diametrically opposed. Indeed, the emergence of the Romantic Sublime inevitably heralds the end of nomenclaturism. In the wake of Herder and Humboldt especially, language comes to be seen not as a means of access to an outside world, but rather as a human activity which confers meaning on the world outside: for Humboldt, 'language is not a work (*ergon*), but an activity (*energeia*).' When Coleridge writes to Godwin in 1800 that 'I would endeavour to destroy the old antithesis of *Words* and *Things*, elevating, as it were, words into Things, and living Things too', he is sounding the death-knell of the old nomenclaturist order.[9]

If the Romantic Sublime signalled the demise of nomenclaturism, the Classical Sublime arose as an early response to nomenclaturist thinking. The 1660s and 1670s were a period of renewed preoccupation with the idea of the linguistic sign and with the notion that words are mere tokens designating an external reality. This mimetic model of language, nomenclaturism, underlies the poetic theory of classicism, and ultimately undermines it. The drive to consider language as a nomenclature generates tensions which strain to breaking point any attempt to found a thorough-going theory of poetry. Linguists demand that words be adequate to the objects they would depict; moralists condemn words which are so adequate that they blur the line between fiction and truth: linguistic and moral truth are at odds. If words are nothing more than the tokens of preconceived ideas, then poetic language can be nothing more than the arrangement of poetic ideas. The logic of nomenclaturism is to reduce poetic discourse to invisibility, and ultimately to deny poetry altogether, a burdensome inheritance for the poetic language of the eighteenth century.

In the mid-seventeenth century, burlesque writing already calls into question the nomenclaturist model, and the poetic theory of French classicism might be described as a series of attempts (*le je ne sais quoi* is one example, *le délicat* another) to paper over the shortcomings of nomenclaturism. Boileau's theory of *le sublime* is the most ambitious and most coherent of the competing poetic theories of classicism. It achieves coherency by side-stepping the troublesome mimetic model, not clamorously and provocatively in the manner of the burlesque writers, but discreetly, and for a time more effectively. The classical sublime, exploiting a continuing undercurrent of platonism, depends on the notion of poetic enthusiasm to shift the emphasis away from consideration of poetic discourse as reflection of ideas towards a reader-oriented view of poetic language. In this way, the classical sublime transcends nomenclaturism, even while holding to some of the reassuring vocabulary of imitation. The dramatic poetry of Racine triumphantly exemplifies the classical sublime in practice. But even Boileau's relatively modest reassertion of platonism could not hold out against a nomenclaturist model increasingly assertive in the wake of Malebranche and Locke: the result, as Edward Nye has shown, was a prolonged period in the eighteenth century when poetic theory fought shy of inspiration and *la fureur poétique*, and took refuge instead in scintillating verbal playfulness.

NOTES

[1] The edition, which has an engraved frontispiece, was compiled by the publisher, Giovanni Alberto Tumermani, and also contains notes by John Hudson and by Jakob Tollius.

[2] For example, VII, p. 177.

[3] See Wilton, *Turner*, p. 39.

[4] See in particular Lawrence Kerslake, *Essays on the Sublime*, which details French writings on the sublime from Boileau to La Harpe. I have been unable to locate a doctoral thesis by Brian Elkner, 'Le Sublime: de Fénelon à Diderot', supposedly submitted in the late 1960s to the University of Lyon and supervised by Robert Mauzi.

[5] *Correspondence*, D15488.

[6] *Œuvres complètes* (Oxford), Vol. 55, p. 775. Similarly, in his article 'Genre de Style' for the *Encyclopédie* (Vol. 7, 1757), Voltaire speaks of 'le simple et le sublime'; but without the context of classical rhetorical theory, his remarks amount to no more than a discussion of 'le mélange des styles'.

[7] *Œuvres complètes*, ed. Moland, Vol. 18, p. 554 ('Enthousiasme', *Questions sur l'Encyclopédie*).

[8] Diderot, Vol. 7, pp. 182-83.

[9] See Bruns, *Modern Poetry and the Idea of Language*, Chap. 2, '*Energeia*: the development of the Romantic idea of language'. The quotation from Coleridge is taken from this chapter.

BIBLIOGRAPHY

The Bibliography is divided as follows:
I. Manuscripts (pre-1800)
II . Theses
III. Books and articles first published before 1800
IV. Books and articles published since 1800

Place of publication of books is Paris unless otherwise stated.

Square brackets indicate date of first publication.

The following abbreviations have been used:

BHR	*Bibliothèque d'Humanisme et de la Renaissance*
DHS	*Dix-Huitième Siècle*
DS	*Diderot Studies*
DSS	*Dix-Septième Siècle*
EC	*Esprit créateur*
FF	*French Forum*
FS	*French Studies*
JWCI	*Journal of the Warburg and Courtauld Institutes*
MLN	*Modern Language Notes*
MLR	*Modern Language Review*
PFSCL	*Papers on French Seventeenth-Century Literature*
RF	*Romanische Forschungen*
RHLF	*Revue d'histoire littéraire de la France*
RLC	*Revue de littérature comparée*
RR	*Romanic Review*
RSH	*Revue des Sciences Humaines*
SCFS	*Seventeenth-Century French Studies*
SVEC	*Studies on Voltaire and the Eighteenth Century*
YFS	*Yale French Studies*

Bibliography

I. MANUSCRIPTS (PRE-1800)

Clément, 'Regles pour la connoissance des Devises', Bibl. de l'Arsenal, MS 5420, pp. 513-19.

Dacier, André, manuscript notes on text of Longinus, *Traité du sublime* (1694, Greek text with Boileau's French translation), British Library, 871.h.4.

'Discours sur l'art des devises', Bibl. de l'Arsenal, MS 3328, fols 1-46.

Saint-Pierre, abbé de, 'Observations sur l'éloquence', Bibl. publique de la Ville de Neuchâtel, MSR 248.

————, 'Observations sur la beauté des ouvrages d'esprit', Bibl. municipale de Rouen, MS 949, pp. 295-314.

Sala, Pierre, 'Emblesmes et devises d'amour', British Library, Stowe MS 955.

II. THESES

Aggeler, William Ford, 'La Conception du sublime dans la littérature française de 1660 à 1720' (Ph.D, University of California, 1939).

Cronk, Nicholas, 'The Classical Sublime: Boileau's *Traité du sublime* in the context of contemporary poetic theory, 1650-1720' (D.Phil, Oxford, 1990).

Dray, J. P., 'Neoplatonism and French religious thought in the seventeenth century' (D.Phil, Oxford, 1987).

Le Boulengé, Marc, 'Dominique Bouhours, *Les Entretiens d'Ariste et d'Eugène*: Troisième entretien, Le Secret: Edition critique' (Mémoire de maîtrise, Montréal, 1974).

Poirson, Etiennette, 'Le sublime et le beau chez les grands préromantiques et romantiques français' (Thèse d'état, Paris IV, 1975).

III. BOOKS AND ARTICLES FIRST PUBLISHED BEFORE 1800

Ablancourt, Nicolas Perrot d', *Lettres et préfaces critiques*, ed. R. Zuber (1972).

Abrégé de rhétorique (1674).

L'Antiphyllarque ou réfutation des lettres de Phyllarque à Ariste (Lyon, 1630).

Arnauld, Antoine, and Lancelot, *Grammaire générale et raisonnée* [1660], Republications Paulet (1969).

————, and Pierre Nicole, *La Logique ou l'art de penser* [1662], ed. P. Clair and Fr. Girbal, seconde édition revue (1981).

Aubignac, François Hedelin d', *La Pratique du théâtre* [1657], ed. P. Martino (Alger, 1927).

————, *Discours académique sur l'éloquence* (1668).

Baillet, Adrien, *Jugemens des savans sur les principaux ouvrages des auteurs*, 9 pts in 4 vols (1685-86).

Balzac, Jean-Louis Guez de, *Œuvres*, 2 vols (1665).

Barbier d'Aucour, Jean, *Sentimens de Cléante sur les Entretiens d'Ariste et d'Eugène* (1671).

Bary, *La Rhetorique françoise* (1659).

Batteux, abbé Charles, *Les Quatre Poëtiques: d'Aristote, d'Horace, de Vida, de Despréaux*, 2 vols (1771).

Baudoin, Jean, *Recueil d'emblemes divers* (1638).

Bellegarde, abbé Jean-Baptiste Morvan de, *Réflexions sur l'élégance et la politesse du stile* (1695).

————, *Lettres curieuses de littérature et de morale* (1702).

————, *Le Sublime des auteurs, ou pensées choisies* (1705).

Besnier, Pierre, *La Réunion des langues, ou l'art de les apprendre toutes par une seule* (1674).

Besoigne, Jérôme, *Histoire de l'abbaye de Port-Royal* (Cologne, 1752-53).

Boileau, Gilles, *Advis à Monsieur Ménage* (1656).

Boileau, Nicolas, *Œuvres diverses*, 2 vols (1674).

————, *Œuvres*, 5 vols, ed. C.-H. Lefèvre de Saint-Marc (1747).

————, *Œuvres complètes*, 7 vols, ed. Charles-H. Boudhors (1934-43) [references to this edition, unless otherwise indicated].

————, *Œuvres complètes*, ed. Françoise Escal, Pléiade (1966).

————, *Correspondance entre Boileau Despréaux et Brossette*, ed. A. Laverdet (1858).

————, *Arte poetica*, ed. Patrizia Oppici, introd. Fausta Garavini (Venice, 1995).

Bossuet, 'Dissertatio de Psalmis', *Liber Psalmorum* (Lyon, 1691).

————, *Œuvres*, 43 vols (Versailles: Lebel, 1815-19).

Bouhours, Dominique, *Les Entretiens d'Ariste et d'Eugène* [1671], presented by F. Brunot (1962) [references to this edition].

————, *Les Entretiens d'Ariste et d'Eugène*, Quatrième édition (1673).

————, *Remarques nouvelles sur la langue françoise* (1675).

————, *La Manière de bien penser dans les ouvrages d'esprit* [1687] (1715, Nouvelle édition, reprint Brighton, 1971) [references to this edition].

————, *La Manière de bien penser dans les ouvrages d'esprit*, Nouvelle édition (1705), reprint, ed. Suzanne Guellouz (1988).

————, 'Explication de divers termes françois que beaucoup de gens confondent faute d'en avoir une notion nette', *Mémoires pour l'histoire des sciences et des beaux arts* (Trévoux, Septembre-Octobre, 1701), 170-94.

Bremond d'Ars, Pierre de, *De l'éloquence*, ed. H. de Bremond d'Ars-Migré (Macon, 1938).

Brossette, Claude, 'Mémoires de Brossette sur Boileau Despréaux', in *Correspondance entre Boileau Despréaux et Brossette*, ed. A. Laverdet (1858).

Burke, Edmund, *A Philosophical Enquiry into the Origin of our Ideas of the Sublime and Beautiful* [1757], ed. J. T. Boulton (London, 1958).

————, *Recherche philosophique sur l'origine de nos idées du sublime et du beau*, introd. and trad. Baldine Saint Girons (1990).

Bussy-Rabutin, *Correspondance avec le Père René Rapin*, ed. C. Rouben (1983).

Camus, Jean-Pierre, *Diversitez* (1609)

Chapelain, Jean, *Lettres*, 2 vols, ed. Ph. Tamizey de Larroque (1880-83).

———, *Opuscules critiques*, ed. A. C. Hunter (1936).

Charpentier, François, *Deffense de la langue françoise pour l'inscription de l'arc de triomphe* (1676).

Cicero, [Rhetorica ad Herennium] *La rhétorique de Cicéron*, trans. Jacob (1652).

———, [De optimo genere oratorum] *Du meilleur genre d'orateurs*, trans. Pierre du Ryer (1654).

———, [De oratore] *La Rhétorique de Ciceron*, trans. abbé J. Cassagnes (1673).

Colletet, Guillaume, 'Discours de l'éloquence, et de l'imitation des Anciens', 'Discours de la poésie morale et sententieuse', in *L'Art poétique* (1658).

———, *Traité de l'épigramme et Traité du sonnet* [first two treatises of *Art poétique*], ed. P. A. Jannini (Geneva, 1965).

Condillac, *Essai sur l'origine des connaissances humaines* [1746] (1973).

Cordemoy, Gerauld de, *Œuvres philosophiques*, ed. P. Clair and Fr. Girbal (1968).

Cotin, Charles, 'Discours sur les Enigmes' and 'Lettre à Damis', in *Recueil des énigmes de ce temps* (1646).

———, 'Discours en général sur les métamorphoses', preface to *L'Uranie* (pp.3-8), in *Œuvres meslées* (1659).

Cyrano de Bergerac, *Œuvres complètes*, ed. J. Prévot (1977).

Dacier, André, 'Remarques' (1683) [on *Traité du sublime*], in Boileau, ed. Boudhors, *Traité du sublime*, 183-228.

———, *La Poétique d'Aristote, [...] avec des remarques critiques sur tout l'ouvrage*, 12^0 (1692).

Deimier, Pierre de, *L'Académie de l'art poétique* (1610).

Descartes, René, *Œuvres*, 13 vols, ed. Ch. Adam and P. Tannery (1897-1913), reprint (1957-76) [references to this edition indicated 'AT'].

———, *Œuvres philosophiques*, 3 vols, ed. F.Alquié (1963-73) [references to this edition unless otherwise indicated].

Diderot, Denis, *Lettre sur les sourds et muets*, ed. Paul Hugo Meyer, *DS*, 7 (1965).

———, *Œuvres complètes*, 15 vols, presented by Roger Lewinter (1969-73).

———, *Lettre sur les aveugles; Lettre sur les sourds et muets*, eds. Marian Hobson and Simon Harvey (2000).

Dinet, Pierre, *Cinq Livres des hieroglyphiques, où sont contenus les [...] secrets de la nature* (1614).

Du Bellay, Joachim, *La Deffence et illustration de la langue francoyse* [1549], ed. H. Chamard (1948).

Du Bos, abbé Jean-Baptiste, *Réflexions critiques sur la poésie et sur la peinture* [1719], 3 vols (1770, reprint Geneva, 1982).

Du Plaisir, *Sentiments sur les lettres, et sur l'histoire, avec des scrupules sur le stile* [1683], ed. Philippe Hourcade (Geneva, 1975).

Duret, Claude, *Trésor de l'histoire des langues de cet univers* [Cologny, 1613], seconde édition (Yverdon, 1619).

Fardoil, Nicolas, 'Sur le style des énigmes', *Harangues, discours et lettres* (1665), 100-105.

Félibien, André, *Entretiens sur les vies des peintres* (1685-88).

Fénelon, *Lettre à l'Académie* [1716], ed. E. Caldarini (Geneva, 1970).

———, *Œuvres*, Vol. I, ed. J. Le Brun, Pléiade (1983).

Fleury, Claude, *Opuscules*, 4 vols (Nîmes, 1780-83).

Fontenelle, *Œuvres*, 3 vols [ed. G.-B. Depping] (1818).

Furetière, Antoine, *Nouvelle allégorique* [1658], ed. Eva van Ginneken (Geneva, 1967).

Gardien, 'Discours sur les devises, emblesmes, et revers de medailles', *Mercure galant* (Extraordinaire d'octobre, 1678), 214-64.

Gibert, Balthazar, *Réflexions sur la rhétorique, où l'on répond aux objections du P. Lamy*, 3 pts (1705-07).

Girard, abbé Gabriel, *La Justesse de la langue françoise*, ed. M. G. Adamo (Fasano and Paris, 1999) [1718].

Goulu, Dom Jean, *Lettres de Phyllarque à Ariste, où il est traité de l'éloquence françoise*, 2 vols [1627-28], 3rd ed. (1628).

Gournay, Marie Le Jars de, *Les Idées littéraires de Mlle de Gournay*, ed. Anne Uildriks (Groningen, 1962).

Gracián, Baltasar, *Agudeza y arte de ingenio* [1642], ed. Evaristo Correa Calderón, 2 vols (Madrid, 1969).

Guéret, Gabriel, *Entretiens sur l'éloquence de la chaire et du barreau* (1666).

Guérin de Bouscal, Daniel, *Le Gouvernement de Sanche Pansa* [1642], ed. C. E. J. Caldicott (Geneva, 1981).

Helvétius, *De l'esprit* [1758], presented by Fr. Châtelet (Verviers, 1973).

Huet, Pierre Daniel, *Demonstratio evangelica* (1679).

La Bruyère, *Les Caractères*, ed. R. Garapon (1962).

La Fontaine, *Œuvres diverses*, ed. Pierre Clarac, Pléiade (1958).

———, *Œuvres complètes: Fables et Contes*, ed. Jean-Pierre Collinet, Pléiade (1991).

La Forge, Louis de, *Œuvres philosophiques*, ed. P. Clair (1974).

La Mothe Le Vayer, *Œuvres*, 2 vols (1654).

La Motte, Antoine Houdar de, 'Discours sur la Poësie en général, et sur l'Ode en particulier' [1707], *Œuvres*, 10 vols (1754), I, Pt. 1, 13-60.

Lamy, Bernard, Cong. Orat., *Nouvelles Réflexions sur l'art poétique* (1668).

———, *La Rhétorique ou l'art de parler*, ed. B. Timmermans (1998) [first published as *De l'art de parler*, 1675].

Lamy, Dom François, OSB, *De la connoissance de soi-mesme* (1697).

———, *La Rhétorique de collège trahie par son apologiste* (1704).

Le Clerc, Jean, *Parrhasiana, ou pensées diverses* (1699).

Le Fèvre, Tanneguy, *Les Vies des poètes grecs, en abrégé* (1665).

Le Grand, Jean-François, 'Discours sur la rhetorique françoise', preface to R. Bary, *La Rhetorique françoise* (1659).

Le Gras, avocat au Parlement, *La Réthorique françoise ou les préceptes de l'ancienne et vraye éloquence* (1671).

Le Maître de Sacy, Louis Isaac, *La Genèse traduite en françois avec l'explication du sens litteral et du sens spirituel*, 2 vols [1682] (1683).

Le Moyne, Pierre, 'Discours de la poésie' [1641], in *Hymnes de la sagesse divine et de l'amour divin*, ed. A. Mantero (1986).

———, *Devises heroiques et morales* (1649).

———, *De l'art de régner* (1665).

———, *De l'art des devises* (1666).

Leonardo da Vinci, *Traitté de la peinture*, trans. Roland Fréart, sieur de Chambray (1651).

———, *The Notebooks*, ed. Irma A. Richter (Oxford, 1980).

Locke, John, *An Essay concerning Human Understanding* [1690], ed. P. H. Nidditch (Oxford, 1975).

'Longinus', *Peri hupsous*, ed. Tanneguy Le Fèvre (Saumur, 1663).

———, *Peri hupsous* (Verona, 1733).

———, *On the sublime*, ed. with introduction and commentary D. A. Russell (Oxford, 1964) [referred to as *OTS*].

———, [French translation] *Traité du sublime*, trans. Boileau [1674], ed. Ch.-H. Boudhors (1942) [referred to as *TS*].

———, [French translation] *Traité du sublime*, trans. Boileau, ed. Francis Goyet (1995).

———, [English translation] *On sublimity*, trans. D. A. Russell, in *Ancient Literary Criticism*, ed. D. A. Russell and M. Winterbottom (Oxford, 1972), 460-503 [referred to as *OS*].

Mairet, J., *La Silvanire*, ed. Daniela Dalla Valle (Rome, 1976).

Malebranche, *Œuvres*, Pléiade, Vol I, ed. G. Rodis-Lewis and G. Malbreil (1979).

Malherbe, François de, *Œuvres complètes*, 5 vols, ed. L. Lalanne (1862-69).

Marivaux, *Journaux et Œuvres diverses*, ed. F. Deloffre and M. Gilot (1969).

Marolles, Michel de, abbé de Villeloin, *Traité du poème épique pour l'intelligence de l'Enéide de Virgile* (1662).

Ménage, Gilles, *Les Origines de la langue françoise* (1650).

———, *Dictionnaire étymologique, ou Origines de la langue françoise*, nouv. éd. (1694).

Menestrier, Claude-François, *L'Art des emblemes ou s'enseigne la morale par les figures de la fable, de l'histoire, et de la nature* [first version, 1662] (Mittenwald, 1981: reprint of 1684 edition).

———, *La Science et l'art des devises* (1686).

———, *La Philosophie des images énigmatiques* [1682] (Lyon, 1694).

Méré, chevalier de, *Œuvres complètes*, 3 vols, ed. Charles-H. Boudhors (1930).

Molière, *Œuvres complètes*, 2 vols, ed. G. Couton, Pléiade (1971).

Montaigne, *Œuvres complètes*, ed. A. Thibaudet and M. Rat, Pléiade (1962).

Montesquieu, *Œuvres complètes*, 3 vols, ed. A. Masson (1950-55).

———, *Essai sur le goût*, ed. Charles-Jacques Beyer (Geneva, Droz, 1967).

Nicole, Pierre, *Traité de la comédie* [1667], ed. G. Couton (1961).

Nicot, Jean, *Thrésor de la langue françoyse* (1606).

Pascal, *Œuvres complètes*, ed. L. Lafuma (1963).

Patrizi da Cherso, Francesco, *Della Poetica* [1586, Pts. 3-7 unpublished], 3 vols, ed. Danilo Aguzzi Barbagli (Florence, 1969-71).

Pellisson, Paul, *Histoire de l'Académie françoise* [1653], 2 vols, ed. Ch.-L. Livet (1858).

Perrault, Charles, *Le Génie: Epistre à M. de Fontenelle* [1686], included in 1964 Munich reprint of *Parallèle*, 172-74.

———, *Parallèle des anciens et des modernes*, 4 vols (1688-97); reprint, introd. H. R. Jauss (Munich, 1964).

———, *Le Cabinet des beaux arts* (1690).

Petit, Pierre, *Selectorum poematum libri duo: accessit dissertatio de furore poetico* (1683).

Piles, Roger de, *Conversations sur la connoissance de la peinture* (1677).

———, *L'Idée du peintre parfait* (1699).

———, *Cours de peinture par principes* (1708).

Pliny, *Natural History*, Loeb Classical Library, Vol. 9 (Cambridge, Mass. and London, 1952).

———, *Histoire naturelle, Livre XXXV: La Peinture*, introd. Pierre-Emmanuel Dauzat (1997).

Pons, abbé Jean-François de, 'Dissertation sur les langues en général, et sur la langue françoise en particulier', *Le Nouveau Mercure* (Mars, 1717), 7-47 [reprinted in *Œuvres* (1738)].

———, 'Réflexions sur l'éloquence', *Le Nouveau Mercure* (Mai, 1718), 5-26 [reprinted in *Œuvres* (1738)].

Poussin, Nicolas, *Lettres et propos sur l'art*, ed. Anthony Blunt (1964).

Pradon, Nicolas, *Le Triomphe de Pradon* [1684] (1686).

———, *Nouvelles Remarques sur tous les ouvrages du sieur D**** (1685).

———, *Réponse à la Satire X du sieur D**** (1694).

Quintilian, *De l'institution de l'orateur*, trans. Michel de Pure (1663).

Racine, *Œuvres complètes*, 2 vols, ed. R. Picard, Pléiade (1950-60).

Rapin, René, *Œuvres*, dernière édition, 3 vols (La Haye, 1725).

———, *Les Réflexions sur la poétique de ce temps*, ed. E. T. Dubois (Geneva, 1970).

Regnault, Charles, 'Discours sur les métamorphoses françoises' [1641], in F. Lachèvre, *Bibliographie des recueils collectifs de poésies publiés de 1597 à 1700*, 4 vols (1901-05), II, pp. 10-12.

Richelet, N., *Les Odes de P. de Ronsard [...] commentes par N. Richelet* (1604).

Ripa, Cesare, *Iconologia* [1593], 3rd edition (Rome, 1603); reprint Georg Olms, introd. Erna Mandowsky (Hildesheim, 1984).

———, *Iconologie*, trans. Jean Baudoin (1644); reprint Garland (New York, 1976).

———, *Iconologie*, trans. Jean Baudoin, 2 vols (Amsterdam, 1698).

Ronsard, *Œuvres complètes*, Pléiade, Vol. I, ed. J. Céard, D. Ménager and M. Simonin (1993).

Rousseau, Jean-Baptiste, *Correspondance de J.-B. Rousseau et de Brossette*, 2 vols, ed. P. Bonnefon (1910-11).

Saint-Amant, *Œuvres*, 5 vols, eds. J. Bailbé and J. Lagny (1969-79).

Saint-Evremond, *Œuvres en prose*, 4 vols, ed. René Ternois (1962-69).

———, *Lettres*, 2 vols, ed. René Ternois (1967-68).

Saint-Pierre, abbé de, 'Observations sur la beauté des ouvrages d'esprit', *Mercure de France* (juin, second volume, 1726), 1306–37.

———, 'Observations sur l'éloquence', ed. L. Kerslake, *DHS*, 31 (1999), 305-28.

Salabert, Jean, *Les Fleurs de la rhetorique françoise* (1636).

Scudéry, Georges de, *Alaric ou Rome vaincue* (1654).

Segrais, *Nouvelles françaises* (1656-57).

Sévigné, Mme de, *Correspondance*, 3 vols, ed. Roger Duchêne, Pléiade (1972-78).

Somaize, *Le Dictionnaire des précieuses*, 2 vols, ed. Ch.-L. Livet (1856).

Tesauro, Emanuele, *Idea delle perfette imprese: testo inedito* [written 1620s], ed. Maria Luisa Doglio (Florence, 1975).

———, *Il cannocchiale aristotelico* [1654], ed. August Buck (Turin, 1670, reprint Bad Homburg, 1968).

Théâtre du xviiᵉ siècle, 2 vols, ed. Jacques Schérer, Pléiade (1975-86).

Théophile de Viau, *Œuvres complètes*, 4 vols, ed. Guido Saba, (Rome, 1978-87).

Thomassin, Louis, Cong. Orat., *La Méthode d'étudier et d'enseigner chrétiennement et solidement les lettres humaines par rapport aux lettres divines et aux Ecritures [...]: De l'étude des poètes*, 3 vols (1681-82).

Tristan L'Hermite, *La Mort de Sénèque* [1645] (1984).

Valeriano Bolzani, Giovanni Pierio, *Hieroglyphica sive de sacris Aegyptiorum aliarumque gentium litteris* (Basel, 1556).

———, *Commentaires hieroglyphiques ou images des choses de Jan Pierius Valerian*, trans. Gabriel Chappuys, 2 vols (Lyon, 1576).

Vaugelas, *Remarques sur la langue française* (1647).

Vaux, Adrien Montluc de, comte de Cramail, *Tombeau de l'orateur français ou Discours de Tircis pour servir de réponse à la lettre de Periandre touchant l'Apologie de M. de Balzac* (1628).

Villars, Montfaucon de, *Le Comte de Gabalis; La Critique de Bérénice* [1670; 1671], ed. R. Laufer (1963).

———, *De la délicatesse* (1671).

Voltaire, *Œuvres complètes*, 52 vols, ed. L. Moland (1877-85).

————, *Œuvres complètes* (Geneva and Oxford, 1968-).

————, *Correspondence and related documents*, ed. Theodore Besterman, definitive edition (Geneva and Oxford, 1968-77).

IV. BOOKS AND ARTICLES PUBLISHED SINCE 1800

Abraham, C. K., *Enfin Malherbe: the influence of Malherbe on French lyric prosody, 1605-1674* (Lexington, Ky., 1971).

Abrams, M. H., *The Mirror and the Lamp: Romantic theory and the critical tradition* [1953] (Oxford, 1977).

Adam, Antoine, 'La théorie mystique de l'amour dans *L'Astrée* et ses sources italiennes', *Revue d'Histoire de la Philosophie et d'Histoire générale de la Civilisation*, 4 (1936), 193-206.

————, 'Note sur le burlesque', *DSS*, Nº. 4 (1949), 81-91.

————, *Histoire de la littérature française au xviiᵉ siècle*, 5 vols (1949-56).

Allut, P., *Recherches sur la vie et sur les Œuvres du P. Claude-François Ménestrier* (Lyon, 1856).

Apostolidès, Jean-Marie, *Le Roi-Machine: spectacle et politique au temps de Louis XIV* (1981).

Arduini, Stefano, 'La *Hypnerotomachia Poliphili* e il sogno linguistico dell'Umanesimo', *Lingua e stile*, 22 (1987), 197-219.

Ashfield, Andrew, and Peter de Bolla, *The Sublime: a reader in British eighteenth-century aesthetic theory* (Cambridge, 1996).

Bakhtin, M. M., 'Discourse in the novel' [1934-35], in *The Dialogic Imagination*, ed. M. Holquist (Austin, 1981).

Bannister, Mark, *Privileged Mortals: the French heroic novel 1630-1660* (Oxford, 1983).

Bar, Francis, *Le Genre burlesque en France au xviiᵉ siècle: étude de style* (1960).

Barnwell, H. T., *Les Idées morales et critiques de Saint-Evremond* (1957).

————, 'Saint-Evremond et la tragédie classique', *DSS*, Nº. 57 (1962), 24-42.

————, 'Racine vu par Saint-Evremond', *Bulletin de liaison racinienne*, 4 (1965), 71-81; reprinted in *Jeunesse de Racine*, (1969), 77-91.

Barthes, Roland, *Le Degré zéro de l'écriture* (1953).

————, 'L'ancienne rhétorique' [1970] in *L'Aventure sémiologique* (1985).

————, 'La Rochefoucauld: *Réflexions ou Sentences et Maximes*' [1961] in *Le Degré zéro de l'écriture, suivi de Nouveaux Essais critiques* (1972).

————, *L'Obvie et l'obtus: Essais critiques III* (1982).

Baudelaire, *Œuvres complètes*, 2 vols, ed. C. Pichois, Pléiade (1975-76).

Bayley, Peter, *French Pulpit Oratory 1598-1650* (Cambridge, 1980).

————, 'Fixed form and varied function: reflections on the language of French classicism', *SCFS*, 6 (1984), 6-21.

Becq, Annie, *Genèse de l'esthétique française moderne: de la raison classique à l'imagination créatrice 1680-1814*, 2 vols (Pisa, 1984).

Bénichou, Paul, *Morales du grand siècle* (1948).

Benjamin, Walter, 'On language as such' [1916], in *One-Way Street and Other Writings* (London, 1979).

Berlioz, Hector, *Mémoires* [1870] (1969).

Bertière, André, *Le Cardinal de Retz mémorialiste* (1977).

Beugnot, Bernard, *L'Entretien au xviie siècle* (Montreal, 1971).

———, 'Boileau, une esthétique de la lumière', *Studi francesi*, 15 (1971), 229-37.

———, 'Prolégomènes à une édition critique des *Entretiens d'Ariste et d'Eugène*', in *Langue, littérature du xviie et du xviiie siècle: Mélanges offerts à Frédéric Deloffre*, ed. R. Lathuillère (1990), 171-86.

———, *La Mémoire du texte: Essais de poétique classique* (1994).

———, *Les Muses classiques: Essai de bibliographie rhétorique et poétique (1610-1716)* (1996).

Beyer, C., 'Du cartésianisme à la philosophie des lumières', *RR*, 34 (1943), 18-39.

Bialostocki, Jan, 'Une idée de Léonard réalisée par Poussin', *La Revue des Arts*, 4 (1954), 130-36.

———, 'Poussin et le Traité de la peinture de Léonard', *Nicolas Poussin* (Colloque, 1958), ed. A. Chastel, 2 vols (1960), I, 133-40.

Blunt, A., 'The Hypnertomachia Poliphili in seventeenth-century France', *JWCI*, 1 (1937-38), 117-37.

Boisclair, Marie-Nicole, *Gaspard Dughet (1615-1675)* (1986).

Bolzoni, Lina, 'La *Poetica* di Francesco Patrizi da Cherso: il progetto di un modello universale della poesia', *Giornale Storico*, 151 (1974), 357-82, and 152 (1975), 33-56.

Borgerhoff, E. B. O., *The Freedom of French Classicism* (Princeton, 1950).

Bosco, Gabriella, 'Boileau e il trattato del sublime di Longino', in *Dicibilità del sublime*, ed. T. Kemeny and E. Cotta Ramusino (Udine, 1990), 115-21.

Bouvier, Michel, 'Le naturel', *DSS*, N°. 156 (1987), 229-40.

Bray, René, *La Formation de la doctrine classique en France* (1927).

Bredvold, Louis I., 'The tendency toward platonism in neo-classical esthetics', *ELH*, 1 (1934), 91-119.

Brockliss, L. W. B., *French Higher Education in the Seventeenth and Eighteenth Centuries: a cultural history* (Oxford, 1987).

Brody, Jules, *Boileau and Longinus* (Geneva, 1958).

———, 'Platonisme et classicisme', *Lectures classiques*, 1-16 [first published in *Saggi e ricerche di letteratura francese*, 2 (1961); and reprinted in *French Classicism: a critical miscellany*, ed. J. Brody (Englewood Cliffs, N.J., 1966)].

———, 'What *was* French Classicism?', *Continuum*, 1 (1989), 51-77 [later republished as 'Que fut le classicisme français?' in *Lectures classiques*].

———, *Lectures classiques* (Charlottesville, 1996).

Brunot, F., *Histoire de la langue française des origines à 1900*, Nouvelle édition, 13 vols in 23 pts (1966-79).

Bruns, Gerald L., *Modern Poetry and the Idea of Language: a critical and historical study* (New Haven, 1974).

Bruyne, Edgar de, *Etudes d'esthétique médiévale*, 3 vols (Bruges, 1946).

Burke, Peter, 'The two faces of Calvinism', *French Literature and its Background: 1 The Sixteenth Century*, ed. J. Cruickshank (Oxford, 1968), 47-62.

Bury, Emmanuel, 'Le classicisme et le modèle philologique: La Fontaine, Racine et La Bruyère', *L'Information littéraire*, 1990, N°. 3, 20-24.

———, 'Traduction et classicisme', *Littératures classiques*, 19 (1993), 129-43.

———, 'Hellénisme et rhétorique: François Cassandre traducteur d'Arioste', in *Un Classicisme ou des classicismes?*, ed. G. Forestier and J.-P. Néraudau (Pau, 1995), 119-29.

Caldicott, C. E. J., 'Baroque or burlesque? Aspects of French comic theatre in the early seventeenth century', *MLR*, 79 (1984), 797-809.

Carchia, Gianni, *Retorica del sublime* (Rome and Bari, 1990).

Carr, Thomas M., 'François Lamy and the rhetoric of attention of Malebranche', *Romance Notes*, 22 (1981), 197-201.

———, 'The rhetorical theories of Malebranche: persuasion through imitation or attention?', *Zeitschrift für französische Sprache und Literatur*, 93 (1983), 14-24.

———, *Descartes and the Resilience of Rhetoric: Varieties of Cartesian Rhetorical Theory* (Carbondale and Edwardsville, 1990).

Castor, Grahame, *Pléiade Poetics* (Cambridge, 1964).

Cave, Terence, *The Cornucopian Text: problems of writing in the French Renaissance* (Oxford, 1979).

Chantalat, Claude, *A La Recherche du goût classique* (1992).

Charles, Michel, *Rhétorique de la lecture* (1977).

———, 'Claude-François Ménestrier, Poétique de l'énigme', *Poétique*, 45 (1981), 25-52.

Chevalier, Jean-Claude, 'La Grammaire générale de Port-Royal et la critique moderne', *Langages*, 7 (1967), 16-33.

———, 'L'analyse du discours et sa signification', *Littérature*, 18 (1975), 63-78.

———, 'Les *Entretiens* du Père Bouhours: soit la littérature et l'idéologie', in *Langue et langages de Leibniz à l'Encyclopdie*, ed. Michèle Duchet and Michèle Jalley (1977), 25-43.

Chinard, Gilbert, *En lisant Pascal* (Lille and Geneva, 1948).

Chomsky, Noam, *Cartesian Linguistics* (New York, 1966).

Chouillet, Jacques, 'La promenade Vernet', *Recherches sur Diderot et sur l'Encyclopdie*, 2 (1987), 123-63.

Clarke, D. M., 'The ambiguous role of experience in Cartesian science', *PSA*, 2 (1976), Pt. 1, 151-64.

Coleman, D. G., *The Gallo-Roman Muse* (Cambridge, 1979).

———, 'Montaigne and Longinus', *BHR*, 47 (1985), 405-13.

Colotte, P., *Pierre de Deimier* (Gap, 1953).

Conisbee, Philip, *Claude-Joseph Vernet, 1714-1789*, exhibition catalogue (London, 1976).

Cornelius, Paul, *Languages in Seventeenth- and Early Eighteenth-Century Imaginary Voyages* (Geneva, 1965).

Cosnier, Colette, 'Jodelet: un acteur du xviie siècle devenu un type', *RHLF*, 62 (1962), 329-52.

Couton, Georges, 'La Fontaine et l'art des emblèmes', *La Poétique de La Fontaine* (1957), 5-21.

———, *Ecritures codées: Essais sur l'allégorie au xviie siècle* (1990).

Croce, Benedetto, *Estetica* [1902], tenth edition (Bari, 1958).

Cronk, Nicholas, 'Metaphor and metamorphosis', *SCFS*, 6 (1984), 179-89.

———, 'Une poétique platonicienne à l'époque classique: le *De furore poetico* de Pierre Petit (1683)', *DSS*, N°. 146 (1985), 99-102.

———, 'The enigma of French classicism: a platonic current in seventeenth-century poetic theory', *FS*, 40 (1986), 269-86.

———, 'La querelle du sublime: théories anciennes et modernes du discours poétique', *D'un siècle à l'autre, Actes du xvie colloque du CMR 17* (Marseille, 1987), 9-17.

———, 'La défense du dialogisme: vers une poétique du burlesque', *Burlesque et formes parodiques, Actes du Colloque du Mans (1986)*, ed. I. Landy-Houillon and M. Menard (1987), 321-38.

———, 'The singular voice: monologism and French classical discourse', *Continuum*, 1 (1989), 175-202.

———, 'Aristotle, Horace, and Longinus: the conception of reader response', in *The Cambridge History of Literary Criticism*, Vol. III, 'The Renaissance', ed. Glyn P. Norton (Cambridge, 1999), 199-204.

Crowther, Paul, *The Kantian Sublime: From morality to art* (Oxford, 1989).

Culler, Jonathan, 'Paradox and the language of morals in La Rochefoucauld', *MLR*, 68 (1973), 28-39.

Curtius, E. R., *European Literature and the Latin Middle Ages* [1948] (London, 1953).

Dagens, Jean, *Bérulle et les origines de la restauration catholique* (1952).

———, 'Hermétisme et cabale en France de Lefèvre d'Etaples à Bossuet', *RLC*, 35 (1961), 5-16.

Dandrey, Patrick, 'Les deux classicismes', *Littératures classiques*, 19 (1993).

Davidson, Hugh M., 'The literary arts of Longinus and Boileau', *Studies in Seventeenth-Century French Literature presented to Morris Bishop*, ed. J.-J. Demorest (Ithaca, 1962), 247-64.

———, 'Yet another view of French classicism', *Bucknell Review*, 13 (1965), 51-62.

———, 'Fontenelle, Perrault and the realignment of the arts', *Literature and History in the Age of Ideas: Essays on the French Enlightenment presented to George R. Havens*, ed. C. G. S. Williams (Columbus, 1975), 3-13.

———, 'Disciplinary options and the discussion of literature in seventeenth-century France', *New Literary History*, 17 (1985-86), 281-94.

Declercq, Gilles, 'Représenter la passion: la sobriété racinienne', *Littératures classiques*, 11 (1989), 69-93.

——, 'Boileau-Huet, la Querelle du *Fiat Lux*', in *Pierre-Daniel Huet (1630-1721)*, ed. S. Guellouz (Tübingen, 1994), 237-62.

——, 'Usage et bel usage: l'éloge de la langue dans les *Entretiens d'Ariste et d'Eugène*', *Littératures classiques*, 28 (1996).

——, 'Aux confins de la rhétorique: sublime et ineffable dans le classicisme français', in *Dire l'évidence* (1997), 403-35. Revised *DSS*, 52 (2000), 199–220.

——, 'La rhétorique classique entre évidence et sublime', dans M. Fumaroli (ed.), *Histoire de la rhétorique* (1999), 629-706.

——, 'Simplicité corrosive et simplicité polémique: de Descartes à Racine', in *La Simplicité*, forthcoming.

Deguy, Michel, 'Le Grand-dire: pour contribuer à une relecture du pseudo-Longin', J.-F. Courtine and others, *Du sublime* (1988), 11-35 (first published in *Poétique*, 58 (1984), 197-214).

DeJean, Joan, *Ancients against Moderns: Culture Wars and the Making of a Fin de Siècle* (Chicago, 1997).

Delon, Michel, 'Le Sublime et l'idée d'énergie: de la théologie au matérialisme', *RHLF*, 86 (1986), 62-70.

——, *L'Idée d'énergie au tournant des Lumières (1770-1820)* (1988).

——, 'Joseph Vernet et Diderot dans la tempête', *Recherches sur Diderot et sur l'Encyclopédie*, 15 (1993), 31-39.

——, 'Le sublime de la nature dans ses horreurs et ses beautés', *L'Histoire des deux Indes: réécriture et polygraphie*, éd. H.-J. Lüsebrink et A. Strugnell, *SVEC*, 333 (Oxford, 1995), 251-61.

De Mauro, Tullio, *Introduzione alla semantica* (Bari, 1965).

De Mourgues, Odette, *Quelques paradoxes sur le classicisme*, The Zaharoff Lecture for 1980-81 (Oxford, 1981).

Dens, Jean-Pierre, *L'Honnête Homme et la critique du goût: esthétique et société au xviie siècle* (Lexington, Ky., 1981).

Dobbs, B. J. T., *The Foundations of Newton's Alchemy* (Cambridge, 1975).

Donzé, Roland, *La Grammaire générale et raisonnée de Port-Royal: contribution à l'histoire des idées grammaticales en France* (Berne, 1967).

Dorival, Bernard, 'Expression littéraire et expression picturale du sentiment de la nature au xviie siècle français', *La Revue des Arts*, 3 (1953), 44-53.

Dubois, Claude-Gilbert, *Mythe et langage au seizième siècle* (Bordeaux, 1970).

Dubois, Elfreida T., 'Some definitions of the sublime in seventeenth-century French literature', *Essays presented to C. M. Girdlestone* (Newcastle upon Tyne, 1960), 75-91.

——, '*Ingenium* et *iudicium*, quelques réflexions sur la nature de la création poétique', in *Critique et création littéraires en France au xviie siècle* (1977), 311-24.

————, 'La vacation lettrée: conceptions et jugements littéraires chez les Jésuites du dix-septième siècle', in *Recherches sur l'histoire de la poétique*, ed. M.-M. Münch (Berne, 1984), 83-104.

Elkner, Brian A., 'Diderot and the sublime: the artist as hero', *Studies in the Eighteenth Century*, II, ed. R. F. Brissenden (Canberra, 1973), 143-62.

Faisant, Claude, 'Lieux communs de la critique classique et post-classique', *Etudes françaises*, 13 (1977), 143-62.

Faral, Edmond, *Les Arts poétiques du XIIe et du XIIIe siècle: recherches et documents sur la technique littéraire du Moyen Age* (1924).

√ Ferguson, Frances, 'A commentary on Suzanne Guerlac's "Longinus and the subject of the sublime"', *New Literary History*, 16, N°. 2 (1985), 291-97.

Floeck, Wilfried, *Die Literarästhetik des französischen Barock: Entstehung - Entwicklung - Auflösung* (Berlin, 1979).

Fogel, Herbert, *The Criticism of Cornelian Tragedy* (New York, 1967).

Forestier, Georges, *Le Théâtre dans le théâtre sur la scène française du xviie siècle* (Geneva, 1981).

———— and Jean-Pierre Néraudau (eds), *Un Classicisme ou des classicismes? Actes du colloque de Reims 1991* (Pau, 1995).

Foucault, Michel, *Les Mots et les choses* (1966).

————, *L'Ordre du discours* (1971).

France, Peter, *Racine's Rhetoric* (Oxford, 1965).

————, 'The language of literature', in *French Literature and its Background 2: The Seventeenth Century*, ed. J. Cruickshank (Oxford, 1969), 1-16.

————, *Rhetoric and Truth in France: Descartes to Diderot* (Oxford, 1972).

————, 'Between prose and verse', in *The Classical Tradition in French Literature: essays presented to R. C. Knight* (London, 1977), 145-55.

Fumaroli, Marc, 'La querelle de la moralité du théâtre avant Nicole et Bossuet', *RHLF*, 70 (1970), 1007-30.

————, 'Crépuscule de l'enthousiasme au xviie siècle' [1976], in *Héros et orateurs* (Geneva, 1996), 349-77.

————, *L'Age de l'éloquence: rhétorique et res literaria de la Renaissance au seuil de l'époque classique* (Geneva, 1980); paperback edition with new preface (1994).

————, 'Le corps éloquent: une somme d'*actio et pronuntiatio rhetorica* au XVIIe siècle, les *Vacationes autumnales* du P. Louis de Cressolles (1620)', *DSS*, N°. 132 (1981), 237-64.

√ ————, 'Apprends, ma confidente, apprends à me connaître: les *Mémoires* de Retz et le traité *Du Sublime*', *Versants*, 1 (1981), 27-56.

√ ————, 'Rhétorique d'école et rhétorique adulte: remarques sur la réception europenne du traité *Du sublime* au xvie at au xviie siècle' [1986], in *Héros et orateurs* (Geneva, 1996), 377-98.

————, 'Hiéroglyphes et lettres: la "sagesse mystérieuse des anciens" au xviie siècle', *DSS*, N°. 158 (1988), 7-20

————, 'La République des Lettres IV. De Descartes à Fontenelle: la Querelle des Anciens et des Modernes', *Annuaire du Collège de France 1990–91. Résumé des cours et travaux* (1991), 505-35.

————, 'L'allégorie du Parnasse dans la Querelle des Anciens et des Modernes,' in *Correspondances. Mélanges offerts à Roger Duchêne* (Tübingen, 1992), 523-34.

————, 'L'Inspiration du poète de Poussin: essai sur l'allégorie du Parnasse', in *L'Ecole du silence: le sentiment des images au xviie siècle* (1994).

————, 'Le grand style', in *Qu'est-ce que le style?*, ed. G. Molinié and P. Cahné (1994), 139-48.

————, *Héros et orateurs: rhétorique et dramaturgie cornéliennes*, 2nd edition (Geneva, 1996).

————, *Le Poète et le Roi: Jean de la Fontaine en son siècle* (1997).

———— (ed.), *Histoire de la rhétorique dans l'Europe moderne 1450-1950* (1999).

————, 'La Querelle des Anciens et des Modernes, sans vainqueurs ni vaincus,' *Le Débat*, 104 (mars-avril 1999), 73-88.

————, 'Les abeilles et les araignées,' in Anne-Marie Lecoq (ed.), *La Querelle des Anciens et des Modernes*, 7-218.

Garapon, Robert, *La Fantaisie verbale et le comique dans le théâtre français du moyen âge à la fin du xviie siècle* (1957).

Genette, Gérard, *Figures I* (1966).

Gillot, H., *La Querelle des anciens et des modernes* (1914).

Gniadek, Stanislaw, 'La théorie sémantique de Port-Royal', *Studia Romanica Posnaniensia*, 2 (1972), 63-75.

Gohin, Ferdinand, *La Fontaine: études et recherches* (1937).

Goldin, Jeanne, *Cyrano de Bergerac et l'art de la pointe* (Montréal, 1973).

Goyet, Francis, 'Le Pseudo-sublime de Longin', *Etudes littéraires*, 24, N°. 3 (1991-92), 105-20.

————, *Le sublime du lieu commun* (1996).

————, 'Longin, le sublime et la guerre', *Studi di letteratura francese*, 22 (1997), 105-18.

Goyet, Thérèse, 'Présence de Platon dans le classicisme français', *Association Guillaume Budé, Actes du Congrès de Tours et de Poitiers* (1954), 364-71.

Graham, David, 'Pour une rhétorique de l'emblème: *L'Art des emblèmes* du Père Claude-François Menestrier', *PFSCL*, 14, N°. 26 (1987), 13-36.

Griffiths, Richard, *The Dramatic Technique of Antoine de Montchrestien: rhetoric and style in French Renaissance tragedy* (Oxford, 1970).

Grosheintz, Oscar, *L'Esthétique oratoire de Bossuet*, doctoral thesis, Berne (Zurich, 1914).

Guellouz, Suzanne, 'Le P. Bouhours et le *je ne sais quoi*', *Les Annales de l'Université de Toulouse - Le Mirail*, 18 (1971), 3-14.

Guerlac, Suzanne, 'Longinus and the subject of the sublime', *New Literary History*, 16, N°. 2 (1985), 275-89.

Guerreiro, Fernando, 'Saint-Evremond et la résistance au sublime, en France, au xviie siècle – une critique de l'idée et du mot de *Vaste*', *Ariane*, 8 (1990), 57-92.

Hache, Sophie, *La Langue du ciel: le sublime en France au XVIIe siècle* (2000).

Haase, Erich, 'Zur Bedeutung von je ne sais quoi im 17. Jahrhundert', *Zeitschrift für französische Sprache und Literatur*, 67 (1956), 47-68.

Hallyn, Fernand, 'Dialectique et rhétorique devant la "nouvelle science" du xviie siècle', dans M. Fumaroli (ed.), *Histoire de la rhétorique*, 601-28.

Harris, Roy, *The Language Makers* (London, 1980).

Harth, Erica, *Ideology and Culture in Seventeenth-Century France* (Ithaca, 1983).

Hartmann, Pierre, *Du Sublime (de Boileau à Schiller)* (Strasbourg, 1997).

Hazard, Paul, *La Crise de la conscience européenne* (1935).

Hepp, Noémi, 'Esquisse du vocabulaire de la critique littéraire de la Querelle du Cid à la Querelle d'Homère', *RF*, 69 (1957), 332-408.

Hertz, Neil, 'A reading of Longinus' [1973], in *The End of the Line. Essays on Psychoanalysis and the Sublime* (New York, 1985).

Higman, Francis M., *The Style of John Calvin in his French polemical treatises* (Oxford, 1967).

Hope, Quentin M., *Saint-Evremond: the* honnête homme *as critic* (Bloomington, 1962).

Hutcheon, Linda, *A Theory of Parody: the teachings of twentieth-century art forms* (New York and London, 1985).

Isherwood, Robert M., *Music in the Service of the King: France in the Seventeenth Century* (Ithaca, 1973).

Iversen, Erik, *The Myth of Egypt and its Hieroglyphs in European Tradition* (Copenhagen, 1961).

Jacoubet, Henri, *Variétés d'histoire littéraire, de méthodologie et de critique d'humeur* (1935).

Jankélévitch, Vladimir, *Le Je-ne-sais-quoi et le presque-rien* (1957).

Johnson, L. W., 'Literary neoplatonism in five French treatises of the early seventeenth century', *RR*, 60 (1969), 233-50.

Jones, Richard Foster, *The Seventeenth Century* (Stanford, 1951).

Josipovici, Gabriel, *The World and the Book*: a study of modern fiction [1971], second edition (London, 1979).

Kapp, Volker, 'La Bible et le sublime dans *Esther* de Racine', *Quaderni del Seicento Francese*, 11 (Paris and Bari, 1994), 157-71.

——, 'Le Sublime est "une chose de sentiment": Silvain, lecteur de Boileau et critique de Longin', *Aspects du classicisme et de la spiritualité: Mélanges en l'honneur de Jacques Hennequin*, ed. A. Cullière (Metz, 1996), 109-26.

——, 'L'apogée de l'atticisme français ou l'éloquence qui se moque de la rhétorique', dans M. Fumaroli (ed.), *Histoire de la rhétorique*, 707-86.

Kerslake, Lawrence, 'Silvain's *Traité du sublime*: authorship and reception', *Romance Notes*, 19 (1978), 38-43.

——, 'An early eighteenth-century theory of the sublime: François Silvain's *Traité du sublime*', *Revue de l'Université d'Ottawa*, 50 (1980), 262-79.

——, 'The sources of some literary articles in the *Encyclopédie*', *SVEC*, 215 (1982), 139-61.

——, *Essays on the Sublime* (Berne, 2000).

Kibédi Varga, Aron, *Rhétorique et littérature: études de structures classiques* (1970).

——, 'La rhétorique et la peinture à l'époque classique', *Rivista di letterature moderne e comparate*, 37 (1984), 105-21.

Klein, Robert, 'La théorie de l'expression figurée dans les traités italiens sur les "imprese", 1555-1612', *BHR*, 19 (1957), 320-42; reprinted in *La Forme et l'intelligible* (1970), 125-50.

Knowlson, James, *Universal Language Schemes in England and France 1600-1800* (Toronto, 1975).

Köhler, Erich, '*Je ne sais quoi*: ein Kapitel aus der Begriffsgeschichte des Unbegreiflichen', *Romanistisches Jahrbuch*, 6 (1953-54), 21-59.

Kortum, Hans, *Charles Perrault und Nicolas Boileau* (Berlin, 1966).

Krantz, Emile, *Etude sur l'esthétique de Descartes* (1882).

Kristeller, Paul, *Eight Philosophers of the Italian Renaissance* (1965).

Lafond, Jean, 'La beauté et la grâce: l'esthétique platonicienne des *Amours de Psyché*', *RHLF*, 80 (1969), 475-90.

Lagarde, François, *La Persuasion et ses effets: Essai sur la réception en France au dix-septième siècle* (Tübingen, 1995).

Land, Stephen K., *From Signs to Propositions: the concept of form in eighteenth-century semantic theory* (London, 1974).

Lanson, Gustave, 'L'influence de la philosophie cartésienne sur la littérature française' [1896], in *Etudes d'histoire littéraire* (1929), 58-98.

Laumaillé, Sophie, 'Le sublime au xviiᵉ siècle: de l'éthique à la rhétorique', *DSS*, 47, Nᵒ. 188 (1995), 381-88.

Le Brun, Jacques, 'Le Père Pierre Lalemant et les débuts de l'Académie Lamoignon', *RHLF*, 61 (1961), 153-76.

Lecoq, Anne-Marie (ed.), *La Querelle des Anciens et des Modernes* (2001).

Lee, Rensselaer W., *Ut Pictura Poesis: the humanistic theory of painting* [1940] (New York, 1967).

Le Guern, Michel, 'La question des styles et des genres dans la rhétorique française de l'âge classique' in *Actualité de l'histoire de la langue française: méthodes et documents*, ed. R. Mathé (Limoges, 1984), 65-70.

——, 'La méthode dans *La Rhetorique ou l'Art de parler* de Bernard Lamy', in *Grammaire et méthode au xviiᵉ siècle*, ed. P. Swiggers (Leuven, 1984), 49-67.

——, 'Sur la place de la question des styles dans les traités de rhétorique de l'âge classique' in *Qu'est-ce que le style?*, ed. G. Molinié and P. Cahné (1994), 175-85.

Levi, A. H. T., 'La disparition de l'héroïsme: étapes et motifs', in *Héroïsme et création littéraire*, ed. Noémi Hepp and Georges Livet (1974), 77-88.

⸻, 'The early seventeenth century: the significance of the *Astrée*', *SCFS*, 5 (1983), 6-17.

⸻, 'The reception of Greek sources in late seventeenth-century France', *FS*, 42 (1988), 408-23.

Lewis, Philip, 'L'anti-sublime, ou la rhétorique du progrès', in *Rhétoriques fin de siècle*, ed. M. Shaw and Fr. Cornilliat (1992), 117-45.

⸻, 'Fragmented text and continuous reading: a Longinian text and some of its implications', in *Discontinuity and Fragmentation*, ed. F. G. Henry (Amsterdam and Atlanta, 1995), 25-33.

Litman, Thodore A., *Le Sublime en France (1660-1714)* (1971).

Loach, Judi, 'L'influence de Tesauro sur le Père Menestrier', in *La France et l'Italie au temps de Mazarin*, ed. J. Serroy (Grenoble, 1986), 167-71.

Löffler, Wilhelm, *Die literarischen Urteile der Frau von Sévigné nach ihren Briefen* (Darmstadt, 1912).

Logan, John L., 'Montaigne et Longin: une nouvelle hypothèse', *RHLF*, 83 (1983), 355-70.

Lombardo, Giovanni, and Francesco Finocchiaro, *Sublime antico e moderno: una bibliografia* (Palermo, 1993).

Loskoutoff, Yvan, *L'Armorial de Calliope: l'œuvre du Père Le Moyne S. J. (1602-1671): littérature, héraldique, spiritualité* (Tübingen, 2000).

Lyons, John D., 'Speaking in pictures, speaking of pictures: problems of representation in the seventeenth century', in *Mimesis: from mirror to method, Augustine to Descartes*, ed. J. D. Lyons and S. G. Nichols (Hanover, 1982), 166-87.

Maber, Richard G., 'Bouhours and the sea: the origins of the first *Entretien d'Ariste et d'Eugène*', *MLR*, 75 (1980), 76-85.

⸻, *The Poetry of Pierre Le Moyne* (Berne, 1982).

⸻, 'Taste, style, and the Jesuits, 1630-1690', *SCFS*, 8 (1986), 53-64.

⸻, 'The search for the sublime: poetic theory and practice in the later seventeenth century' (paper delivered to the French Studies Conference, Oxford, 1984; unpublished to date).

Magné, Bernard, *Crise de la littérature française sous Louis XIV: humanisme et nationalisme*, 2 vols (Lille and Paris, 1976).

Mahon, D., *Studies in Seicento Art and Theory* (London, 1947).

Mâle, Emile, 'La clef des allégories peintes et sculptées au XVIIᵉ et au XVIIIᵉ siècles', *Revue des deux mondes*, 38 (1927), 106-29 (1 mai), 375-94 (15 mai).

Marin, Louis, *Le Portrait du Roi* (1981).

⸻, '*Locus classicus sublimis*: l'orage dans le paysage poussinien', *Esprit créateur*, 25 (1985), 53-72.

⸻, 'Sur une tour de Babel dans un tableau de Poussin', in *Du sublime* (1988), ed. J.-F. Courtine and others, 237-58.

————, 'On the sublime, infinity, je ne sais quoi', in *A New History of French Literature*, ed. D. Hollier (Cambridge, Mass., 1989), 340-45.

————, *Sublime Poussin* (1995).

Marmier, Jean, *Horace en France, au dix-septième siècle* (1962).

Mattioli, Emilio, *Interpretazioni dello Pseudo-Longino* (Modena, 1988).

Maurer, Karl, 'Boileaus Übersetzung der Schrift PERI HUPSOUS als Text des französischen 17. Jahrhunderts', *Entretiens de la Fondation Hardt*, 25 (1978), 213-62.

May, Gita, 'Diderot and Burke: a study in aesthetic affinity', *PMLA*, 75 (1960), 527-39.

McBride, Robert, 'The evolution of the *Querelle du théâtre* during the seventeenth century in France', *SCFS*, 3 (1981), 30-37.

McGowan, Margaret M., 'Moral intention in the fables of La Fontaine', *JWCI*, 29 (1966), 264-81.

Melzer, Sara E., *Discourses of the Fall: a study of Pascal's Pensées* (Berkeley and Los Angeles, 1986).

Menant, Sylvain, *La Chute d'Icare: la crise de la poésie française 1700-1750* (Geneva, 1981).

Mercier, Roger, 'La querelle de la poésie au début du XVIIIe siècle', *RSH*, No. 133 (1969), 19-46.

————, 'La question du langage poétique au début du XVIIIe siècle: la Bible et la critique', *RSH*, No. 146 (1972), 255-82.

Merlin, Hélène, 'Où est le monstre? Remarques sur l'esthétique de l'âge classique', *RSH*, No. 188 (1982), 179-93.

Mérot, Alain, *Eustache Le Sueur (1616-1655)* (1987).

Michel, Alain, 'Sublime et parole de Dieu: de Saint Augustin à Fénelon', *RHLF*, 86 (1986), 52-61.

Miedema, Hessel, 'The term "Emblema" in Alciati', *JWCI*, 31 (1968), 234-50.

Mishra, Vijay, *The Gothic Sublime* (Albany, N.Y., 1994).

Monk, Samuel H., *The Sublime: a study of critical theories in eighteenth-century England* [1935] (Ann Arbor, 1960).

————, 'A grace beyond the reach of art', *Journal of the History of Ideas*, 5 (1944), 131-50.

Moore, W. G., 'Boileau and Longinus', *FS*, 14 (1960), 52-62.

————, 'Montaigne and Lucretius', *YFS*, 28 (1967), 109-14.

Morgan, Janet, 'The meanings of *vraisemblance* in French classical theory', *MLR*, 81 (1986), 293-304.

Mornet, Daniel, *Histoire de la clarté française: ses origines, son évolution, sa valeur* (1929).

Munteano, B., *Constantes dialectiques en littérature et en histoire* (1967).

Natali, G., 'Storia del "non so che"', *Lingua Nostra*, 12 (1951), 45-49.

Naves, Raymond, *Le Goût de Voltaire* (1938; reprint Geneva, 1967).

Néraudau, Jean-Pierre, *L'Olympe du Roi-Soleil: mythologie et idéologie royale au grand siècle* (1986).

Newby, Elizabeth A., *A Portrait of the Artist: the legends of Orpheus and their use in Medieval and Renaissance aesthetics* (New York, 1987).

Niderst, Alain, *Fontenelle à la recherche de lui-même (1657-1702)* (1972).

———, 'Les Gens de Paris et les Gens de Versailles', *D'un siècle à l'autre, Actes du xvf colloque du CMR 17* (Marseille, 1987), 159-69.

Nisbet, H. B. and Claude Rawson (eds.), *The Cambridge History of Literary Criticism*, Vol. IV, 'The Eighteenth Century' (Cambridge, 1997).

✓ Noille, Christine, 'L'analyse du style dans la rhétorique classique', *DSS*, N°. 188 (1995), 389-406.

Norton, Glyn P. (ed.), *The Cambridge History of Literary Criticism*, Vol. III, 'The Renaissance' (Cambridge, 1999).

Nothnagle, John T., 'Poet or hierophant: a new view of the poetic furor', *EC*, 4 (1964), 203-07.

Nye, Edward, *Literary and Linguistic Theories in Eighteenth-Century France: From 'nuances' to 'impertinence'* (Oxford, 2000).

Olson, Elder, 'The argument of Longinus' *On the Sublime*', in *Critics and Criticism: Ancient and Modern*, ed. R. S. Crane (Chicago, 1952), 232-59.

Ong, Walter J., *Ramus, Method, and the Decay of Dialogue* (Cambridge, Mass., 1958).

The Oxford Classical Dictionary, 2nd Edition, ed. N. G. L. Hammond and H. H. Scullard (Oxford, 1970).

Panofsky, Erwin, *Idea: a concept in art theory* [1924] (New York, 1968).

Parker, David, *The Making of French Absolutism* (London, 1983).

Partee, Morriss Henry, *Plato's Poetics: the authority of beauty* (Salt Lake City, 1981).

Pélissier, L. G., 'Les Correspondants du duc de Noailles', *RHLF*, 7 (1900), 624-44.

Perkins, Merle L., 'Unpublished maxims of the abbé de Saint-Pierre', *French Review*, 31 (1958), 498-502.

Peyrache-Leborgne, Dominique, 'Sublime, sublimation et narcissisme chez Diderot', *Recherches sur Diderot et sur l'Encyclopédie*, 13 (1992), 31-46.

———, *La Poétique du sublime de la fin des Lumières au romantisme (Diderot, Schiller, Wordsworth, Shelley, Hugo, Michelet)* (1997).

Phillips, Henry, *The Theatre and its Critics in Seventeenth-Century France* (Oxford, 1980).

Picard, R., *La Carrière de Jean Racine* (1961).

Pizzorusso, Arnaldo, *La poetica di Fénelon* (Milano, 1959).

✓ Pocock, Gordon, *Boileau and the Nature of Neo-classicism* (Cambridge, 1980).

Potts, D. C., '"Une carrière épineuse": Neoplatonism and the poet's vocation in Boileau's *Art poétique*', *French Studies* 47 (1993), 20-32.

Praz, Mario, *Studies in Seventeenth-Century Imagery* [first Italian publication Milan, 1934], 2nd edition, 2 pts (Rome, 1974-75).

Puttfarken, Thomas, *Roger de Piles' Theory of Art* (New Haven, 1985).

Quarré, Pierre, *Les Plus Belles Œuvres des collections de la Côte-d'Or* (Dijon, 1958).

Raymond, Marcel, *L'Influence de Ronsard sur la poésie française (1550-85)*, 2 vols (1927).

Reiss, Timothy J., 'Introduction: the word/world equation', *YFS*, 49 (1973), 3-12.

Renard, Joseph, *Catalogue des Œuvres imprimées de Claude-François Ménestrier de la Compagnie de Jésus*, ouvrage posthume publié par C. Sommervogel (Lyon, 1883).

Rigault, M. H., *Histoire de la Querelle des anciens et des modernes* (1856).

Rivara, Annie, 'Poétique du naïf et du sublime, *La Vie de Marianne*', *Europe* (novembre 1996), 87–106.

————, 'Le comique et le sublime dans le théâtre de Marivaux', in *La Pensée de Marivaux*, forthcoming.

Rizza, Cecilia, 'Avviamento allo studio delle poetiche del barocco letterario in Francia', in *Barocco francese e cultura italiana* (Genoa, 1973).

Rodis-Lewis, Geneviève, 'Un théoricien du langage au xviie siècle: Bernard Lamy', *Le Français Moderne*, 36 (1968), 19-50.

Rohou, Jean, 'Le burlesque et les avatars de l'écriture discordante (1635-1655)', *Burlesque et formes parodiques, Actes du Colloque du Mans (1986)*, ed. I. Landy-Houillon and M. Menard (1987), 349-65.

Rosenberg Henderson, Natalie, 'Le Sueur's decorations for the Cabinet des Muses in the Hôtel Lambert', *Art Bulletin*, 56 (1974), 555-70.

Rosset, T., *Entretien, Doutes, Critique et Remarques du Père Bouhours sur la langue française: 1671-1692* (Grenoble, 1908).

Russell, Daniel S., *The Emblem and Device in France* (Lexington, Ky., 1985).

————, 'Emblems and devices in seventeenth-century French culture', *Word and Image*, ed. D. L. Rubin (*EMF*, 1) (Charlottesville, 1994), 9-30.

Russell, Donald A., *Criticism in Antiquity* (London, 1981).

————, and M. Winterbottom (eds.), *Ancient Literary Criticism* (Oxford, 1972).

Saint Girons, Baldine, *Fiat lux: Une philosophie du sublime* (1993).

Salizzoni, Roberto, 'Il fondo dell'opera. Il sublime secondo N. Hertz', *Rivista di estetica*, 27 (1987), 21-38.

Santangelo, Giovanni Saverio, 'Fra antichi e moderni: l'apogeo del sublime', in *Da Longino a Longino: I luoghi del sublime*, ed. Luigi Russo (Palermo, 1987), 81-101.

Saunders, Alison, *The Seventeenth-Century French Emblem: A study in diversity* (Geneva, 2000).

Saussure, F. de, *Cours de linguistique générale*, ed. T. de Mauro (1972).

Sayce, R. A., 'Boileau and the French baroque', *FS*, 2 (1948), 148-52.

————, 'Racine's style: periphrasis and direct statement', in *The French Mind: studies in honour of Gustave Rudler* (Oxford, 1952), 70-89.

————, *The Biblical Epic in the Seventeenth Century* (Oxford, 1955).

————, *The Essays of Montaigne: a critical exploration* (1972).

Scaglione, A., 'Nicola Boileau come fulcro nella fortuna del "sublime"', *Convivium*, raccolta nuova 18 (Turin, 1950), 161-87.

————, 'La responsabilità di Boileau per la fortuna del "sublime" nel settecento', *Convivium*, raccolta nuova 20 (Torino, 1952), 166-95.

Schalk, Fritz, 'Nochmals zum *je ne sais quoi*', *Romanische Forschungen*, 86 (1974), 131-38.

Schnapper, Antoine, 'A propos d'une récente acquisition: Houasse et le Cabinet des Beaux-Arts de Perrault', *La Revue du Louvre et des Musées de France*, 18 (1968), 241-44.

Seeber, Edward, 'Ideal languages in the French and English imaginary voyage', *PMLA*, 60 (1945), 586-97.

Seicento: le siècle de Caravage dans les collections françaises (1988).

Selig, Karl Ludwig, 'La teoria dell'emblema in Ispagna: i testi fondamentali', *Convivium*, nuova serie, 23 (1955), 409-21.

Seznec, Jean, *La Survivance des dieux antiques* [1940] (1980).

Siguret, Françoise, *L'Œil surpris: perception et représentation dans la première moitié du xviie siècle* (Tübingen, 1985).

Simon, Pierre-Henri, 'Le "je ne sais quoi" devant la raison classique', *CAIEF*, 11 (1959), 104-17.

Slaughter, M. M., *Universal Languages and Scientific Taxonomy in the Seventeenth Century* (Cambridge, 1982).

Smith, Horatio E., *The Literary Criticism of Pierre Bayle*, doctoral dissertation, Johns Hopkins (Albany, N.Y., 1912).

Sommer, Hubert, and Paul Zumthor, 'A propos du mot génie', *Zeitschrift für romanische Philologie*, 66 (1950), 170-201.

Soriano, Marc, *La Brosse à reluire sous Louis XIV: l'Epître au roi de Perrault corrigée par Racine et Boileau* (1989).

————, 'Les contes gais', *Gai Pied*, No. 403 (19 Jan. 1990), 78-81.

Spitzer, Leo, *Essays on Seventeenth-Century French Literature*, trans. and ed. David Bellos (Cambridge, 1983).

Stanton, Domna C., 'Playing with signs: the discourse of Molière's *Dom Juan*', *FF*, 5 (1980), 106-21.

Stegman, André, 'Les théories de l'emblème et de la devise en France et en Italie (1520-1620)', in *L'Emblème à la Renaissance* (1982), 61-77.

Strosetzki, Christoph, 'Pragmatique herméneutique de la traduction d'après la querelle des Anciens et des Modernes', in *Un Classicisme ou des classicismes? Actes du colloque de Reims 1991*, ed. G. Forestier and J.-P. Néraudau (Pau, 1995), 131-41.

Sulzer, Dieter, 'Zu einer Geschichte der Emblemtheorien', *Euphorion*, 64 (1970), 23-50.

Thompson, D. W., 'Montani, Saint-Evremond, and Longinus', *MLN*, 51 (1936), 10-17.

Thuillier, Jacques, 'La notion d'imitation dans la pensée artistique du xviie siècle', in *Critique et création littéraires en France au xviie siècle* (1977), 361-74.

———, 'Introduction', *Histoire et théorie de l'art en France au xviie siècle*, *DSS*, N°. 138 (1983), 3-6.

Tigerstedt, E. N., *The Decline and Fall of the Neoplatonic Interpretation of Plato: an outline and some observations*, Commentationes Humanarum Litterarum: Societas Scientiarum Fennica, 52 (Helsinki, 1974).

Tocanne, Bernard, *L'Idée de nature en France dans la seconde moitié du xviie siècle* (1978).

Todorov, Tzvetan, *Théories du symbole* (1977).

Trethewey, John, '*Le Menteur* and self-conscious theatre', *SCFS*, 6 (1984), 120-30.

Truchet, Jacques, *La Prédication de Bossuet*, 2 vols (1960).

Tunstall, Kate E., 'Hieroglyph and device in Diderot's *Lettre sur les sourds et muets*', *DS*, 28 (2000), 161-72.

Van Tieghem, Paul, *Le Sentiment de la nature dans le préromantisme européen* (1960).

Venesoen, Constant, 'L'Entretien sur le bel esprit de Bouhours: source de l'Art poétique de Nicolas Boileau', *DSS*, N°. 89 (1970), 23-45.

Viala, Alain (ed.), *Qu'est-ce qu'un classique?*, special number of *Littératures classiques*, 19 (1993).

Vicaire, Paul, *Platon: critique littéraire* (1960).

Vitanovic, Slobodan, 'Le problème du génie dans la poétique de Boileau', *Critique et création littéraires en France au xviie siècle* (1977), 195-201.

———, 'La place de la mythologie dans la poétique de Boileau', *La Mythologie au xviie siècle, Actes du xie Colloque du CMR 17* (Marseille, 1982), 25-31.

Vuillemier, Florence, 'Le Père Dominique Bouhours face aux partisans de la Pointe', in *Un Classicisme ou des classicismes? Actes du colloque de Reims 1991*, ed. G. Forestier and J.-P. Néraudau (Pau, 1995), 153-66.

Wadsworth, P. A., 'New views of French classicism in relation to the baroque', *FR*, 25 (1951-52), 172-81.

Walker, D. P., *The Ancient Theology* (London, 1972).

———, 'Esoteric symbolism', *Music, Spirit and Language in the Renaissance* (London, 1985), Chap. 15.

Warnick, Barbara, *The Sixth Canon: Belletristic Rhetorical Theory and its French Antecedents* (Columbia, 1993).

Watts, Derek A., *Cardinal de Retz: the ambiguities of a seventeenth-century mind* (Oxford, 1980).

Wehle, Winfried, 'Vom Erhabenen oder über die Kreativität des Kreatürlichen', in *Frühaufklärung*, ed. S. Neumeister (Munich, 1994), 195-240.

———, 'Das Erhabene: Aufklärung durch Aufregung', *Das 18. Jahrhundert* (1995), 9-22.

Weinberg, Bernard, 'Translations and commentaries of Longinus, On the Sublime, to 1660: a bibliography', *Modern Philology*, 47 (1950), 145-51.

————, *A History of Literary Criticism in the Italian Renaissance*, 2 vols (Chicago, 1961).

————, 'Une traduction française du Sublime de Longin vers 1645', *Modern Philology*, 59 (1962), 159-201.

Weiskel, Thomas, *The Romantic Sublime: studies in the structure and psychology of transcendence* (Baltimore, 1976).

Wencelius, L., *L'Esthétique de Calvin* (1937).

Wentzlaff-Eggebert, Christian (ed.), *Le Langage littéraire au xviie siècle: De la rhétorique à la littérature* (Tübingen, 1991).

Wilton, Andrew, *Turner and the Sublime* (London, 1980).

Wind, Edgar, *Giorgione's 'Tempesta' with comments on Giorgione's poetic allegories* (Oxford, 1969).

Wittgenstein, L., *Philosophical Investigations* (Oxford, 1953).

Wittkower, Rudolf, 'Hieroglyphics in the Early Renaissance', *Allegory and the Migration of Symbols* (London, 1977), 113-28.

Wood, Theodore E. B., *The Word 'Sublime' and its Context, 1650-1760* (The Hague, 1972).

Woolhouse, R. S., *The Empiricists* (Oxford, 1988).

Wright, C. H. C., *French Classicism* (Cambridge, Mass., 1920).

Yates, Frances A., *The French Academies of the Sixteenth Century* (London, 1947).

Zuber, Roger, *Les Belles Infidèles et la formation du goût classique: Perrot d'Ablancourt et Guez de Balzac* (1968).

————, 'La critique classique et l'idée d'imitation' [first published as 'L'idée d'imitation', 1971], in *Les Emerveillements de la raison* (1997), 163-74.

————, 'Boileau traducteur: de la rhétorique à la littérature' [1991], in *Les Emerveillements de la raison* (1997), 255-60.

————, 'La tragédie sublime: Boileau adopte Racine' [1992], in *Les Emerveillements de la raison* (1997), 251-54.

————, *Les Emerveillements de la raison: classicismes littéraires du xviie siècle français* (1997).

INDEX

Ablancourt, Nicolas Perrot d', *Lettres et préfaces critiques*, 37

Abrégé de Rhétorique, 86, 89, 99-100

Académie des Inscriptions et Belles-Lettres, 138

Académie des Sciences, 143

Académie française, 18, 138, 168

académie Lamoignon, 124, 126, 127, 128, 132, 134, 137, 138, 139
    see Boileau; Bossuet; Bouhours; Cordemoy; Fleury; Menestrier; Pellisson; Rapin

Adam, Antoine, 118, 126

Aesop, in La Fontaine, 20, 33

aesthetic theory, 41, 156-57
    and platonism, 108, 110, 169
    and rhetoric, 82-90
    passim, 103, 105
    pragmatic aesthetic, 83, 85, 106-107, 154, 155
    suggestion, 72
    see imitation; platonism

Alciati, Andrea, *Emblemata*, 65

Ancients, 127, 131, 138-39
    and the sublime, chapter 5
    passim, 122-27, 131-39
    see Querelle

Aristotle, 78, 85, 94, 119
    Poetics, 25, 26, 33, 39, 69
    Rhetoric, 78, 130

aristotelianism, 11, 19, 40, 41, 57
    aristotelian poetics, 31, 48, 72, 109

Arnauld, Antoine and Nicole, Pierre, *La*

Logique ou l'art de penser, 4, 5, 6, 12, 155

art theory, 21, 41

Aubignac, abbé d', *Discours académique sur l'éloquence*, 9-10
    La Pratique du théâtre, 24

Aubigné, Agrippa d', 37

St Augustine, 42, 45, 131, 153

Baillet, Adrien, *Jugemens des savans*, 33, 34, 37, 40, 51, 97

Balzac, Jean-Louis Guez de, 8, 27, 62, 168
    Lettres, 88
    Socrate chrétien, 78

Barbier d'Aucour, Jean, *Sentimens de Cléante sur les Entretiens*, 51, 71

Bary, René, *La Rhetorique françoise*, 78, 84-85, 86, 89

Baudoin, Jean, 65
    'Préface' to Ripa's *Iconologia*, 46-47

Bayle, Pierre, 158

Bayley, Peter, 10

le bel esprit, 59, 60, 61, 63, 70, 71, 72-73, 109
    see Bouhours, *Entretiens*

Bellegarde, abbé Morvan de
    Lettres curieuses de littérature et de morale, 137
    Réflexions sur la Genèse, 137
    Réflexions sur l'élégance et la politesse du stile, 137
    Le Sublime des auteurs, 137

Printed in the United States
917800005B